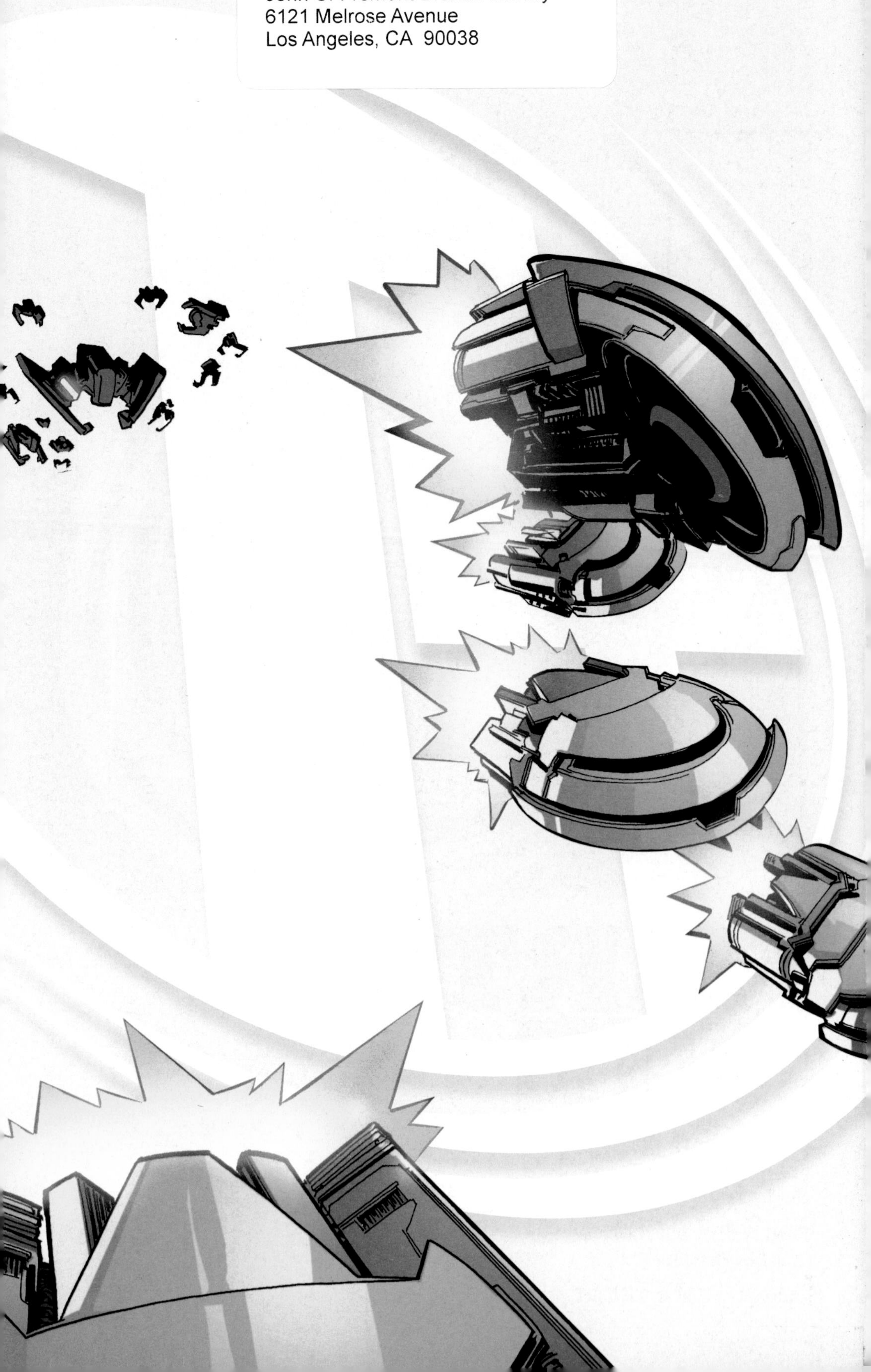

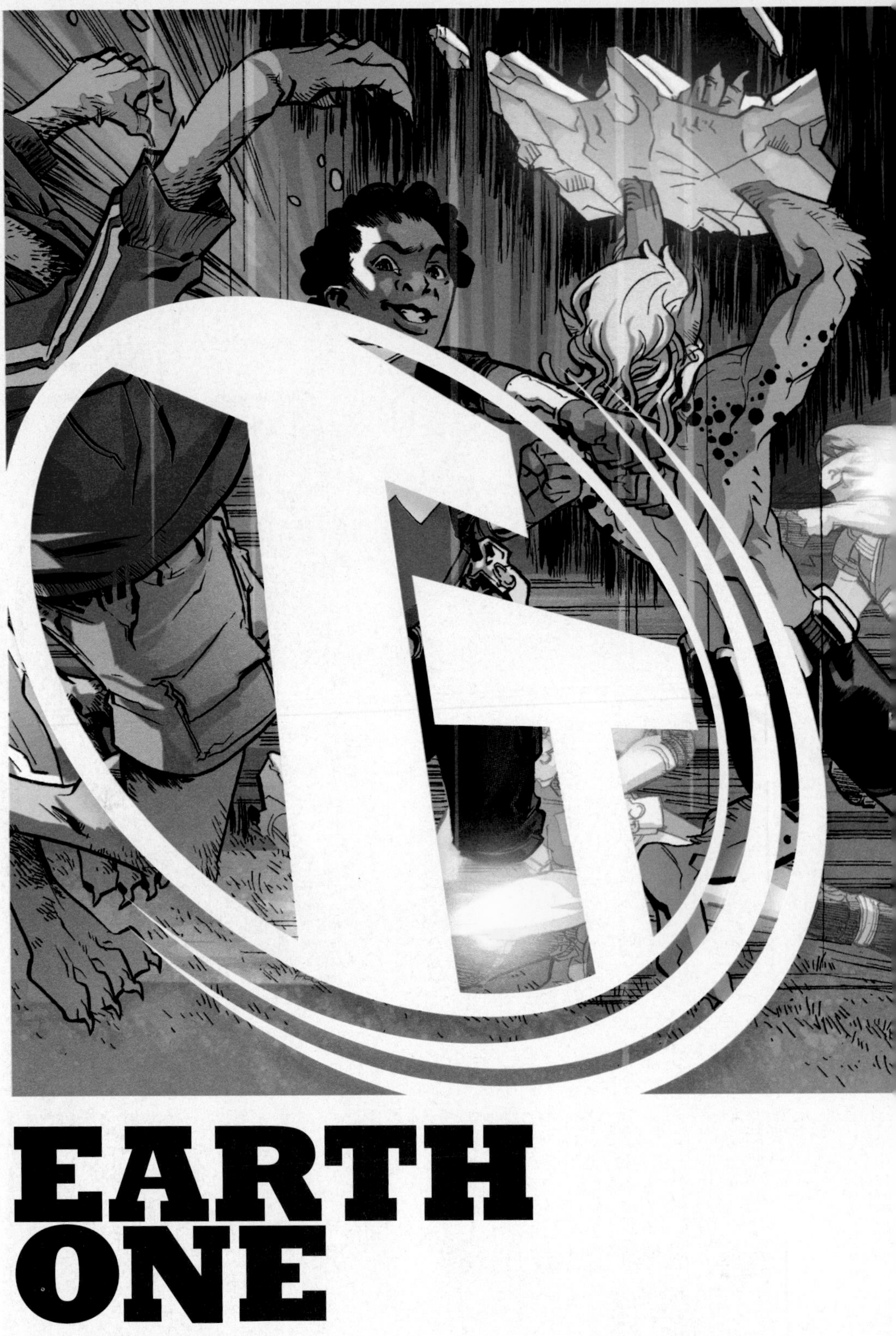

EARTH ONE

Written by Jeff Lemire
Art by Andy MacDonald
Colors by Brad Anderson
with Allen Passalaqua
Lettered by Jared K. Fletcher

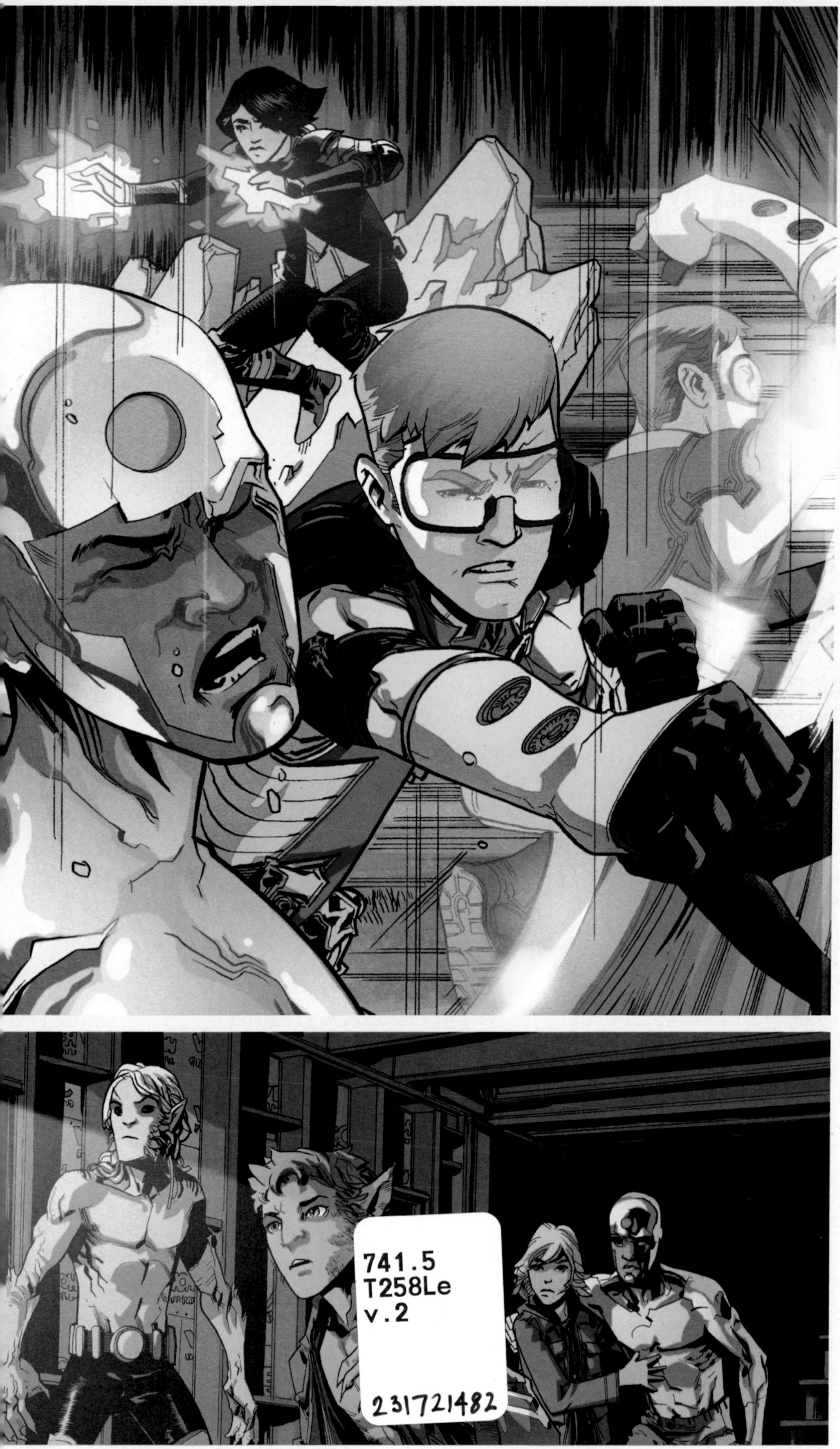

Chris Conroy Editor
Dave Wielgosz Assistant Editor
Steve Cook Design Director – Books
Louis Prandi Publication Design

Bob Harras Senior VP – Editor-in-Chief, DC Comics

Diane Nelson President
Dan DiDio Publisher
Jim Lee Publisher
Geoff Johns President & Chief Creative Officer
Amit Desai Executive VP – Business & Marketing Strategy,
Direct to Consumer & Global Franchise Management
Sam Ades Senior VP – Direct to Consumer
Bobbie Chase VP – Talent Development
Mark Chiarello Senior VP – Art, Design & Collected Editions
John Cunningham Senior VP – Sales & Trade Marketing
Anne DePies Senior VP – Business Strategy, Finance & Administration
Don Falletti VP – Manufacturing Operations
Lawrence Ganem VP – Editorial Administration & Talent Relations
Alison Gill Senior VP – Manufacturing & Operations
Hank Kanalz Senior VP – Editorial Strategy & Administration
Jay Kogan VP – Legal Affairs
Thomas Loftus VP – Business Affairs
Jack Mahan VP – Business Affairs
Nick J. Napolitano VP – Manufacturing Administration
Eddie Scannell VP – Consumer Marketing
Courtney Simmons Senior VP – Publicity & Communications
Jim (Ski) Sokolowski VP – Comic Book Specialty Sales & Trade Marketing
Nancy Spears VP – Mass, Book, Digital Sales & Trade Marketing

Special Thanks to Matt Idelson

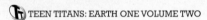 TEEN TITANS: EARTH ONE VOLUME TWO

Published by DC Comics. All new material Copyright © 2017 by DC
Originally published Copyright © 2016 DC Comics. All Rights R
All characters featured in this publication, the distinctive lik
thereof and related elements are trademarks of DC Comics. The
characters and incidents featured in this publication are entirely
DC Comics does not read or accept unsolicited submissions
stories or artwork. Printed by LSC Communications, Salem, VA, USA
First Printing

DC Comics, 2900 W. Alameda Ave., Burbank, CA 91505

ISBN: 978-1-4012-7153-4

Library of Congress Cataloging-in-Publication Data

Names: Lemire, Jeff, author. | MacDonald, Andy (Artist), artist. | A
Brad, colourist. | Passalaqua, Allen, colourist. | Fletcher, Jared K
letterer.
Title: Teen Titans Earth One. Volume two / written by Jeff Lemire ;
Andy MacDonald ; colors by Brad Anderson, with Allen Pas
lettered
by Jared K. Fletcher.
Description: Burbank, CA : DC Comics, [2017]
Identifiers: LCCN 2017025871 | ISBN 9781401271534 (paperbac
Subjects: LCSH: Comic books, strips, etc. | BISAC: COMICS & G
NOVELS /
Superheroes. | COMICS & GRAPHIC NOVELS / Science Fiction
Classification: LCC PN6728.T34 L47 2017 | DDC 741.5/973—dc2
LC record available at https://lccn.loc.gov/2017025871

PEFC Certified
Printed on paper from
sustainably managed
forests, controlled
sources
PEFC/29-31-337   www.pefc.org

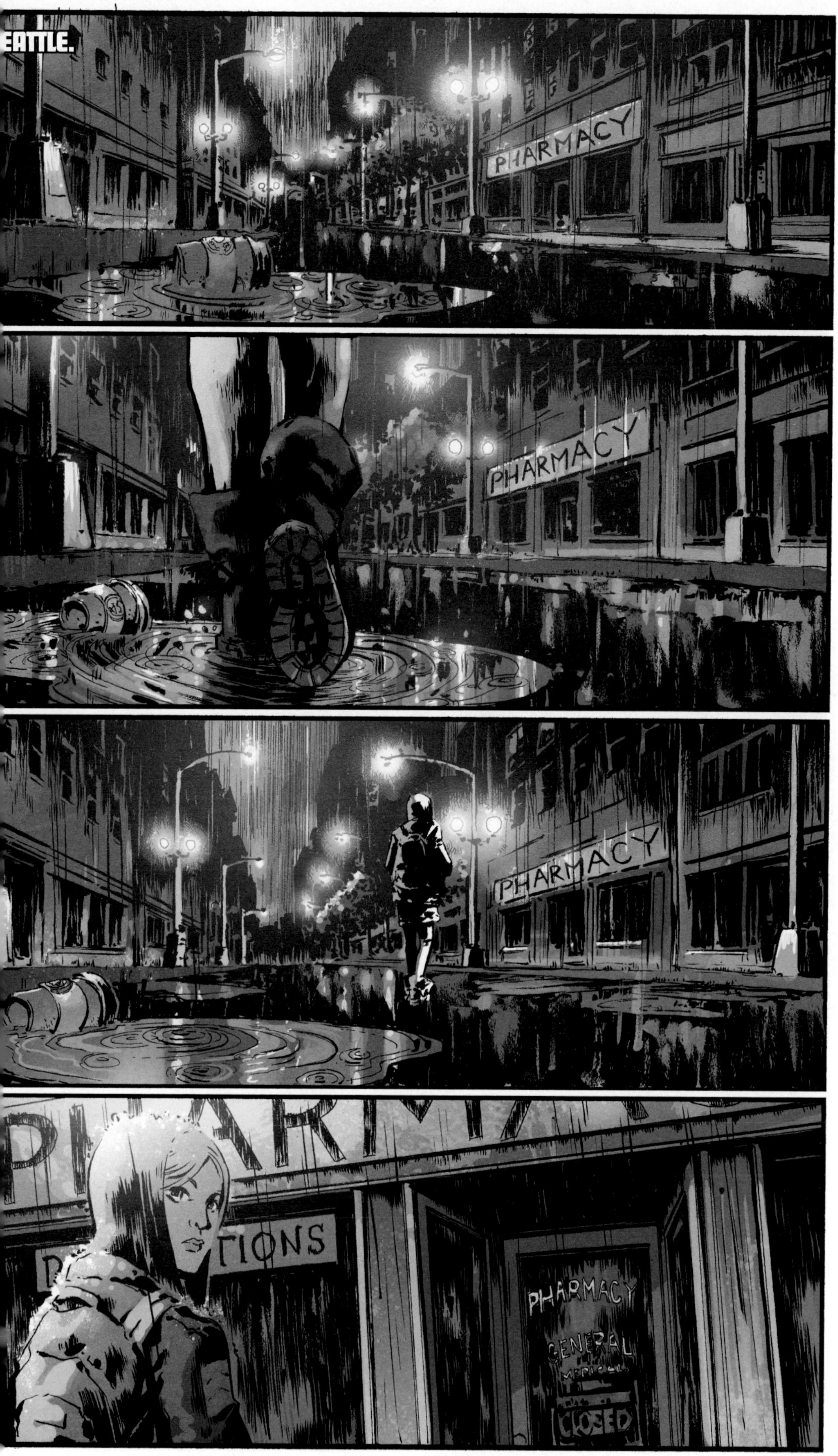

EATTLE.
PHARMACY
PHARMACY
PHARMACY
TIONS
PHARMACY
GENERAL
CLOSED

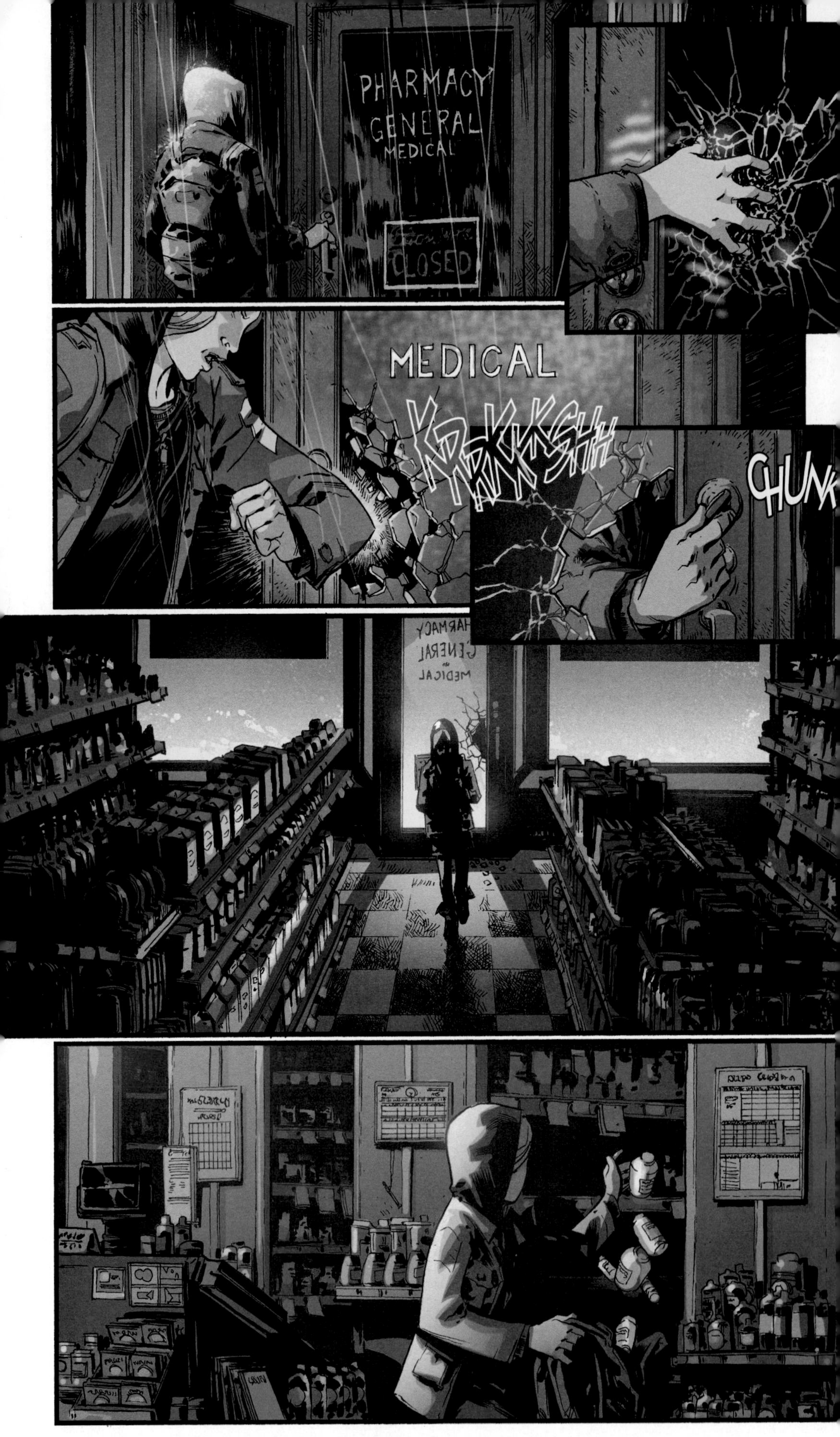
PHARMACY
GENERAL
MEDICAL
CLOSED
MEDICAL
KRRKKKSHH
CHUNK

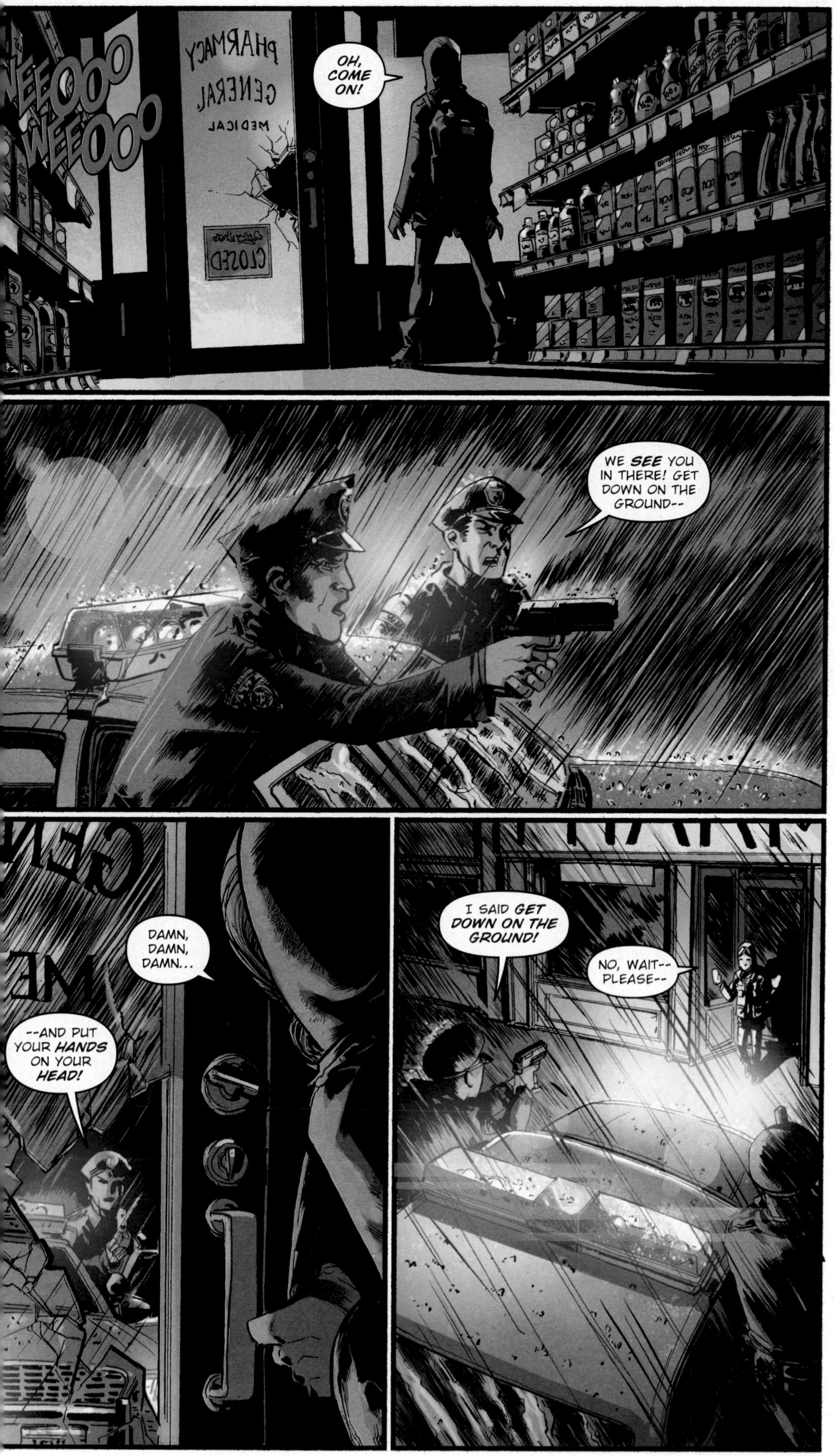
WEEOOO WEEOOO
PHARMACY
GENERAL
MEDICAL
CLOSED
OH, COME ON!
WE SEE YOU IN THERE! GET DOWN ON THE GROUND--
DAMN, DAMN, DAMN...
--AND PUT YOUR HANDS ON YOUR HEAD!
I SAID GET DOWN ON THE GROUND!
NO, WAIT--PLEASE--

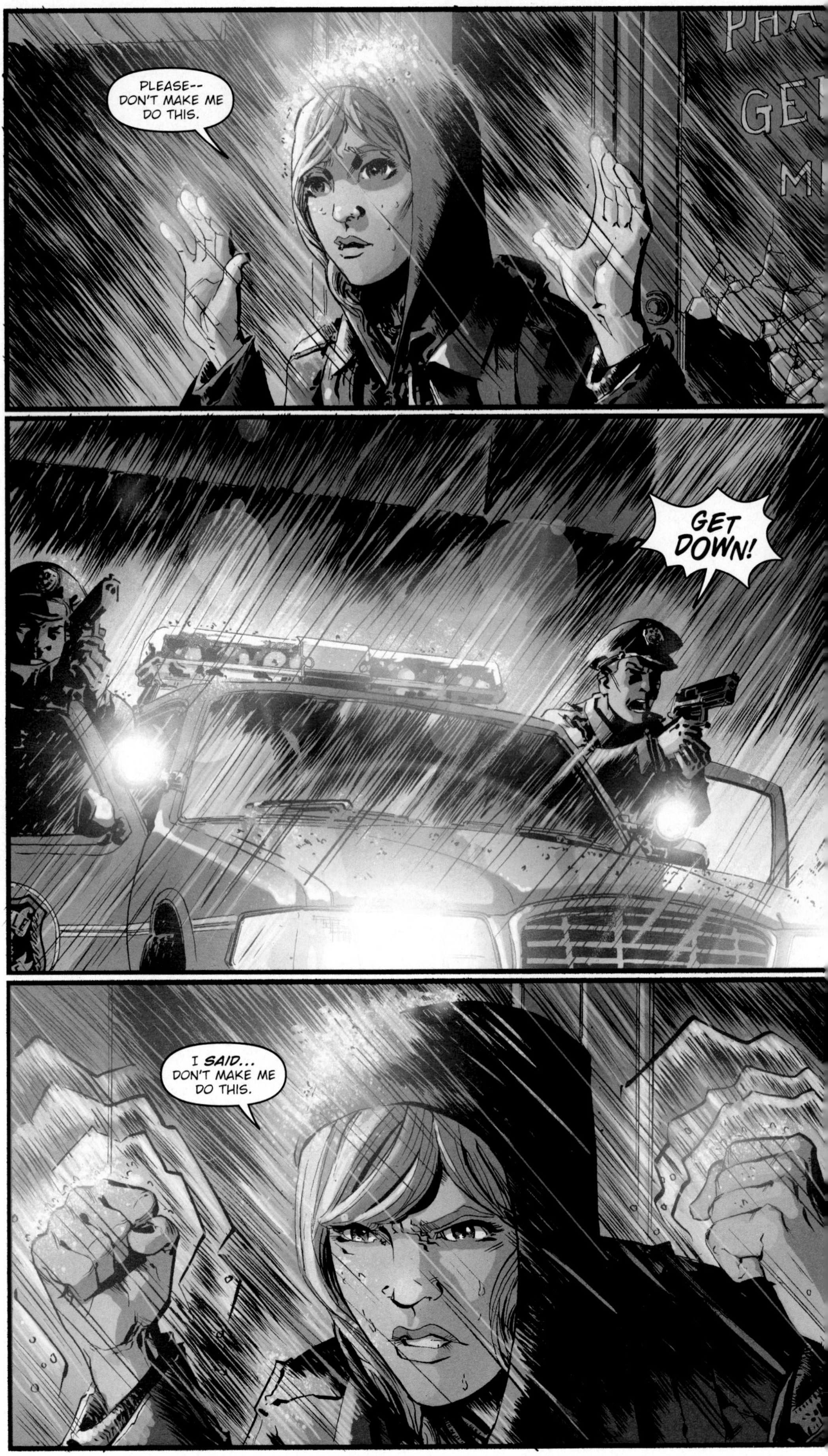
PLEASE--
DON'T MAKE ME
DO THIS.
GET DOWN!
I SAID...
DON'T MAKE ME
DO THIS.

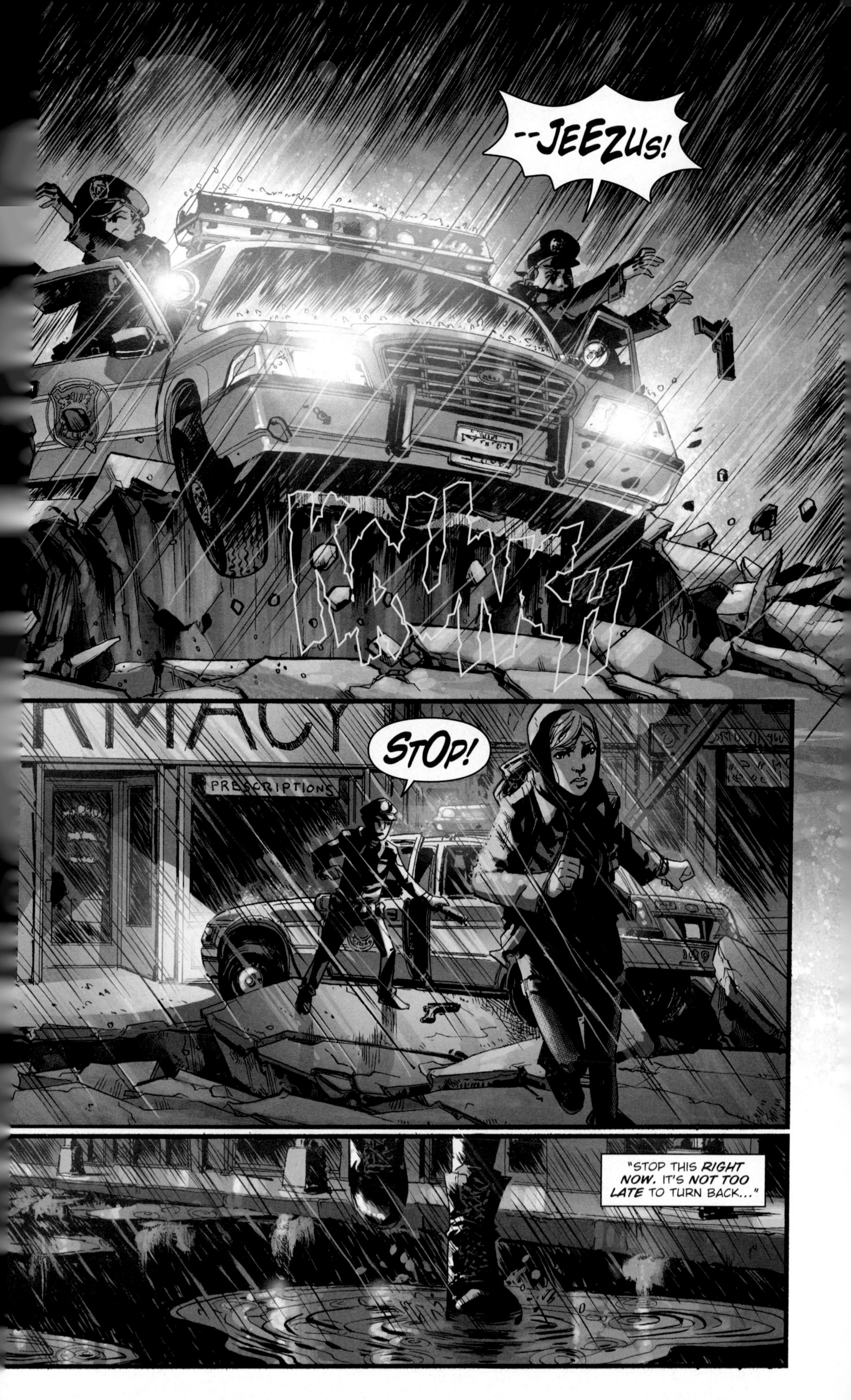
--JEEZUS!
RMACY
PRESCRIPTIONS
STOP!
"STOP THIS RIGHT NOW. IT'S NOT TOO LATE TO TURN BACK..."

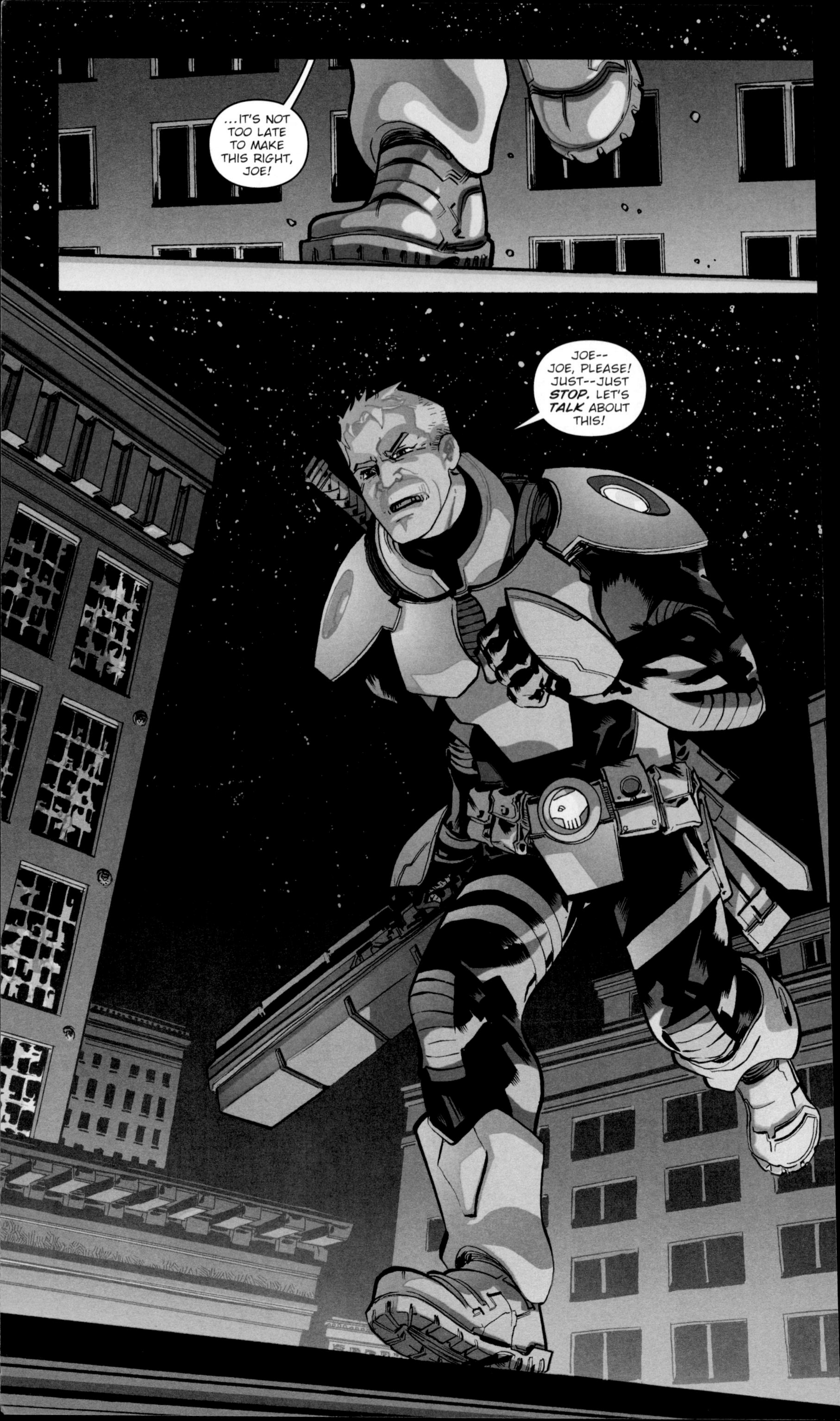
...IT'S NOT TOO LATE TO MAKE THIS RIGHT, JOE!
JOE-- JOE, PLEASE! JUST--JUST STOP. LET'S TALK ABOUT THIS!

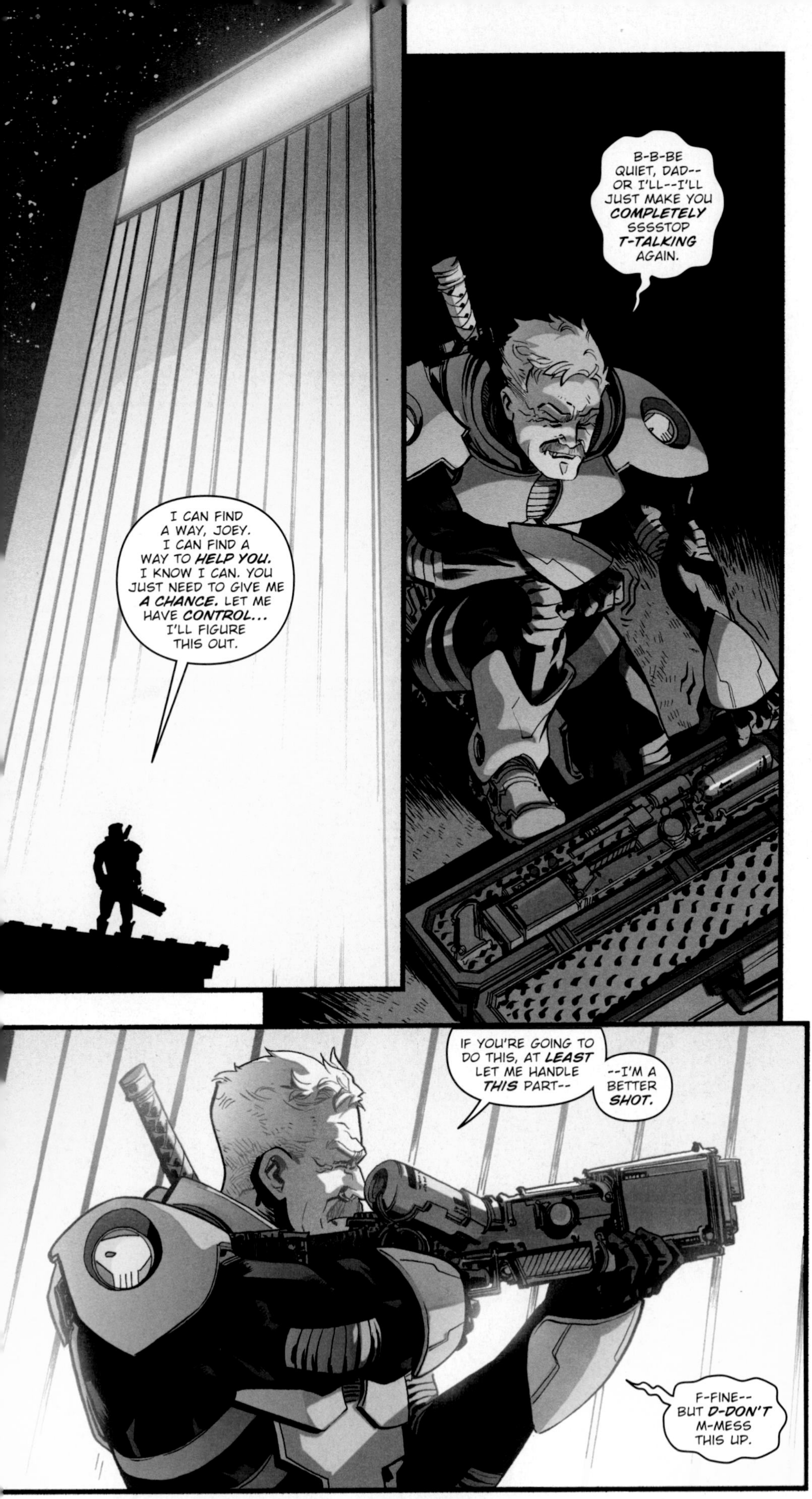
B-B-BE QUIET, DAD-- OR I'LL--I'LL JUST MAKE YOU COMPLETELY SSSSTOP T-TALKING AGAIN.
I CAN FIND A WAY, JOEY. I CAN FIND A WAY TO HELP YOU. I KNOW I CAN. YOU JUST NEED TO GIVE ME A CHANCE. LET ME HAVE CONTROL... I'LL FIGURE THIS OUT.
IF YOU'RE GOING TO DO THIS, AT LEAST LET ME HANDLE THIS PART--
--I'M A BETTER SHOT.
F-FINE-- BUT D-DON'T M-MESS THIS UP.

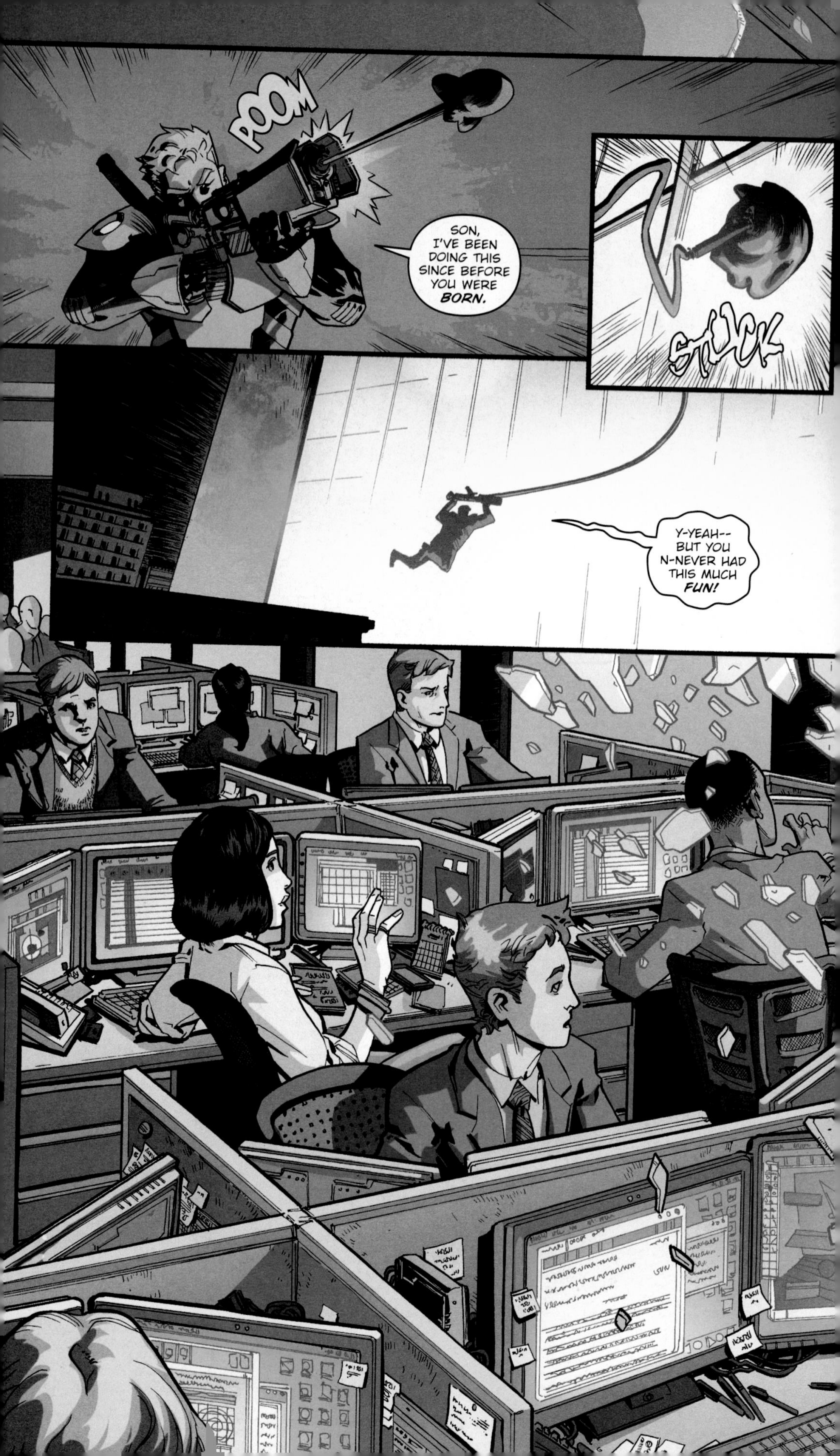
POOM
SON, I'VE BEEN DOING THIS SINCE BEFORE YOU WERE **BORN.**
STUCK
Y-YEAH-- BUT YOU N-NEVER HAD THIS MUCH **FUN!**

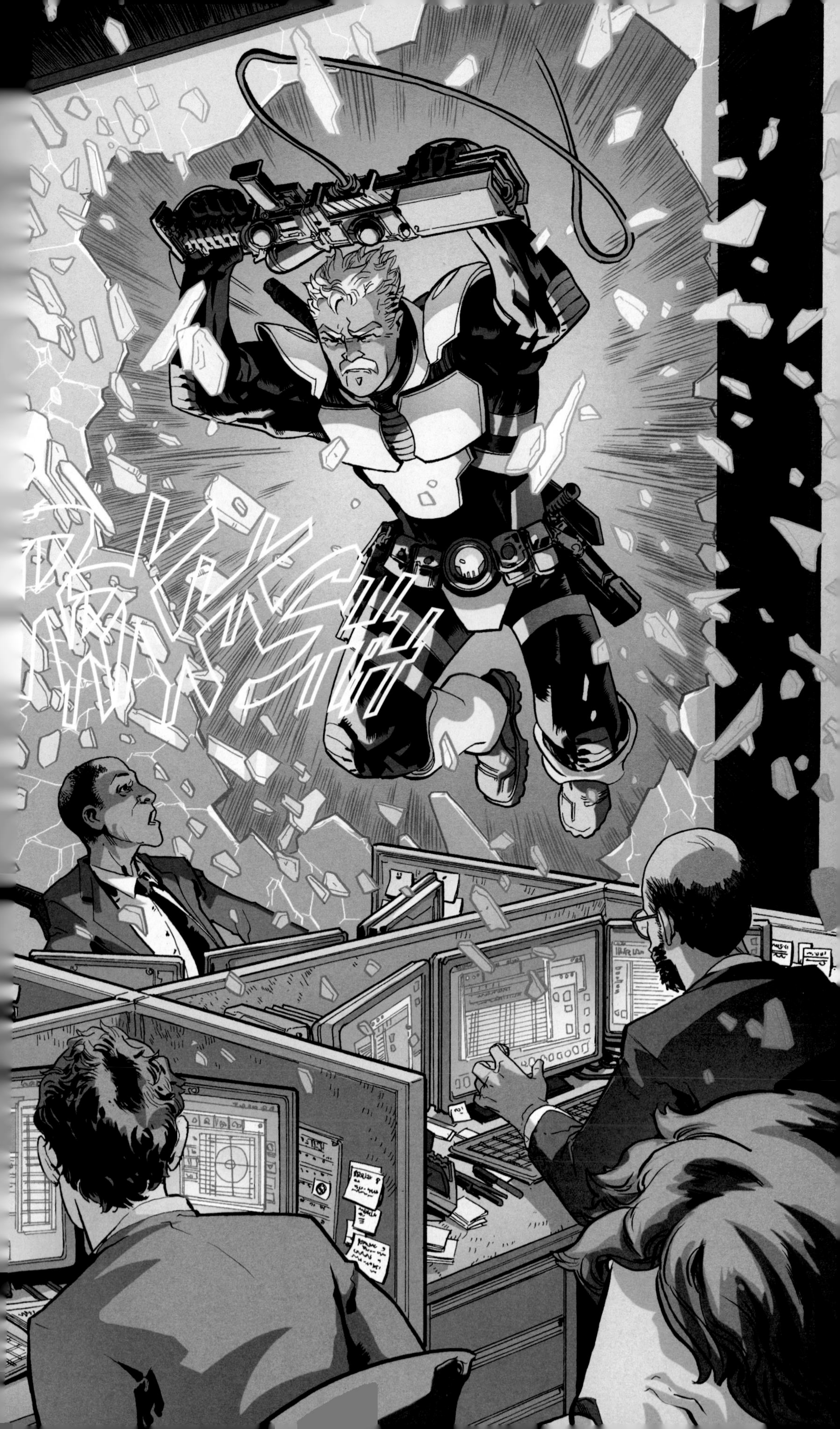

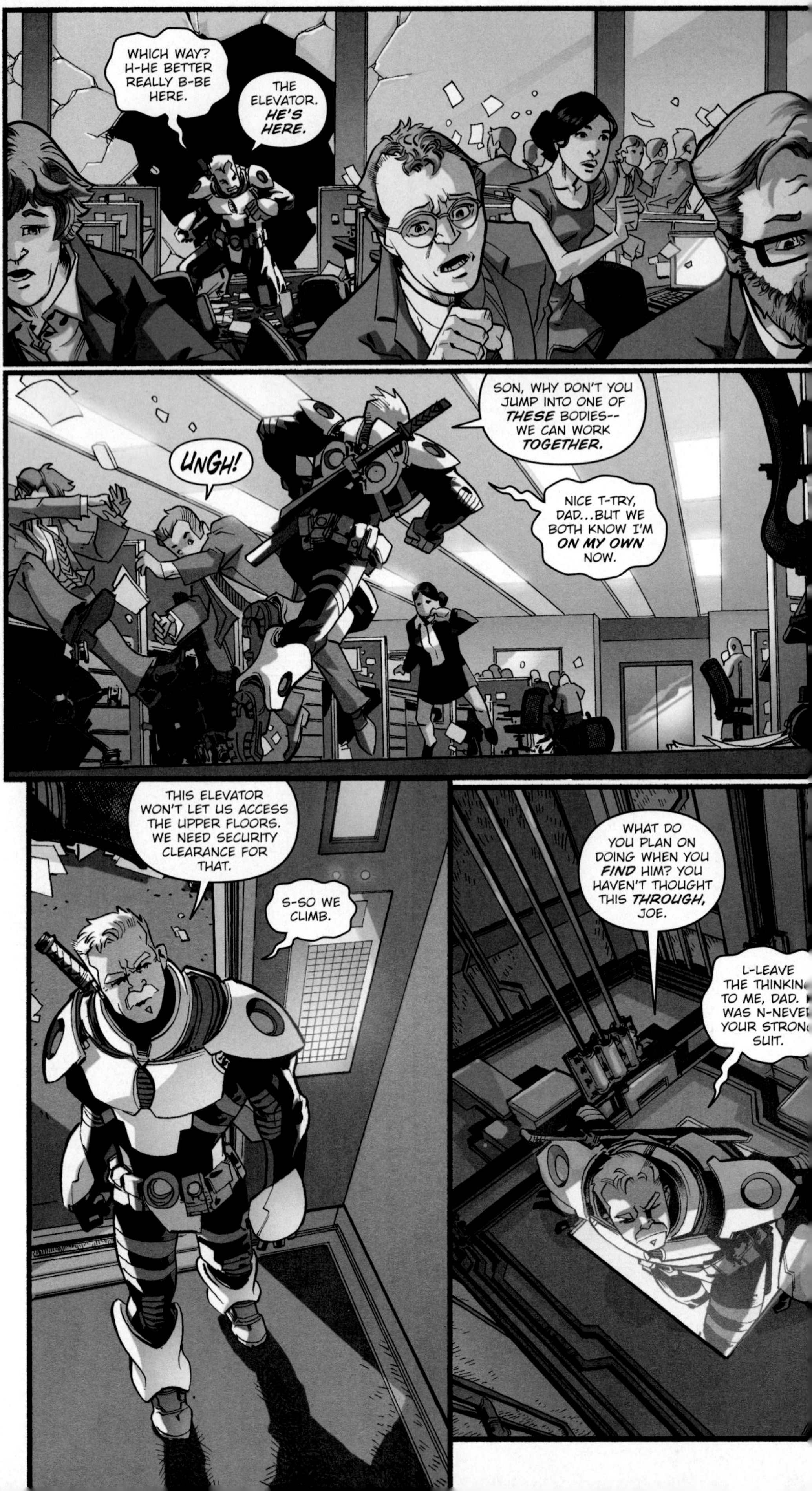
WHICH WAY? H-HE BETTER REALLY B-BE HERE.
THE ELEVATOR. *HE'S HERE.*
SON, WHY DON'T YOU JUMP INTO ONE OF *THESE* BODIES-- WE CAN WORK *TOGETHER.*
UNGH!
NICE T-TRY, DAD...BUT WE BOTH KNOW I'M *ON MY OWN* NOW.
THIS ELEVATOR WON'T LET US ACCESS THE UPPER FLOORS. WE NEED SECURITY CLEARANCE FOR THAT.
S-SO WE CLIMB.
WHAT DO YOU PLAN ON DOING WHEN YOU *FIND* HIM? YOU HAVEN'T THOUGHT THIS *THROUGH,* JOE.

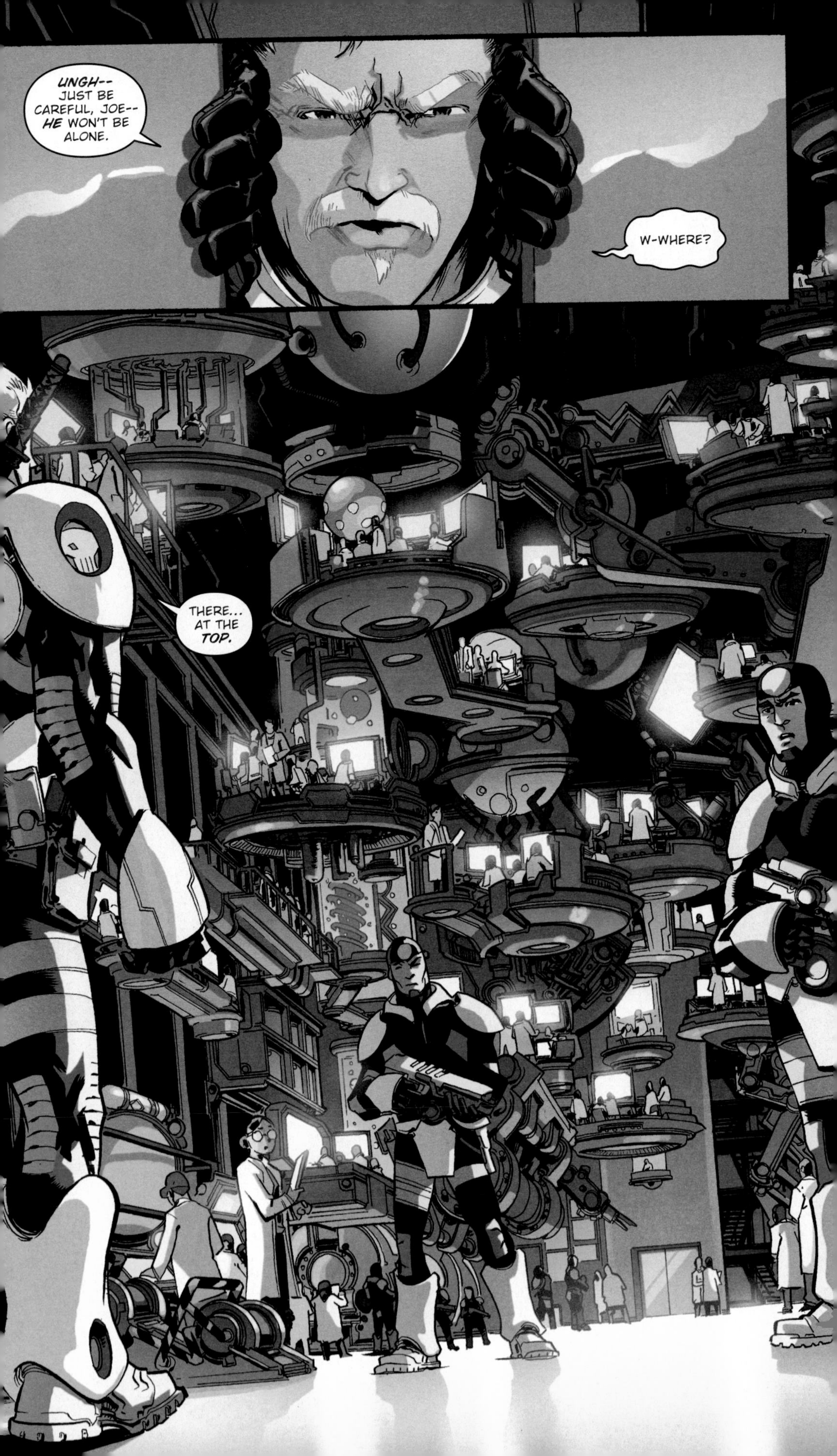
UNGH-- JUST BE CAREFUL, JOE-- HE WON'T BE ALONE.
W-WHERE?
THERE... AT THE TOP.

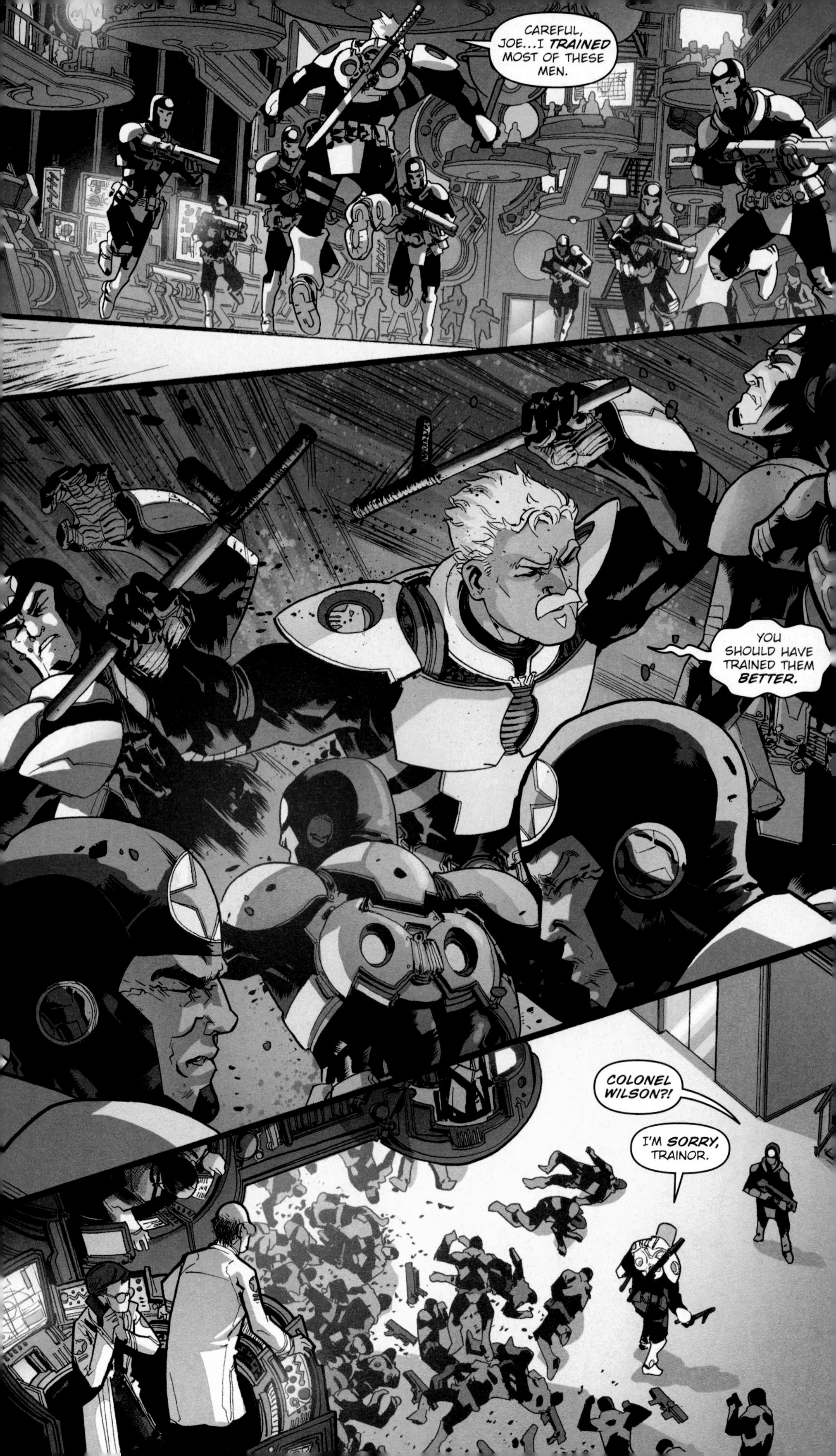
CAREFUL, JOE...I TRAINED MOST OF THESE MEN.
YOU SHOULD HAVE TRAINED THEM BETTER.
COLONEL WILSON?!
I'M SORRY, TRAINOR.

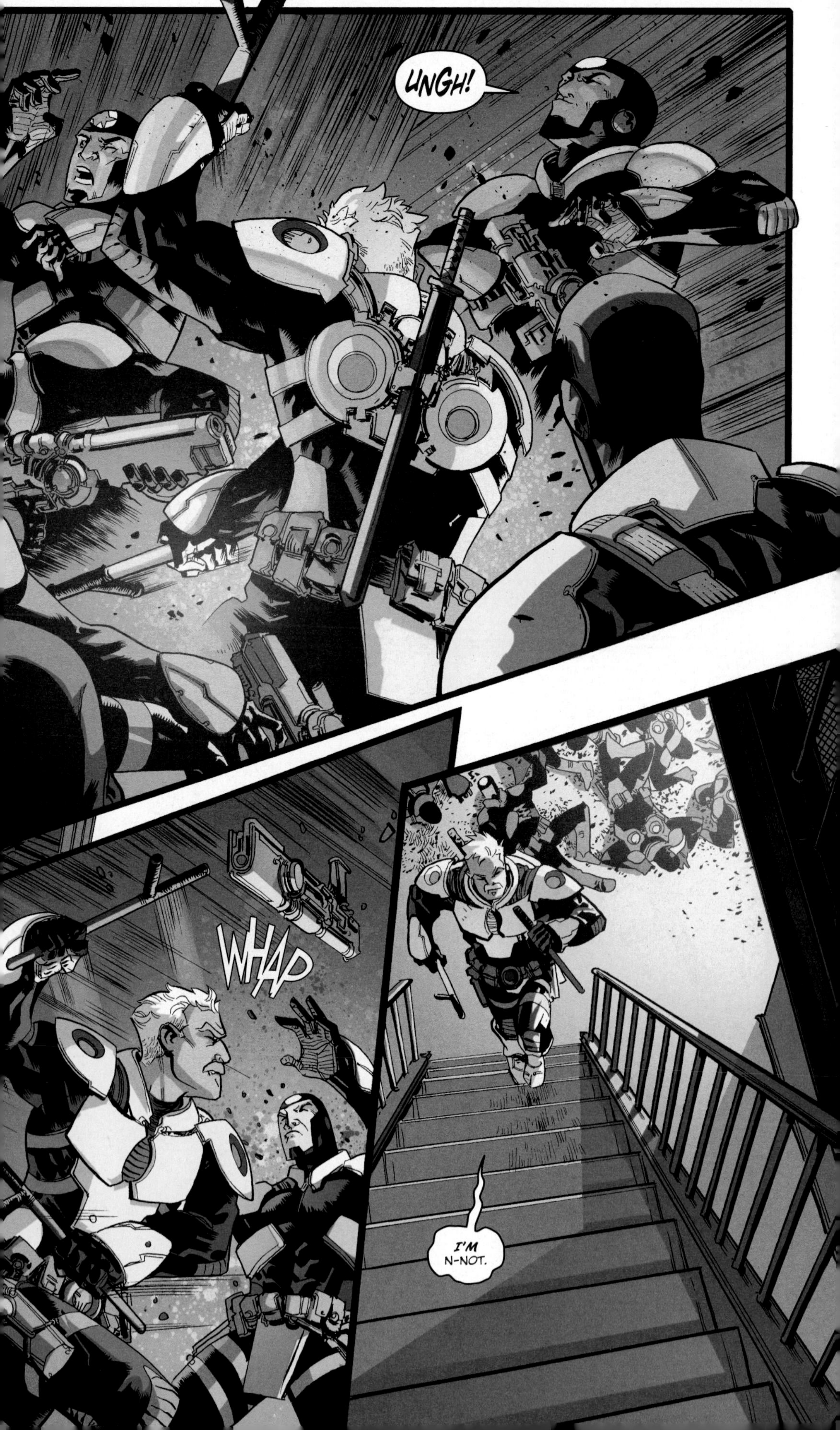
UNGH!
WHAP
I'M N-NOT.

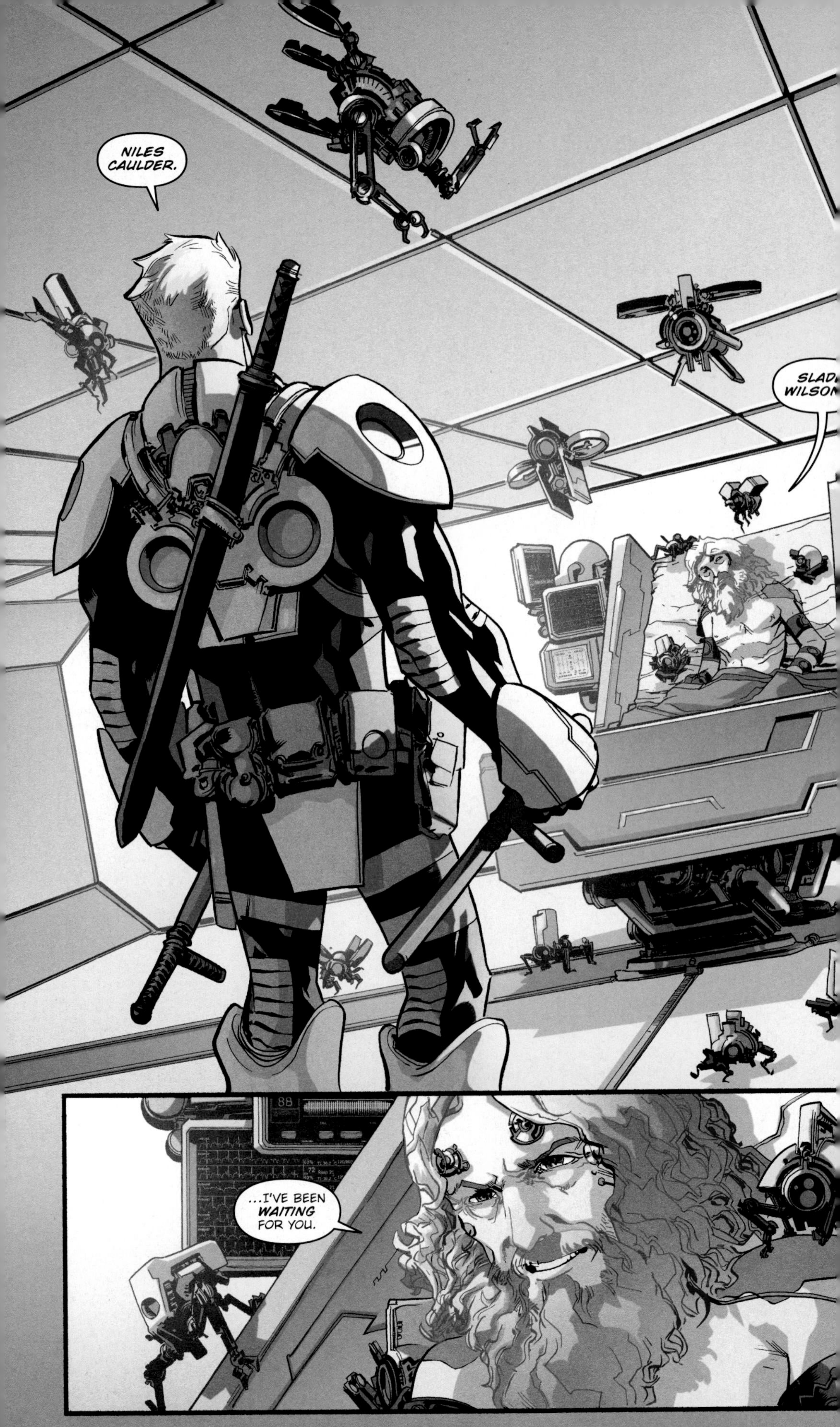
NILES CAULDER.
SLAD WILSON
...I'VE BEEN *WAITING* FOR YOU.

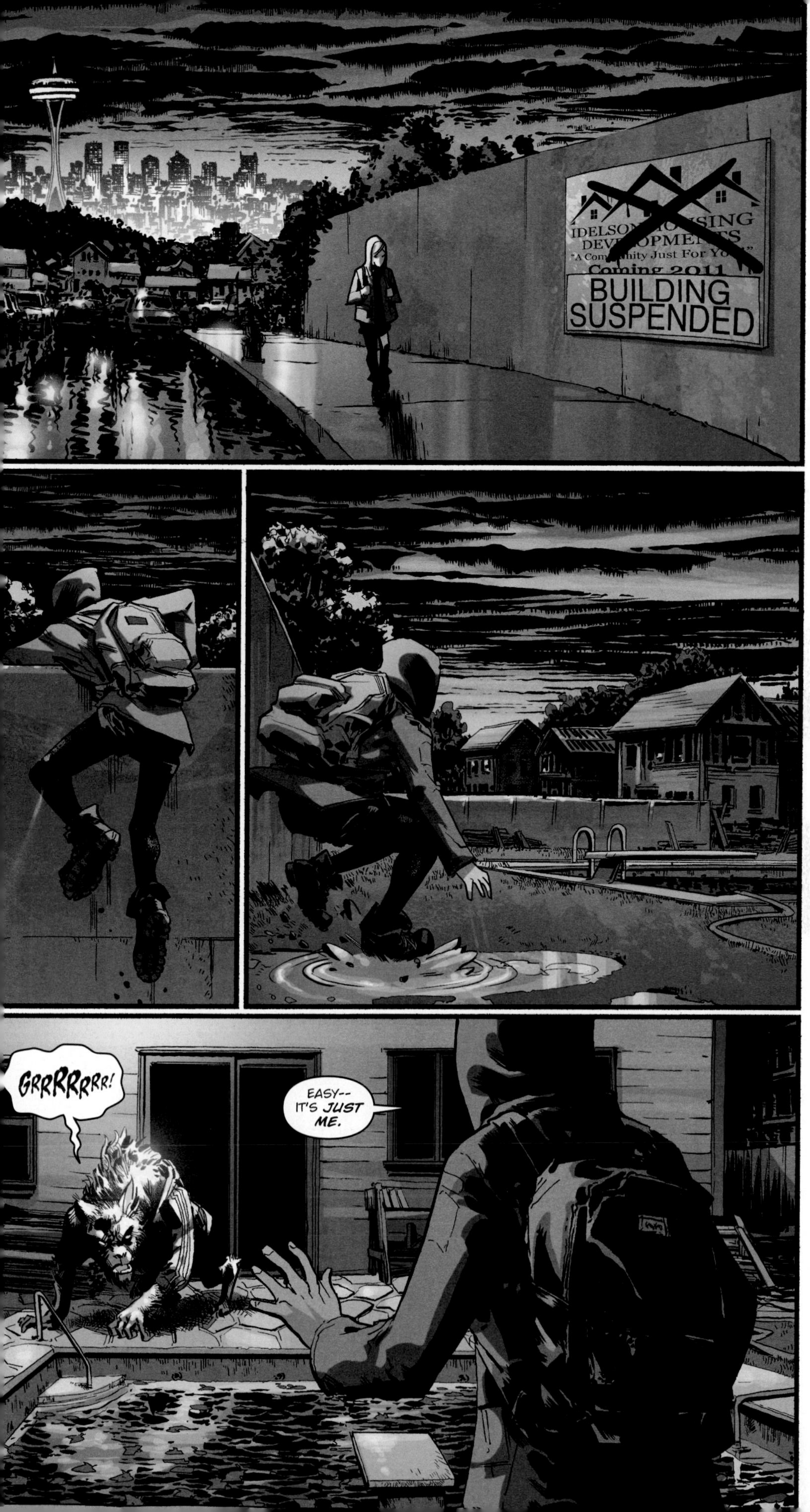
Coming 2011
BUILDING SUSPENDED
GRRRRRRR!
EASY-- IT'S JUST ME.

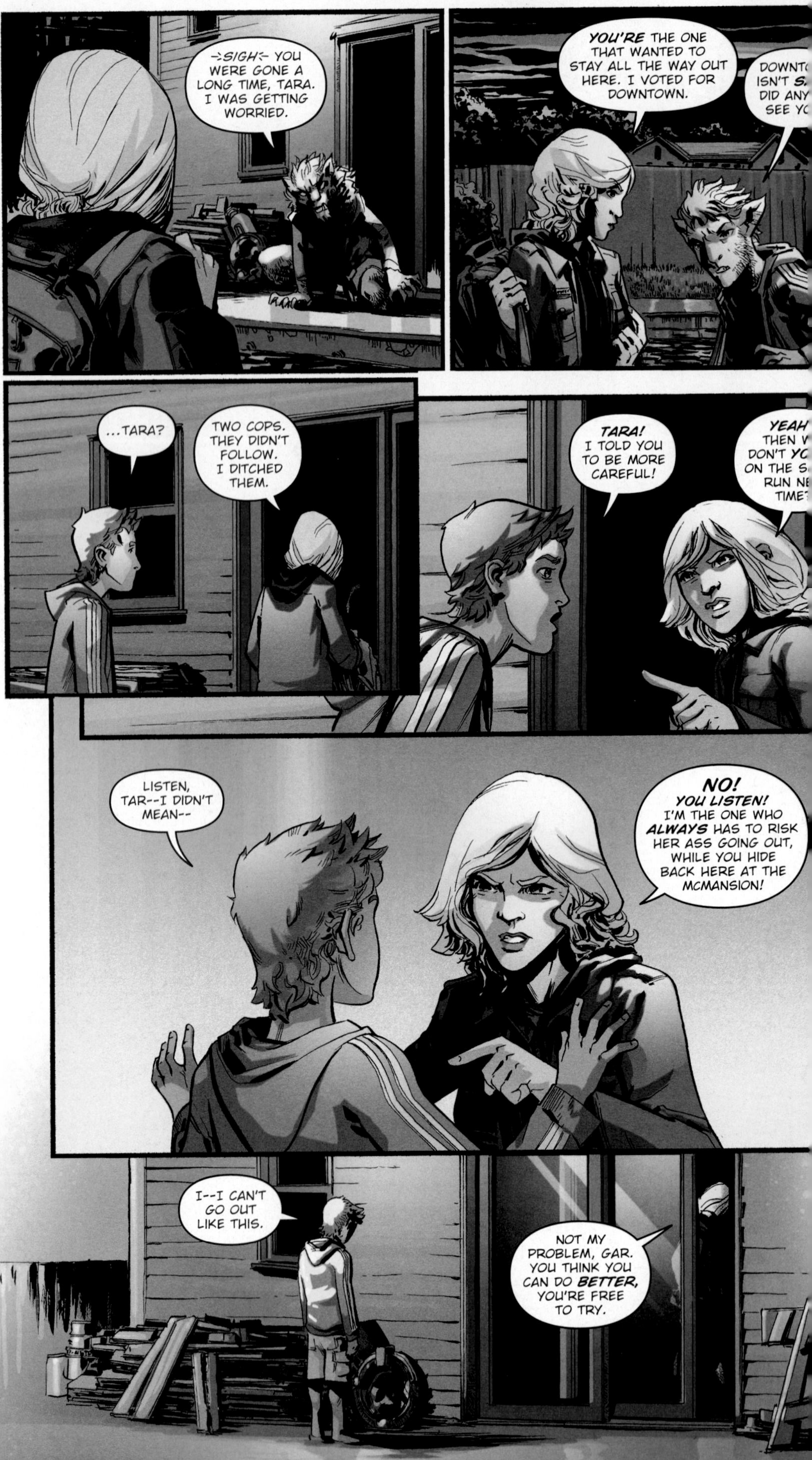

-SIGH- YOU WERE GONE A LONG TIME, TARA. I WAS GETTING WORRIED.
YOU'RE THE ONE THAT WANTED TO STAY ALL THE WAY OUT HERE. I VOTED FOR DOWNTOWN.
DOWNT ISN'T S DID ANY SEE YO
...TARA?
TWO COPS. THEY DIDN'T FOLLOW. I DITCHED THEM.
TARA! I TOLD YOU TO BE MORE CAREFUL!
YEAH THEN DON'T YO ON THE S RUN NE TIME
LISTEN, TAR--I DIDN'T MEAN--
NO! YOU LISTEN! I'M THE ONE WHO ALWAYS HAS TO RISK HER ASS GOING OUT, WHILE YOU HIDE BACK HERE AT THE MCMANSION!
I--I CAN'T GO OUT LIKE THIS.
NOT MY PROBLEM, GAR. YOU THINK YOU CAN DO BETTER, YOU'RE FREE TO TRY.

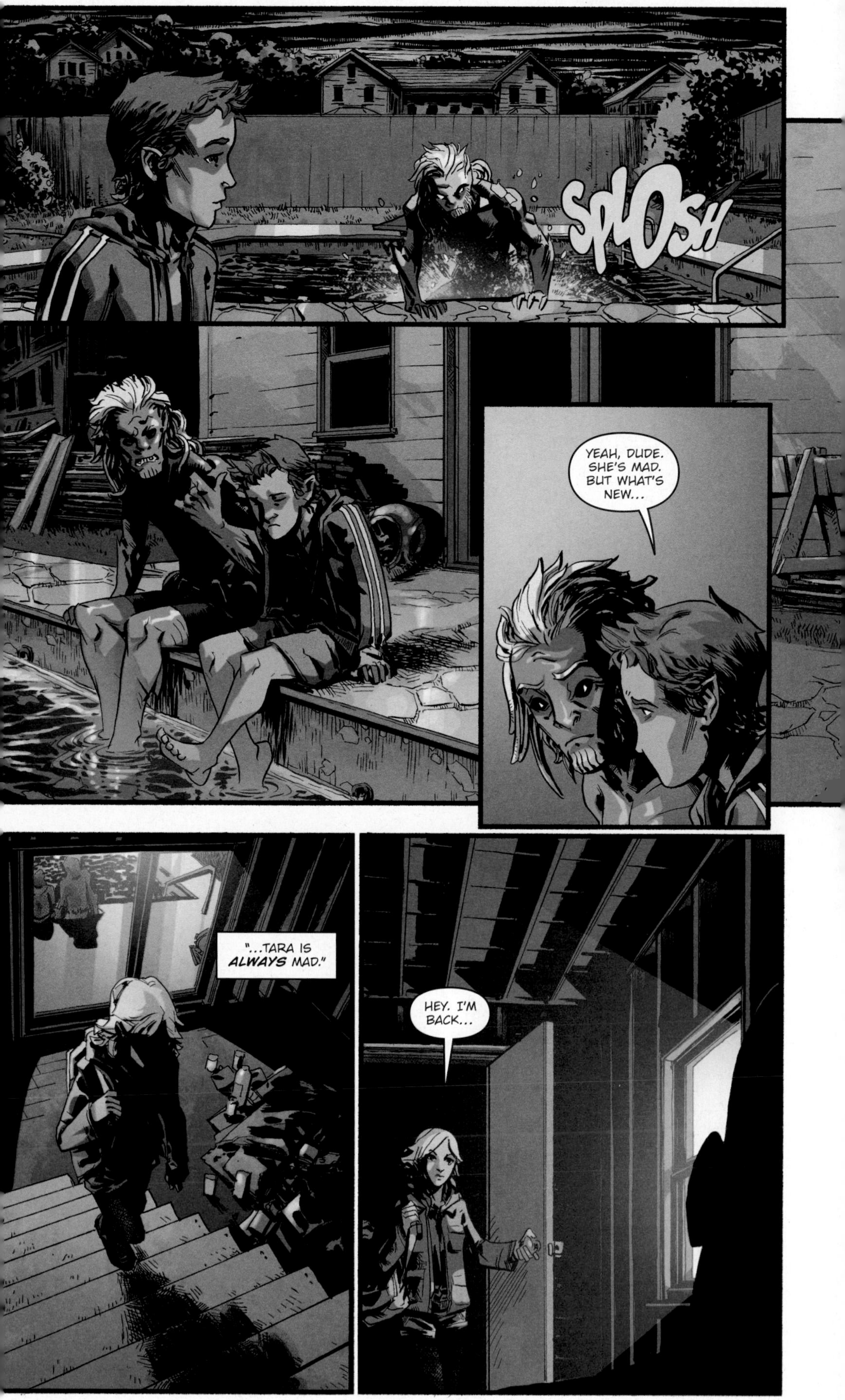
SPLOSH
YEAH, DUDE. SHE'S MAD. BUT WHAT'S NEW...
"...TARA IS ALWAYS MAD."
HEY. I'M BACK...

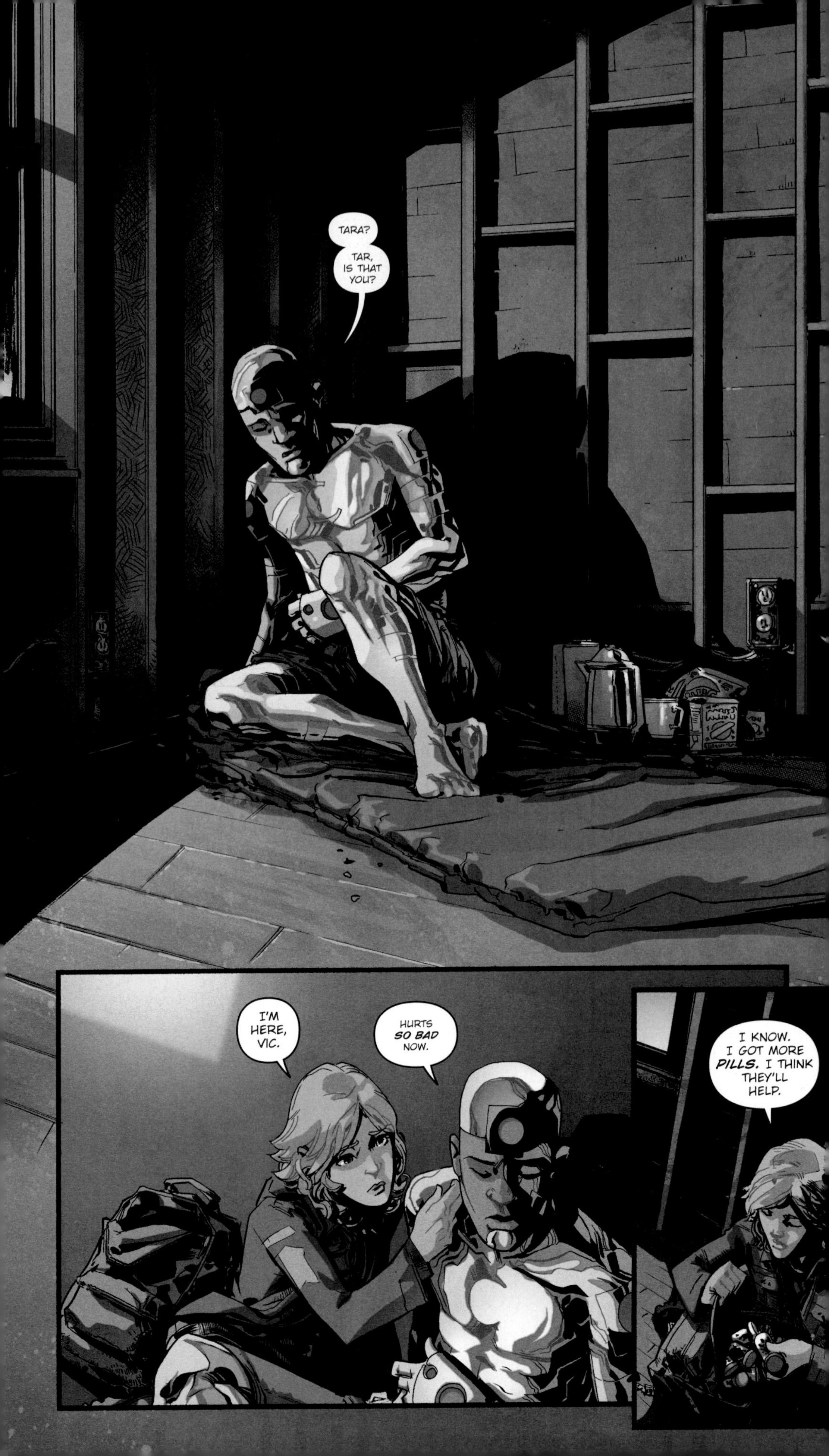

TARA?
TAR, IS THAT YOU?
I'M HERE, VIC.
HURTS SO BAD NOW.
I KNOW. I GOT MORE PILLS. I THINK THEY'LL HELP.

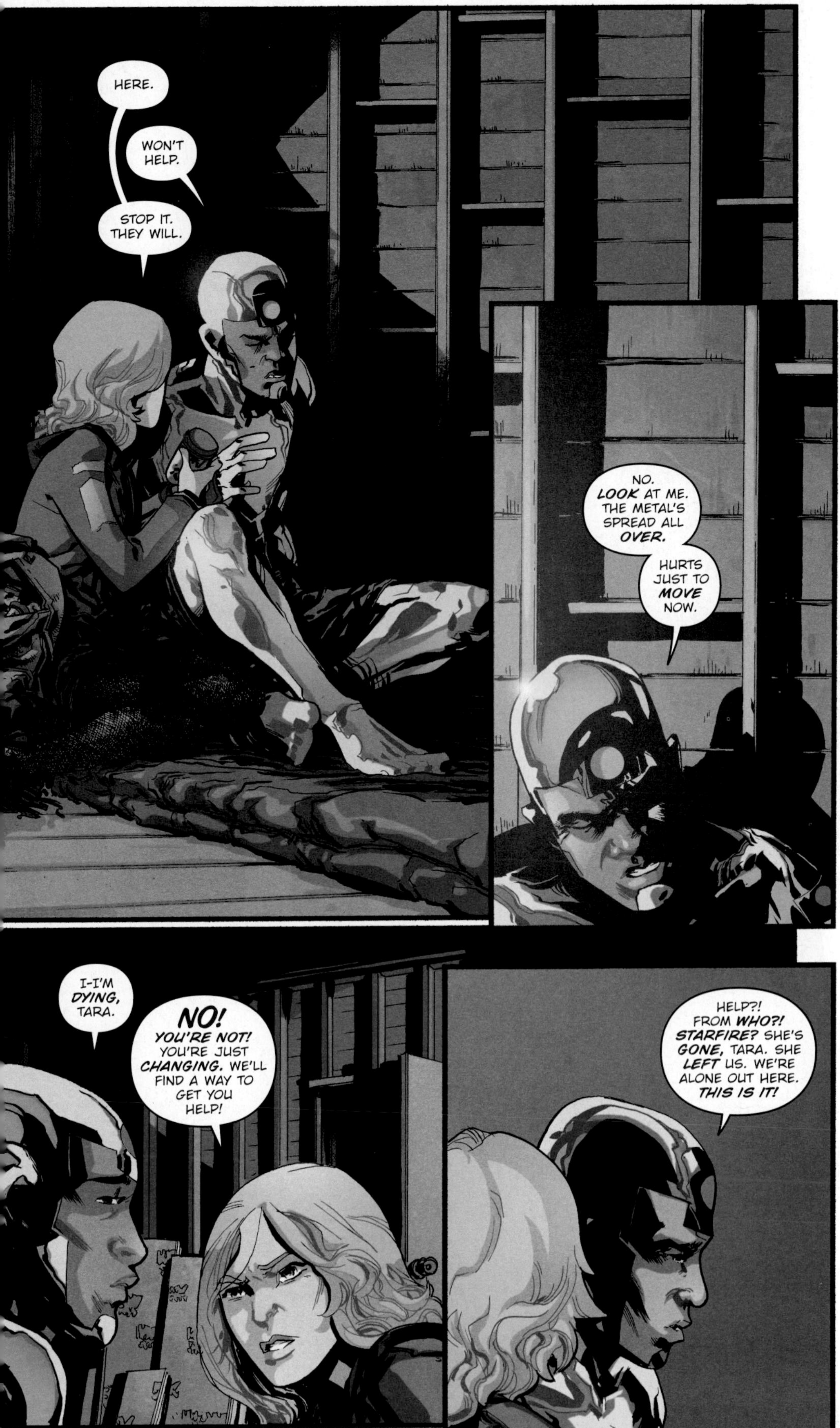
HERE.
WON'T HELP.
STOP IT. THEY WILL.
NO. **LOOK** AT ME. THE METAL'S SPREAD ALL **OVER.**
HURTS JUST TO **MOVE** NOW.
I-I'M **DYING,** TARA.
NO! YOU'RE NOT! YOU'RE JUST **CHANGING.** WE'LL FIND A WAY TO GET YOU HELP!
HELP?! FROM **WHO?! STARFIRE?** SHE'S **GONE,** TARA. SHE **LEFT** US. WE'RE ALONE OUT HERE. **THIS IS IT!**

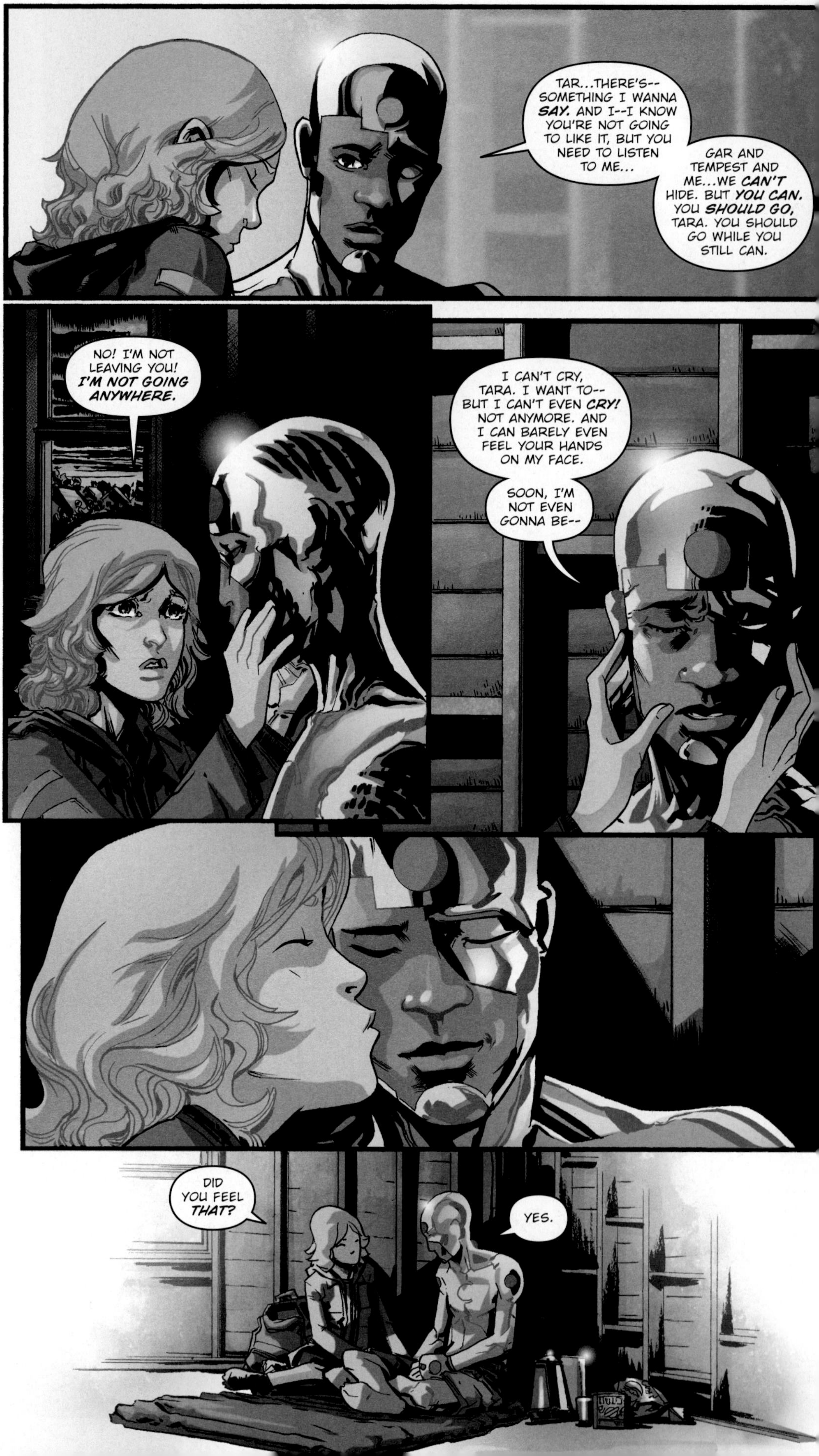
TAR...THERE'S--SOMETHING I WANNA SAY. AND I--I KNOW YOU'RE NOT GOING TO LIKE IT, BUT YOU NEED TO LISTEN TO ME...
GAR AND TEMPEST AND ME...WE CAN'T HIDE. BUT YOU CAN. YOU SHOULD GO, TARA. YOU SHOULD GO WHILE YOU STILL CAN.
NO! I'M NOT LEAVING YOU! I'M NOT GOING ANYWHERE.
I CAN'T CRY, TARA. I WANT TO--BUT I CAN'T EVEN CRY! NOT ANYMORE. AND I CAN BARELY EVEN FEEL YOUR HANDS ON MY FACE.
SOON, I'M NOT EVEN GONNA BE--
DID YOU FEEL THAT?
YES.

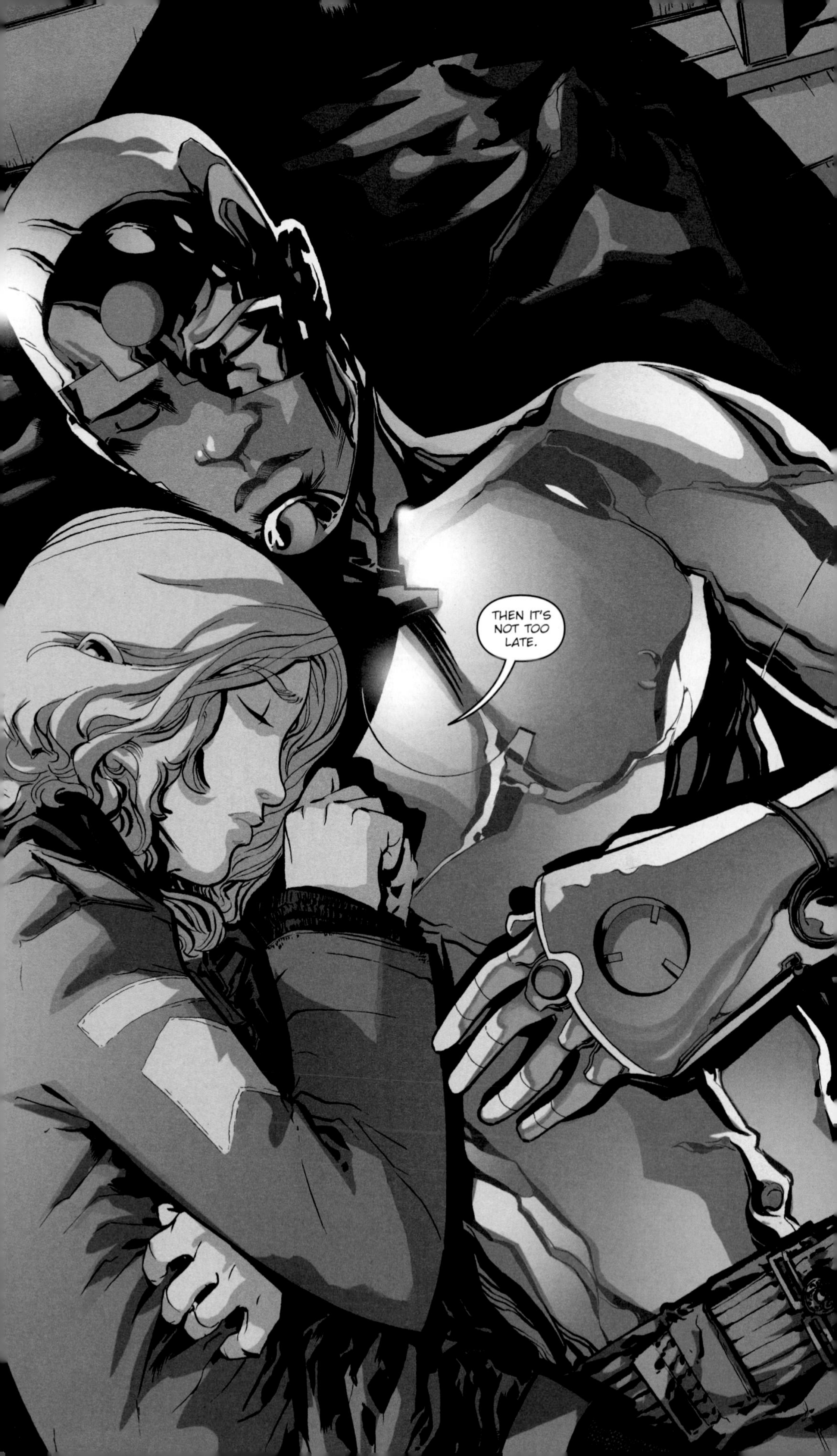
THEN IT'S NOT TOO LATE.

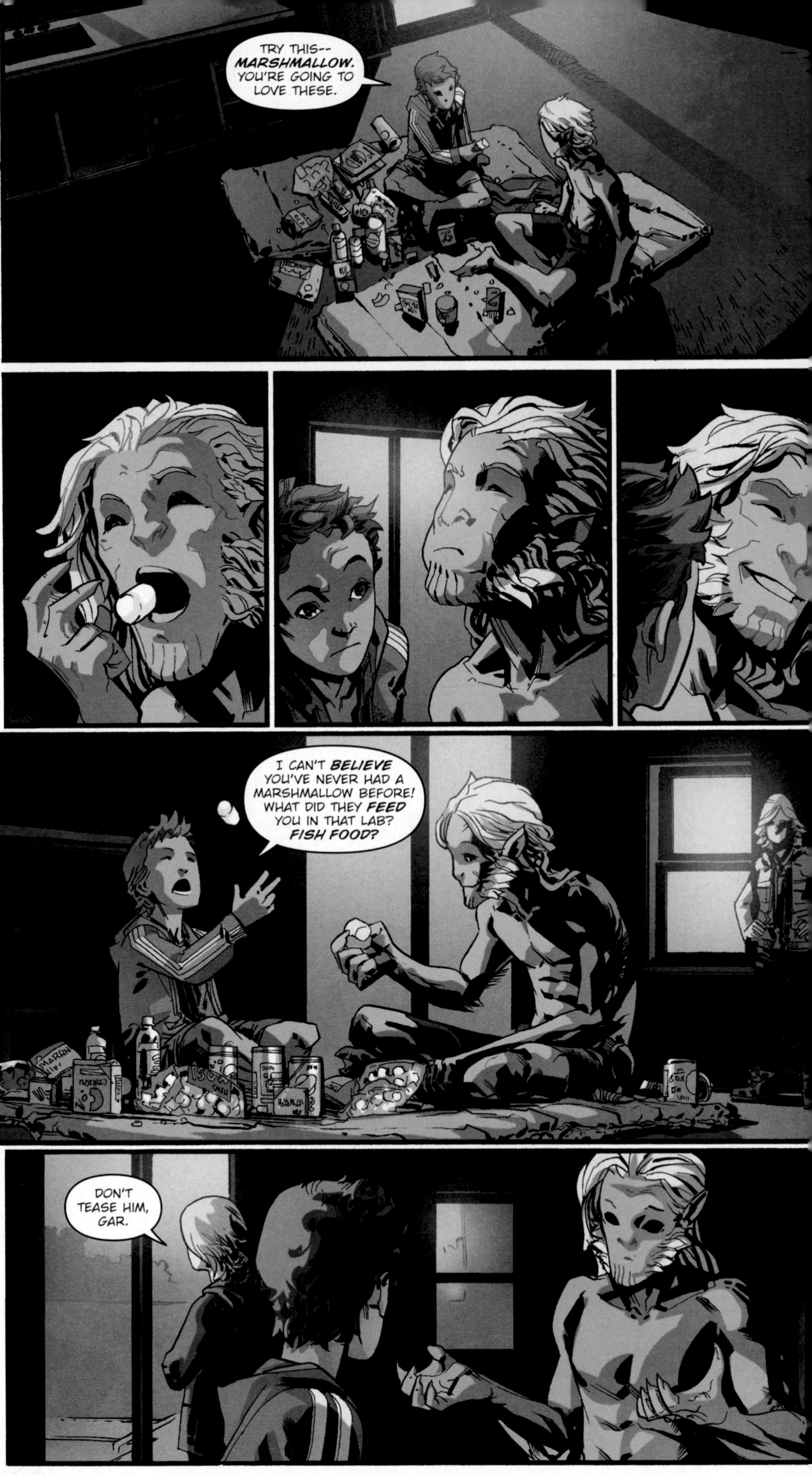
TRY THIS-- MARSHMALLOW. YOU'RE GOING TO LOVE THESE.
I CAN'T BELIEVE YOU'VE NEVER HAD A MARSHMALLOW BEFORE! WHAT DID THEY FEED YOU IN THAT LAB? FISH FOOD?
DON'T TEASE HIM, GAR.

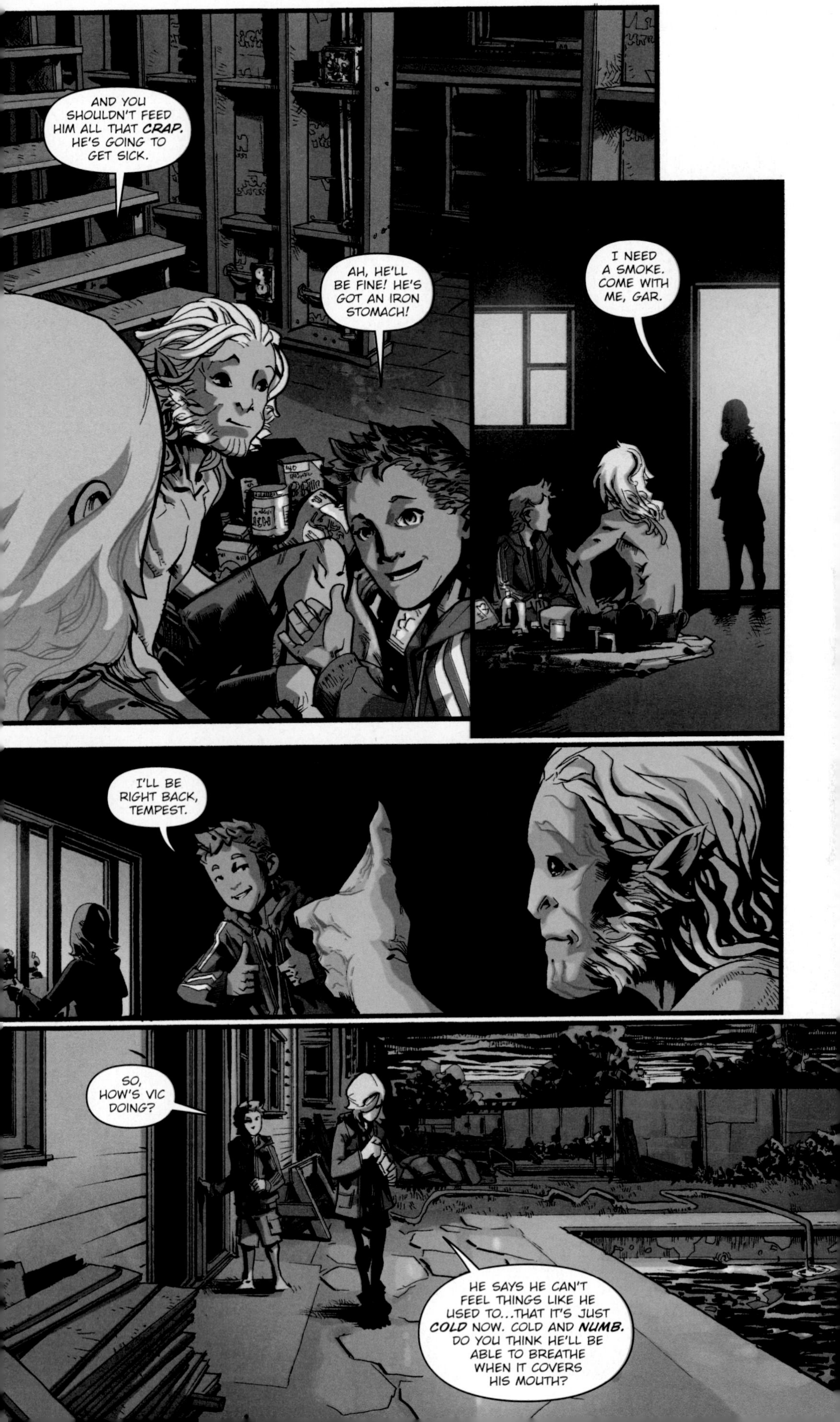
AND YOU SHOULDN'T FEED HIM ALL THAT CRAP. HE'S GOING TO GET SICK.
AH, HE'LL BE FINE! HE'S GOT AN IRON STOMACH!
I NEED A SMOKE. COME WITH ME, GAR.
I'LL BE RIGHT BACK, TEMPEST.
SO, HOW'S VIC DOING?
HE SAYS HE CAN'T FEEL THINGS LIKE HE USED TO...THAT IT'S JUST COLD NOW. COLD AND NUMB. DO YOU THINK HE'LL BE ABLE TO BREATHE WHEN IT COVERS HIS MOUTH?

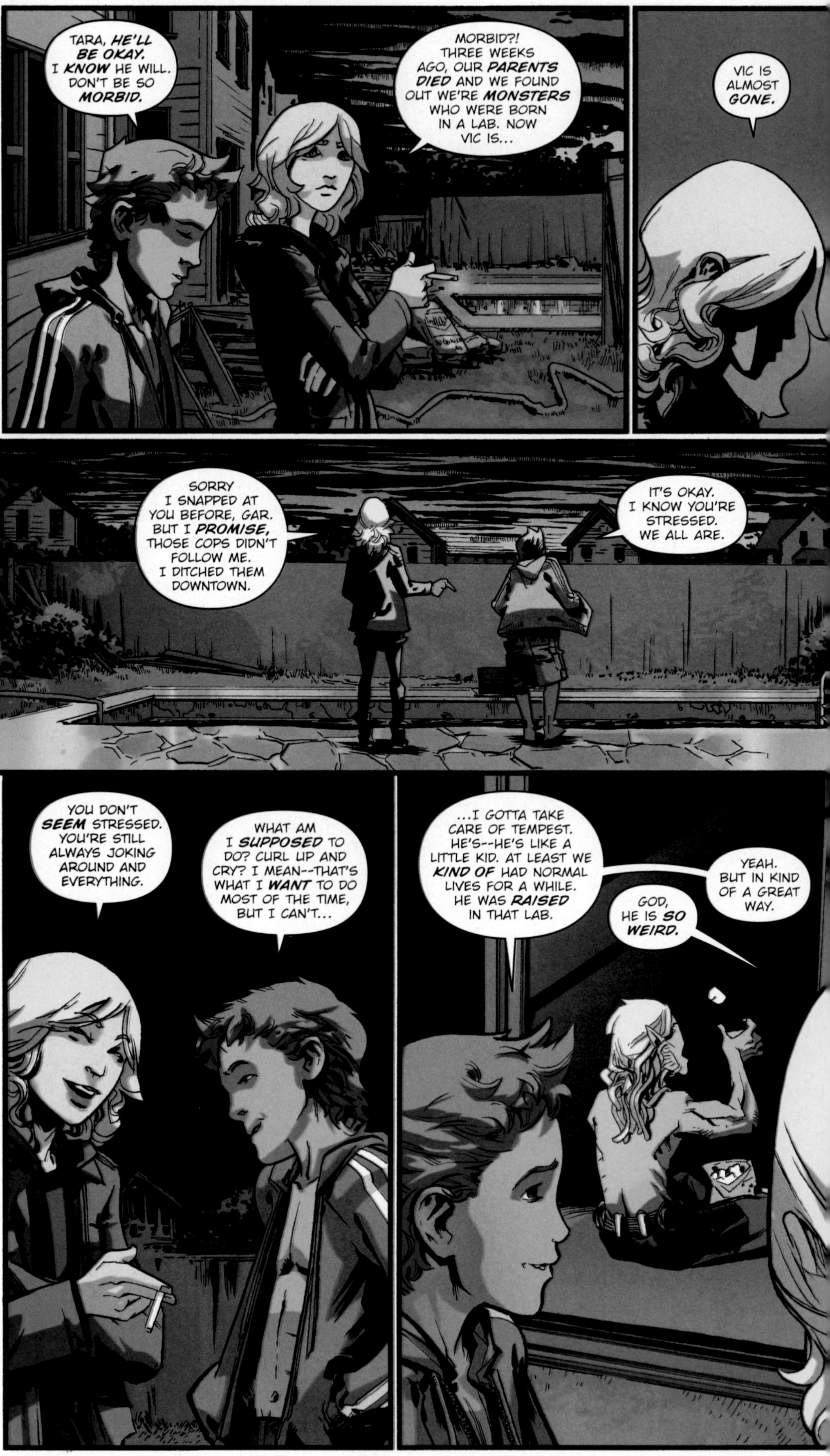
TARA, HE'LL BE OKAY. I KNOW HE WILL. DON'T BE SO MORBID.
MORBID?! THREE WEEKS AGO, OUR PARENTS DIED AND WE FOUND OUT WE'RE MONSTERS WHO WERE BORN IN A LAB. NOW VIC IS...
VIC IS ALMOST GONE.
SORRY I SNAPPED AT YOU BEFORE, GAR. BUT I PROMISE, THOSE COPS DIDN'T FOLLOW ME. I DITCHED THEM DOWNTOWN.
IT'S OKAY. I KNOW YOU'RE STRESSED. WE ALL ARE.
YOU DON'T SEEM STRESSED. YOU'RE STILL ALWAYS JOKING AROUND AND EVERYTHING.
WHAT AM I SUPPOSED TO DO? CURL UP AND CRY? I MEAN--THAT'S WHAT I WANT TO DO MOST OF THE TIME, BUT I CAN'T...
...I GOTTA TAKE CARE OF TEMPEST. HE'S--HE'S LIKE A LITTLE KID. AT LEAST WE KIND OF HAD NORMAL LIVES FOR A WHILE. HE WAS RAISED IN THAT LAB.
GOD, HE IS SO WEIRD.
YEAH. BUT IN KIND OF A GREAT WAY.

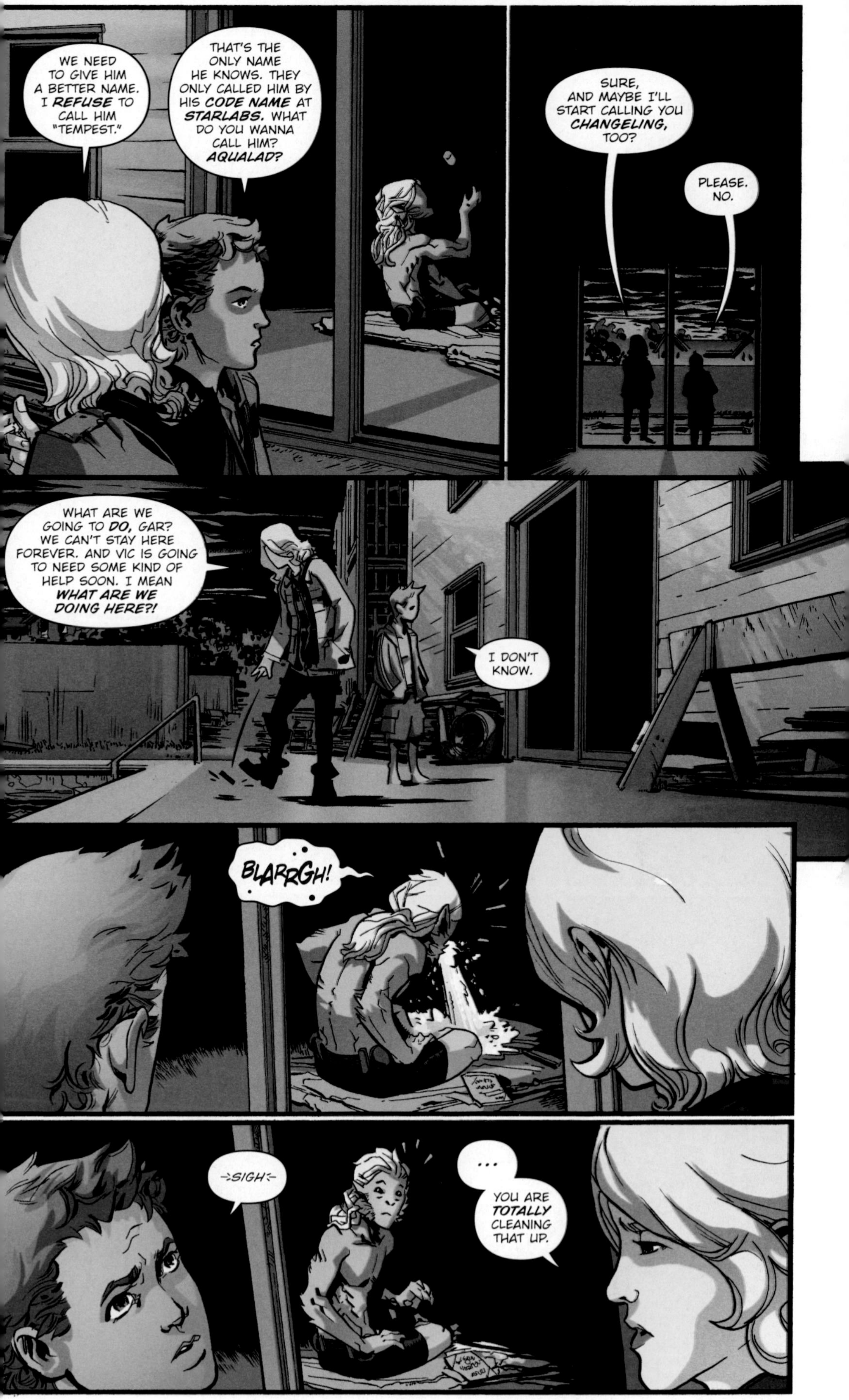

WE NEED TO GIVE HIM A BETTER NAME. I REFUSE TO CALL HIM "TEMPEST."
THAT'S THE ONLY NAME HE KNOWS. THEY ONLY CALLED HIM BY HIS CODE NAME AT STARLABS. WHAT DO YOU WANNA CALL HIM? AQUALAD?
SURE, AND MAYBE I'LL START CALLING YOU CHANGELING, TOO?
PLEASE. NO.
WHAT ARE WE GOING TO DO, GAR? WE CAN'T STAY HERE FOREVER. AND VIC IS GOING TO NEED SOME KIND OF HELP SOON. I MEAN WHAT ARE WE DOING HERE?!
I DON'T KNOW.
BLARRGH!
SIGH
...
YOU ARE TOTALLY CLEANING THAT UP.

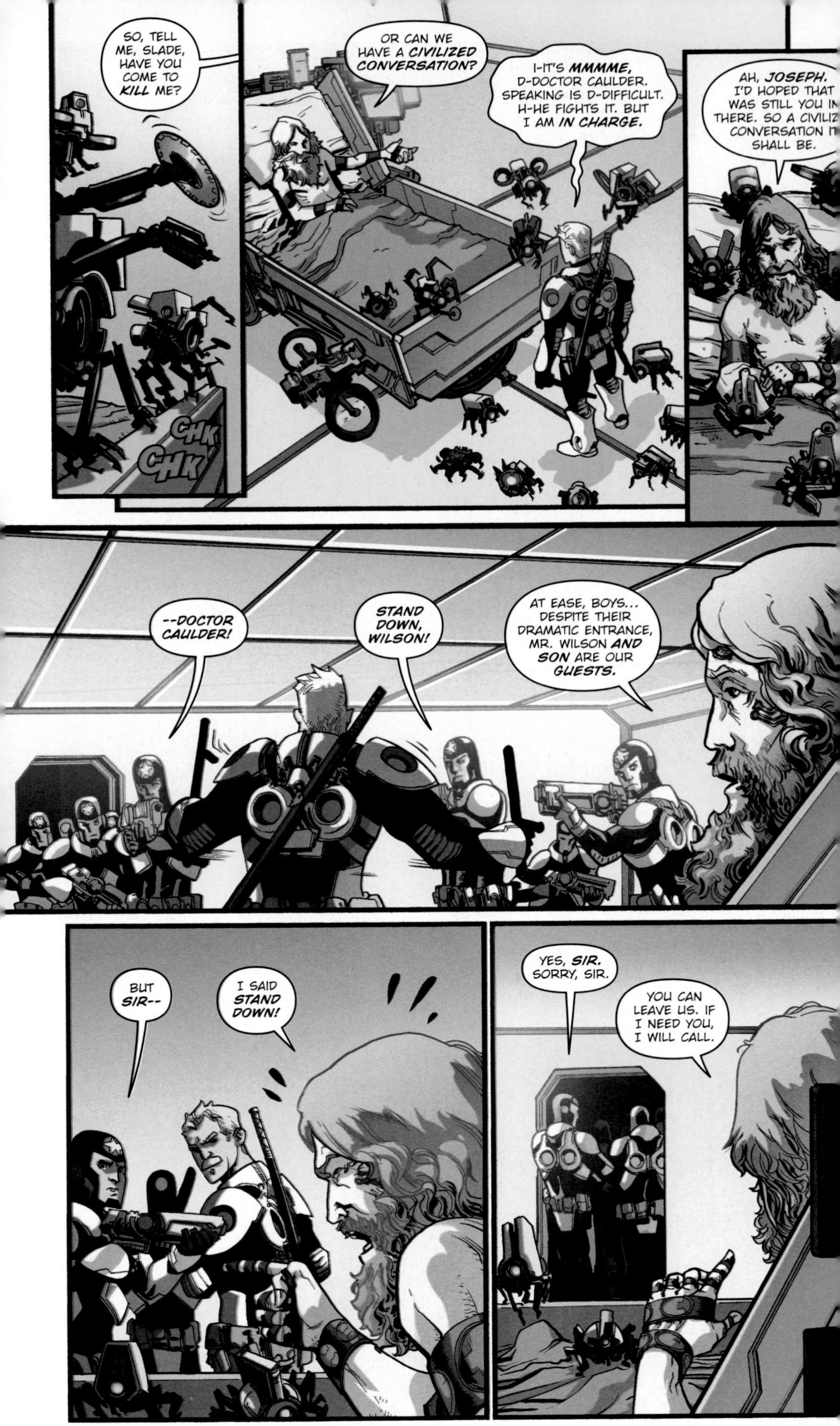
SO, TELL ME, SLADE, HAVE YOU COME TO KILL ME?
CHK CHK
OR CAN WE HAVE A CIVILIZED CONVERSATION?
I-IT'S MMMME, D-DOCTOR CAULDER. SPEAKING IS D-DIFFICULT. H-HE FIGHTS IT. BUT I AM IN CHARGE.
AH, JOSEPH. I'D HOPED THAT WAS STILL YOU IN THERE. SO A CIVILIZ CONVERSATION IT SHALL BE.
--DOCTOR CAULDER!
STAND DOWN, WILSON!
AT EASE, BOYS... DESPITE THEIR DRAMATIC ENTRANCE, MR. WILSON AND SON ARE OUR GUESTS.
BUT SIR--
I SAID STAND DOWN!
YES, SIR. SORRY, SIR.
YOU CAN LEAVE US. IF I NEED YOU, I WILL CALL.

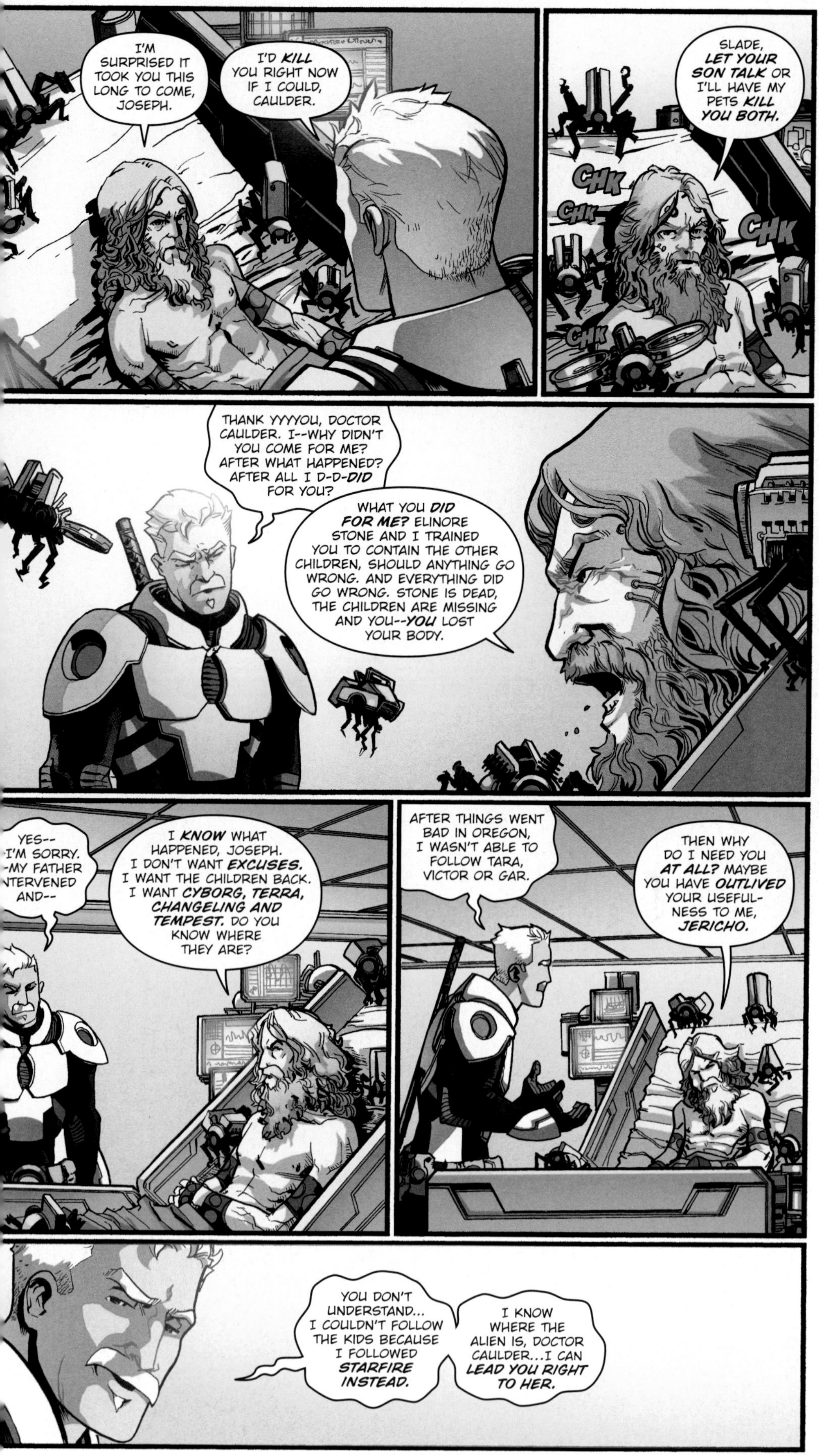

I'M SURPRISED IT TOOK YOU THIS LONG TO COME, JOSEPH.
I'D KILL YOU RIGHT NOW IF I COULD, CAULDER.
SLADE, LET YOUR SON TALK OR I'LL HAVE MY PETS KILL YOU BOTH.
CHK
CHK
CHK
CHK
THANK YYYYOU, DOCTOR CAULDER. I--WHY DIDN'T YOU COME FOR ME? AFTER WHAT HAPPENED? AFTER ALL I D-D-DID FOR YOU?
WHAT YOU DID FOR ME? ELINORE STONE AND I TRAINED YOU TO CONTAIN THE OTHER CHILDREN, SHOULD ANYTHING GO WRONG. AND EVERYTHING DID GO WRONG. STONE IS DEAD, THE CHILDREN ARE MISSING AND YOU--YOU LOST YOUR BODY.
YES-- I'M SORRY. -MY FATHER NTERVENED AND--
I KNOW WHAT HAPPENED, JOSEPH. I DON'T WANT EXCUSES. I WANT THE CHILDREN BACK. I WANT CYBORG, TERRA, CHANGELING AND TEMPEST. DO YOU KNOW WHERE THEY ARE?
AFTER THINGS WENT BAD IN OREGON, I WASN'T ABLE TO FOLLOW TARA, VICTOR OR GAR.
THEN WHY DO I NEED YOU AT ALL? MAYBE YOU HAVE OUTLIVED YOUR USEFUL-NESS TO ME, JERICHO.
YOU DON'T UNDERSTAND... I COULDN'T FOLLOW THE KIDS BECAUSE I FOLLOWED STARFIRE INSTEAD.
I KNOW WHERE THE ALIEN IS, DOCTOR CAULDER...I CAN LEAD YOU RIGHT TO HER.

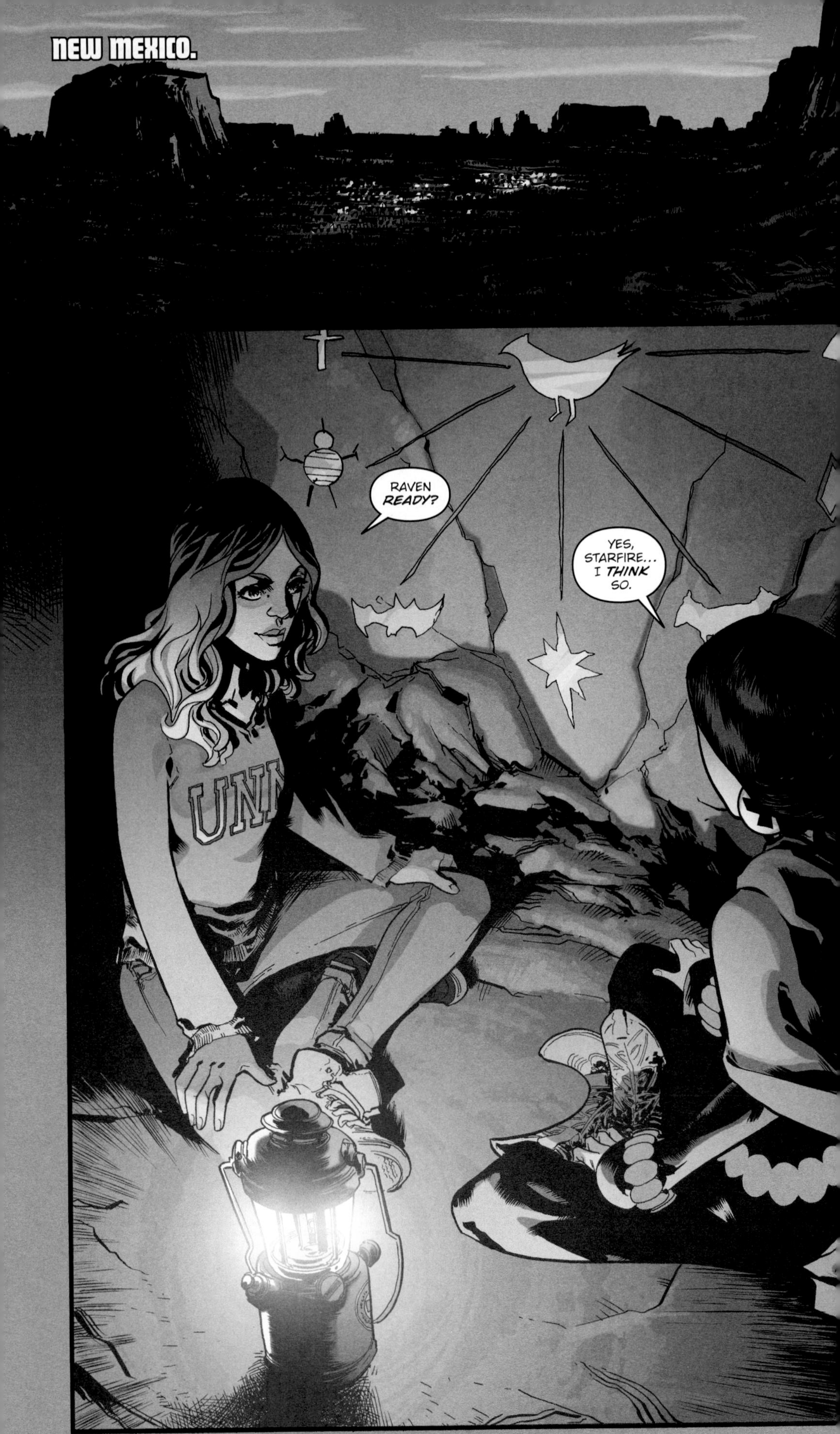
NEW MEXICO.
RAVEN READY?
YES, STARFIRE... I THINK SO.
UNM

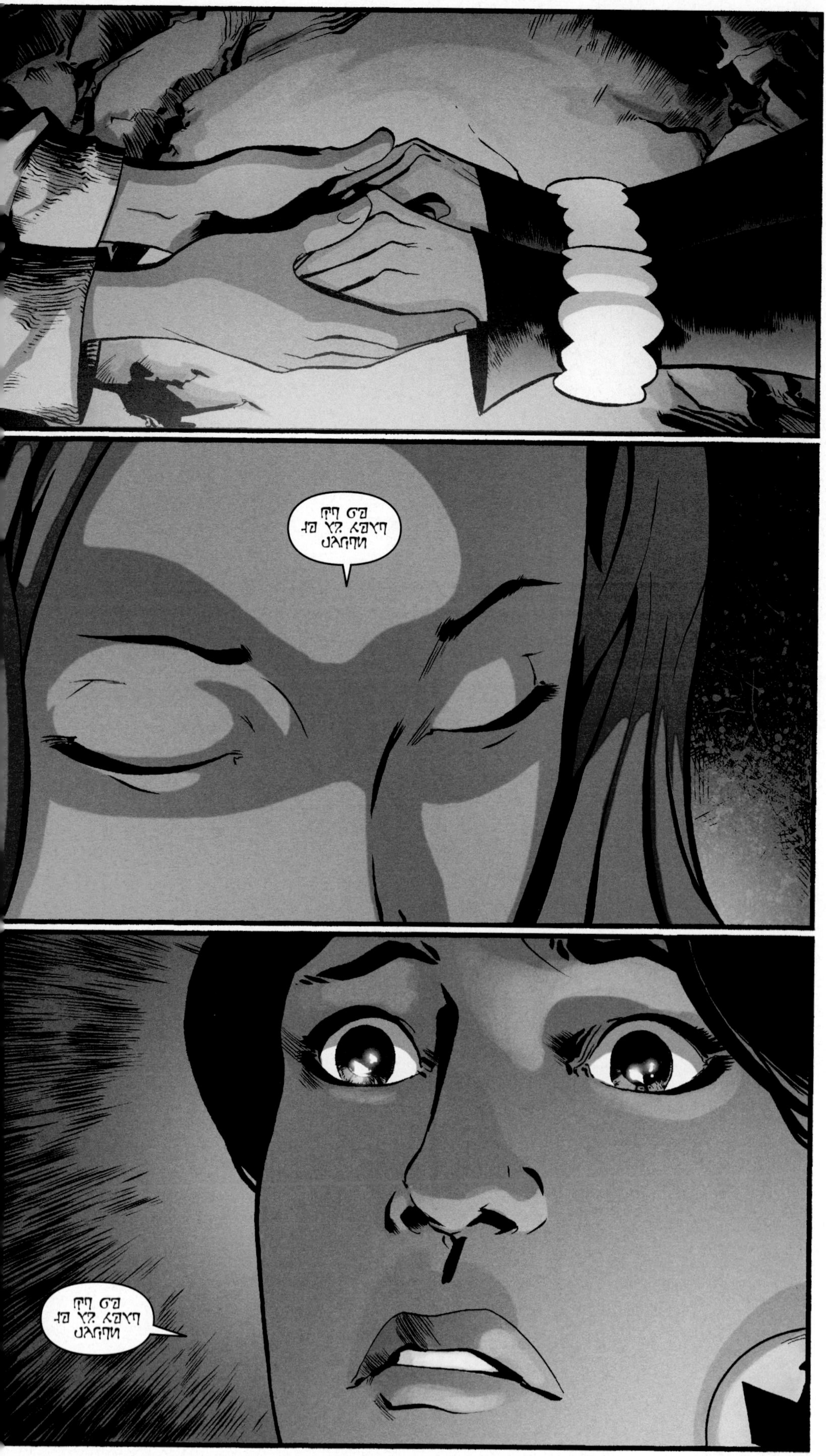

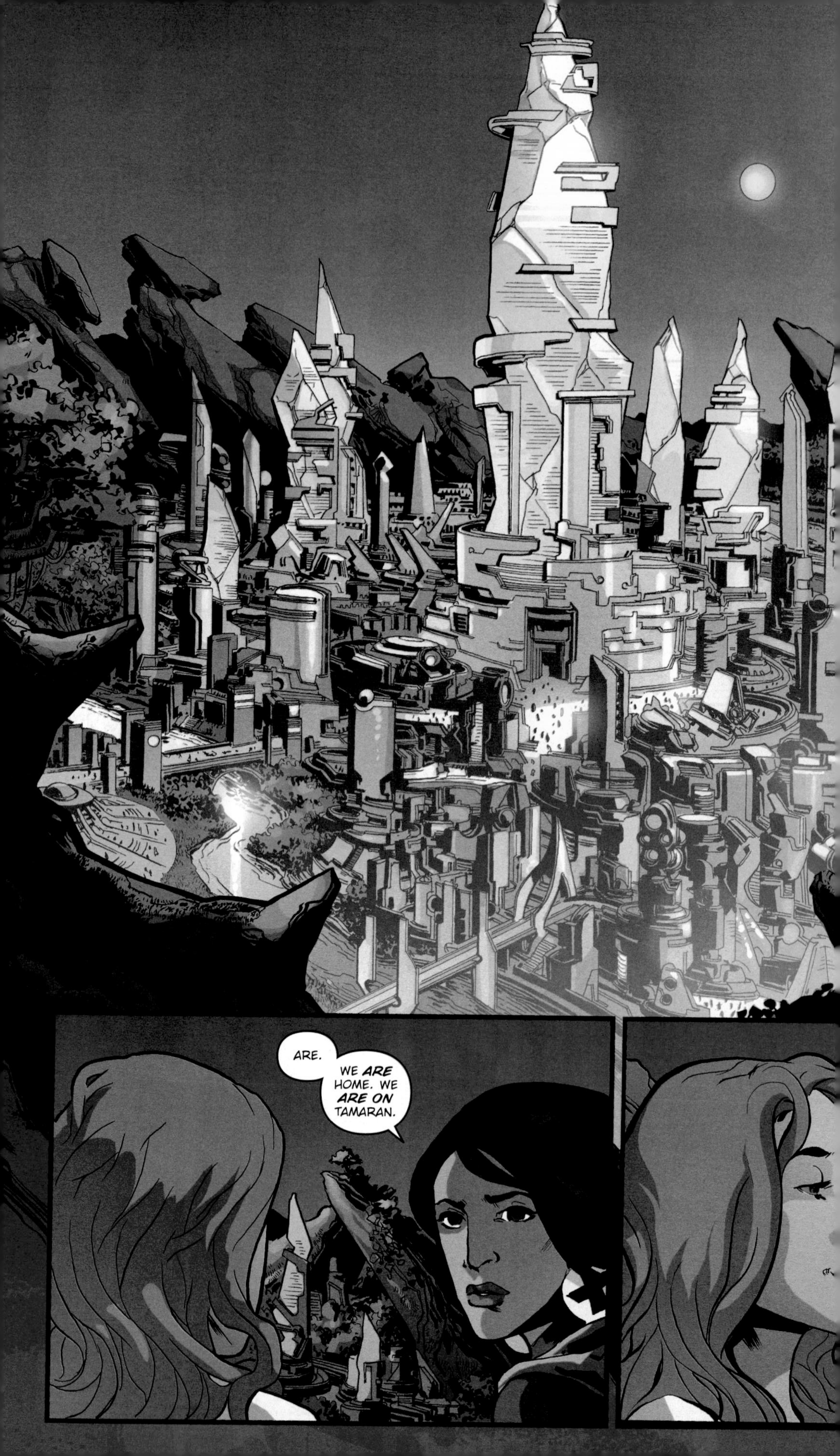
ARE.
WE ARE HOME. WE ARE ON TAMARAN.

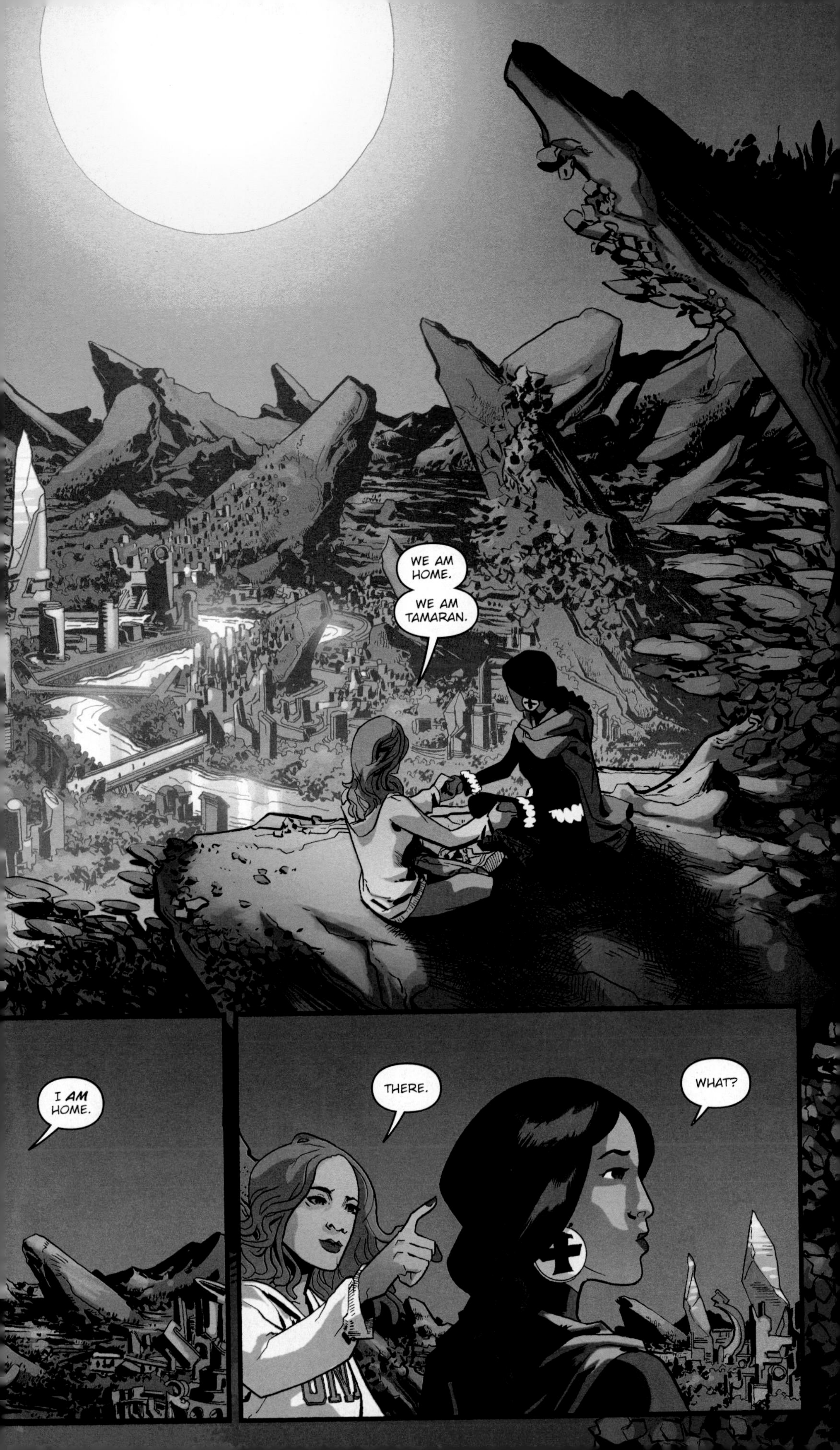
WE AM HOME.
WE AM TAMARAN.
I *AM* HOME.
THERE.
WHAT?

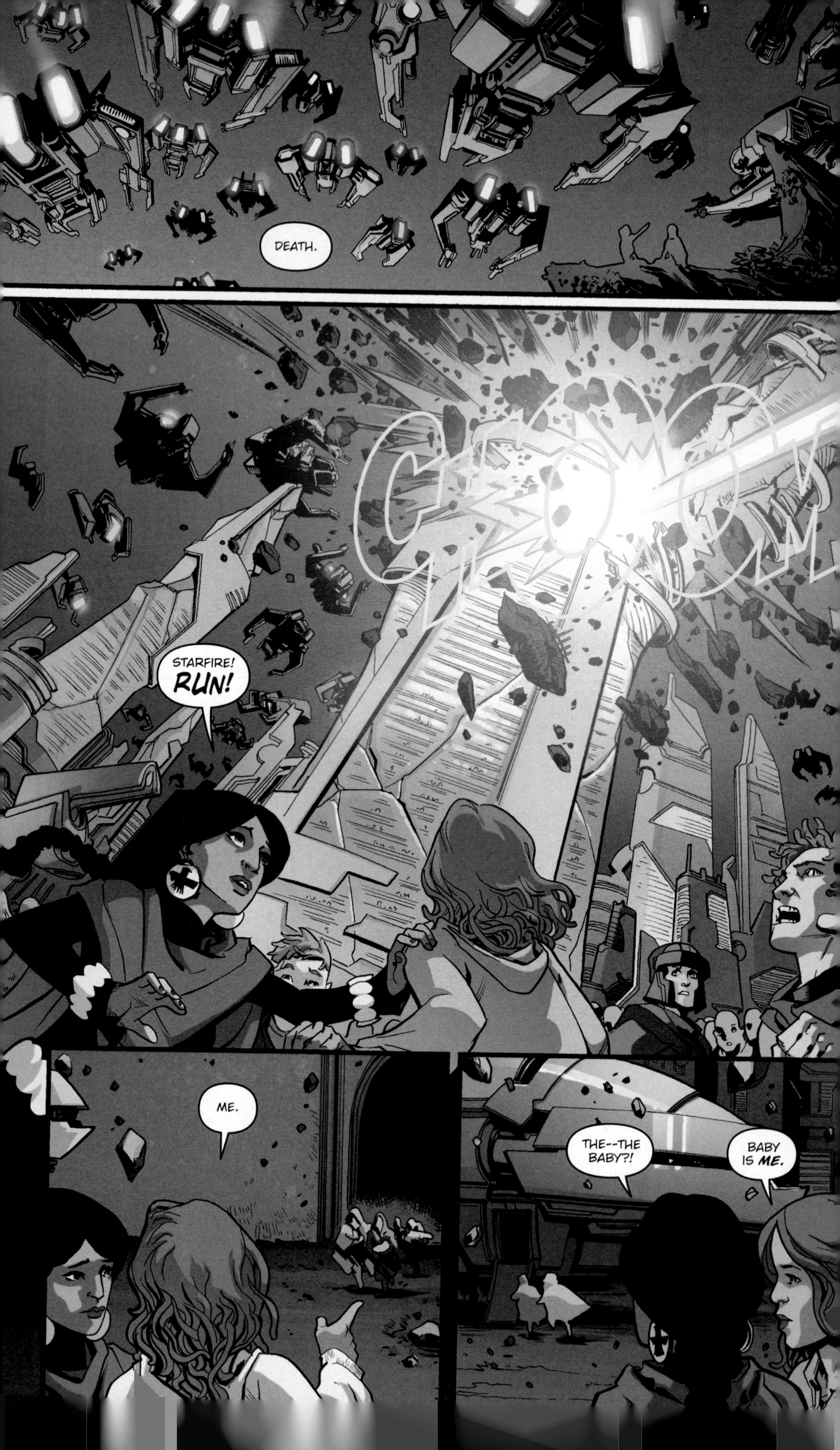
DEATH.
STARFIRE! RUN!
ME.
THE--THE BABY?!
BABY IS ME.

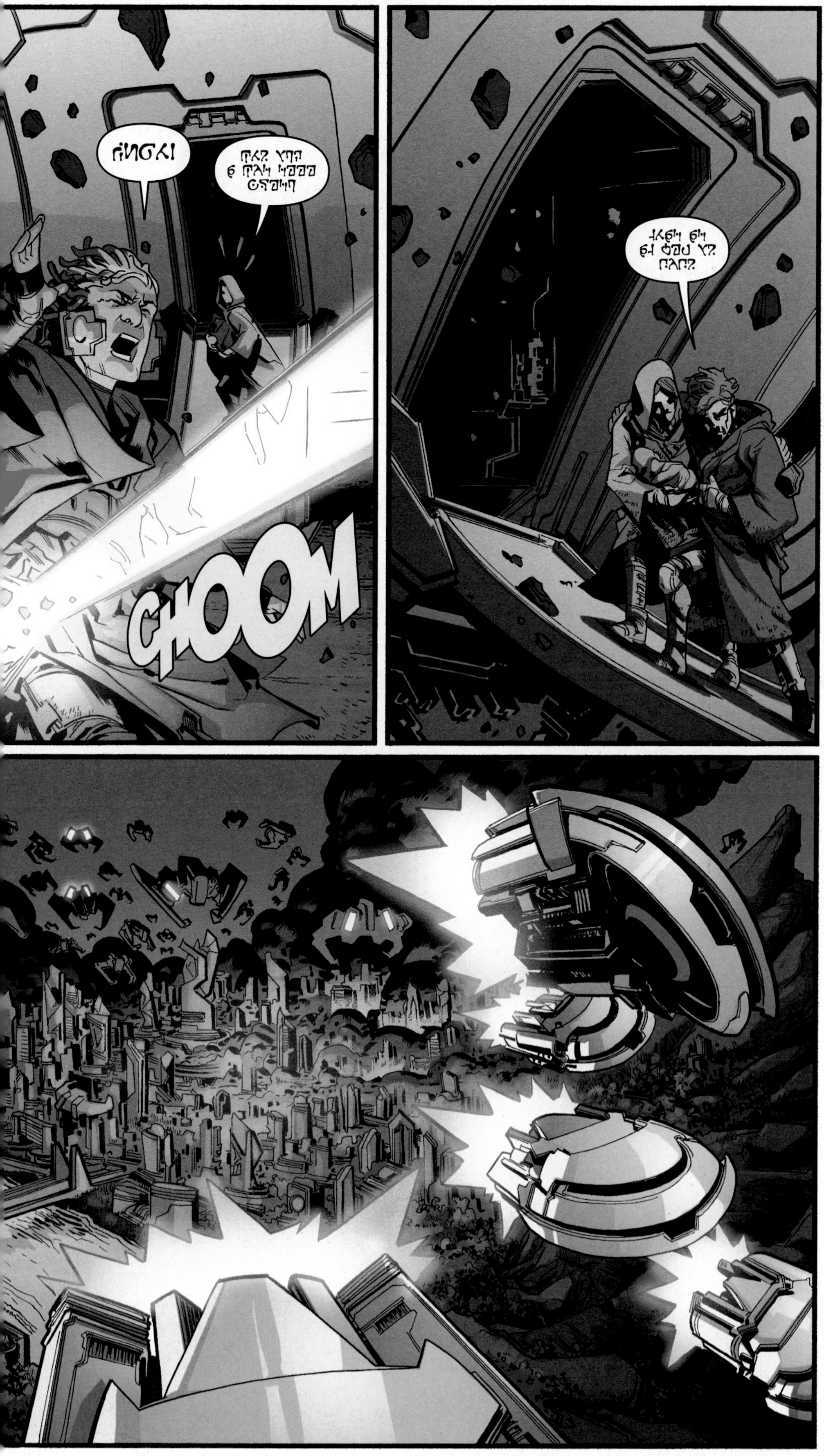
CHOOM

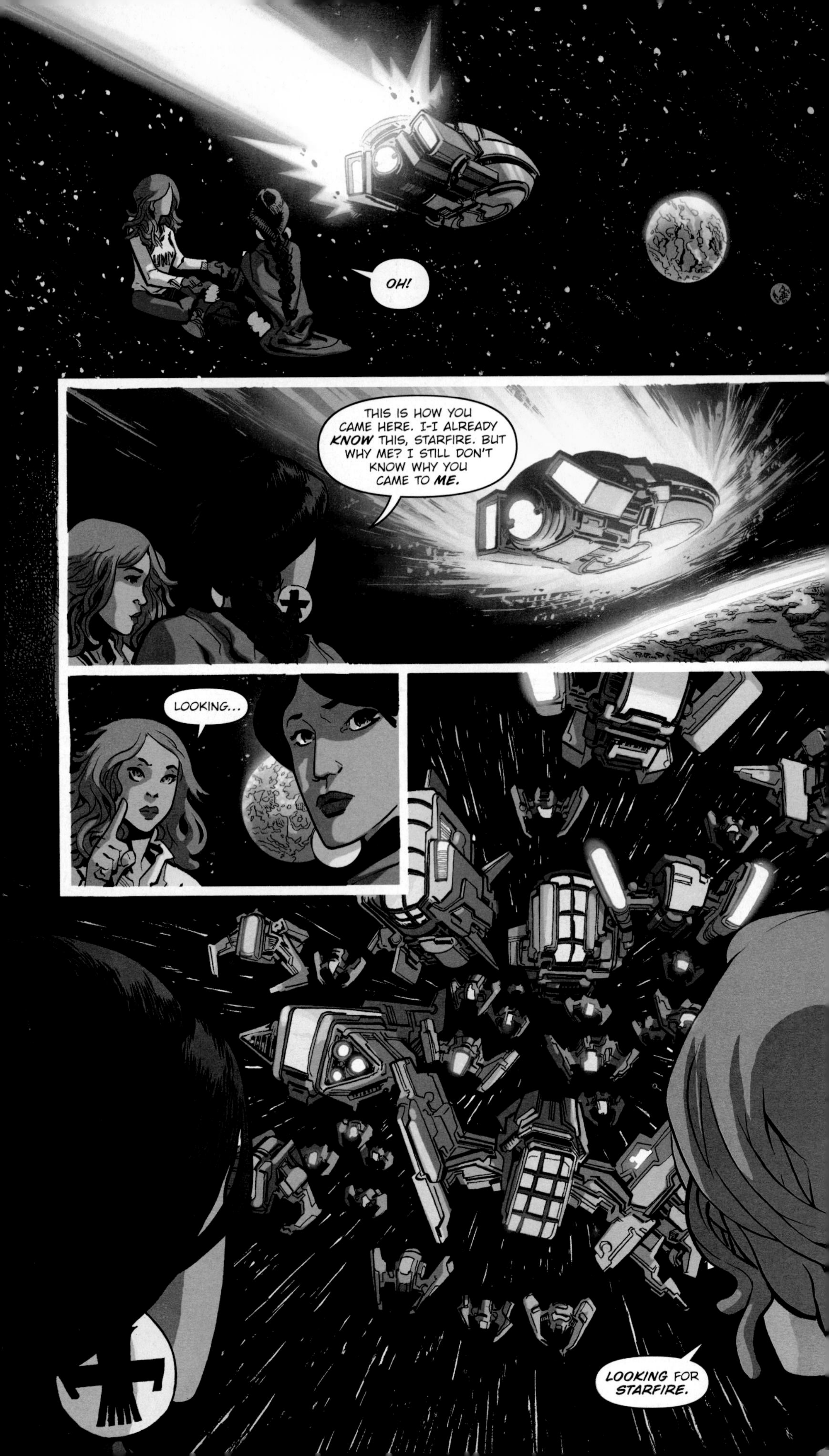
OH!
THIS IS HOW YOU CAME HERE. I-I ALREADY KNOW THIS, STARFIRE. BUT WHY ME? I STILL DON'T KNOW WHY YOU CAME TO ME.
LOOKING...
LOOKING FOR STARFIRE.

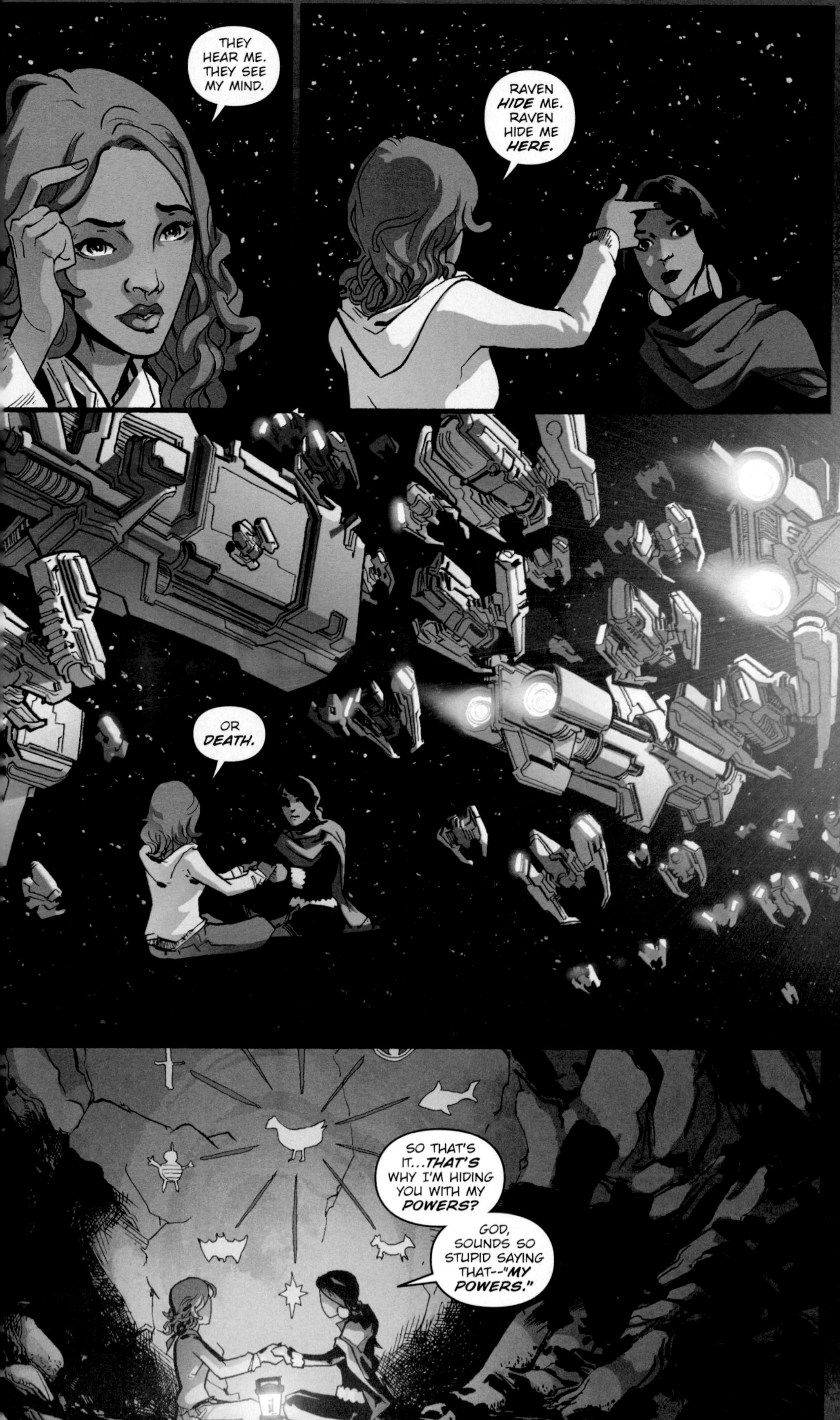
THEY HEAR ME. THEY SEE MY MIND.
RAVEN HIDE ME. RAVEN HIDE ME HERE.
OR DEATH.
SO THAT'S IT...THAT'S WHY I'M HIDING YOU WITH MY POWERS?
GOD, SOUNDS SO STUPID SAYING THAT--"MY POWERS."

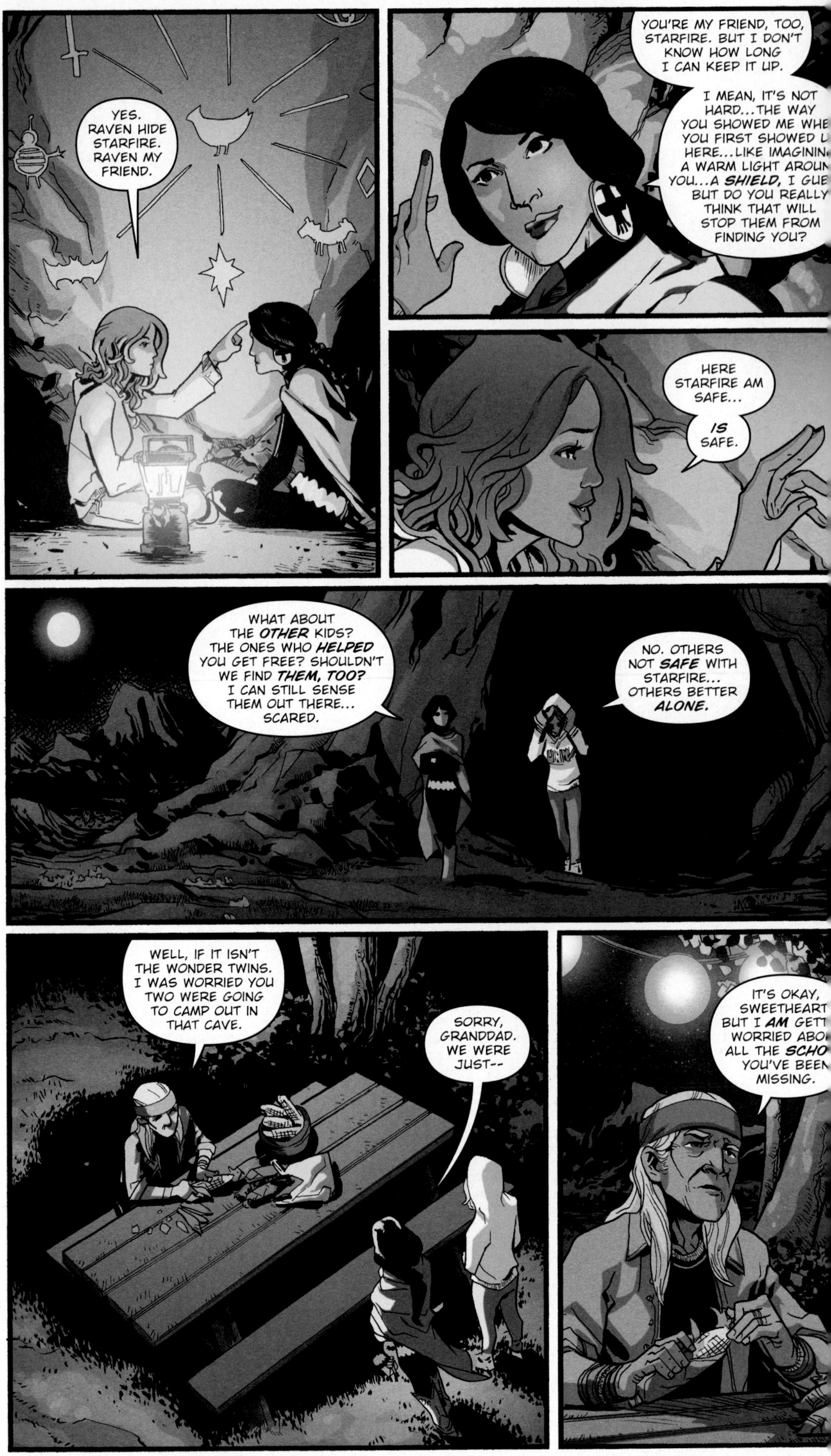
YES. RAVEN HIDE STARFIRE. RAVEN MY FRIEND.
YOU'RE MY FRIEND, TOO, STARFIRE. BUT I DON'T KNOW HOW LONG I CAN KEEP IT UP.
I MEAN, IT'S NOT HARD...THE WAY YOU SHOWED ME WHE YOU FIRST SHOWED U HERE...LIKE IMAGININ A WARM LIGHT AROUN YOU...A *SHIELD,* I GUE BUT DO YOU REALLY THINK THAT WILL STOP THEM FROM FINDING YOU?
HERE STARFIRE AM SAFE...
IS SAFE.
WHAT ABOUT THE *OTHER* KIDS? THE ONES WHO *HELPED* YOU GET FREE? SHOULDN'T WE FIND *THEM, TOO?* I CAN STILL SENSE THEM OUT THERE... SCARED.
NO. OTHERS NOT *SAFE* WITH STARFIRE... OTHERS BETTER *ALONE.*
WELL, IF IT ISN'T THE WONDER TWINS. I WAS WORRIED YOU TWO WERE GOING TO CAMP OUT IN THAT CAVE.
SORRY, GRANDDAD. WE WERE JUST--
IT'S OKAY, SWEETHEART BUT I *AM* GETT WORRIED ABO ALL THE *SCHO* YOU'VE BEEN MISSING.

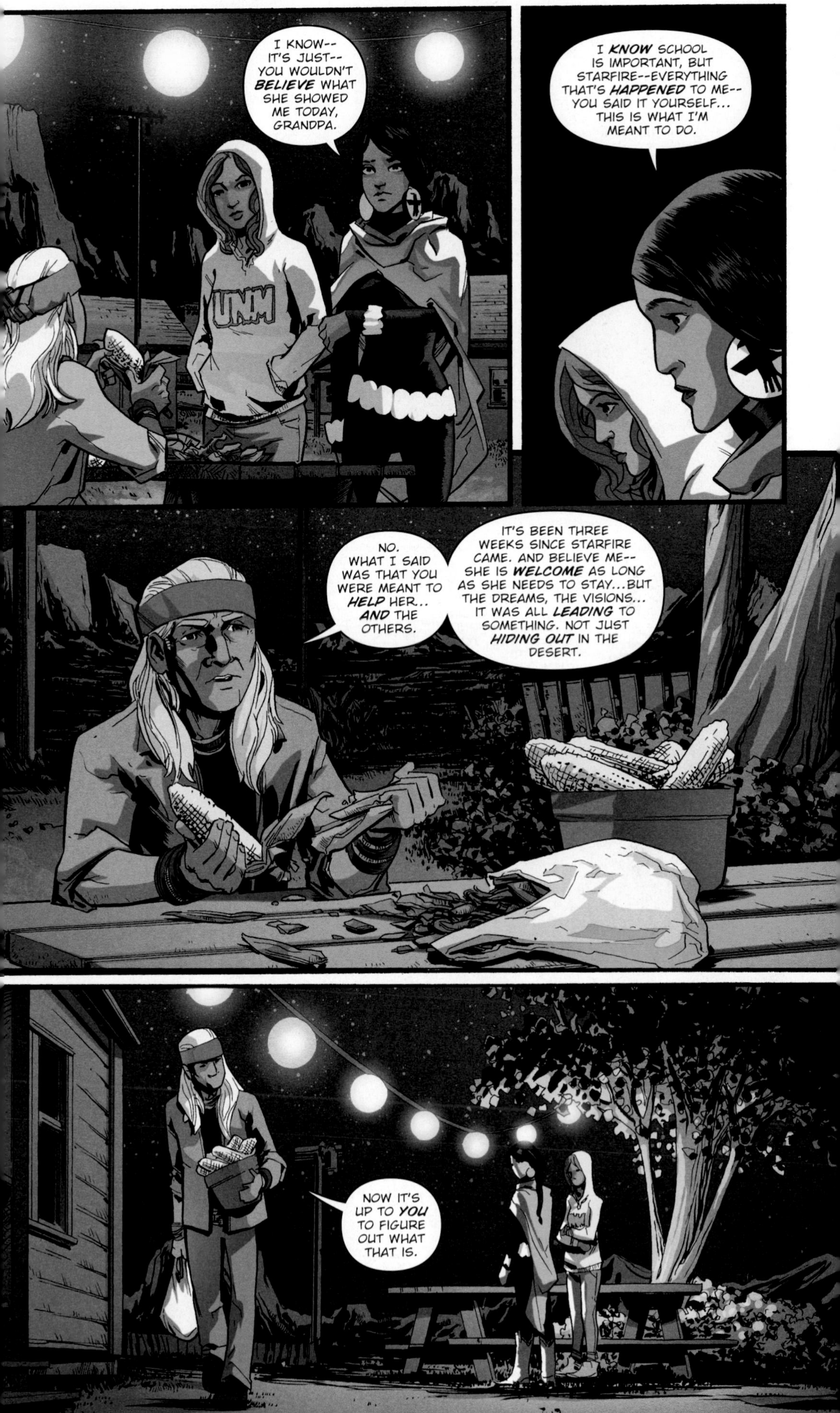
I KNOW--
IT'S JUST--
YOU WOULDN'T BELIEVE WHAT SHE SHOWED ME TODAY, GRANDPA.
I KNOW SCHOOL IS IMPORTANT, BUT STARFIRE--EVERYTHING THAT'S HAPPENED TO ME--
YOU SAID IT YOURSELF... THIS IS WHAT I'M MEANT TO DO.
UNM
NO. WHAT I SAID WAS THAT YOU WERE MEANT TO HELP HER... AND THE OTHERS.
IT'S BEEN THREE WEEKS SINCE STARFIRE CAME. AND BELIEVE ME--SHE IS WELCOME AS LONG AS SHE NEEDS TO STAY...BUT THE DREAMS, THE VISIONS... IT WAS ALL LEADING TO SOMETHING. NOT JUST HIDING OUT IN THE DESERT.
NOW IT'S UP TO YOU TO FIGURE OUT WHAT THAT IS.

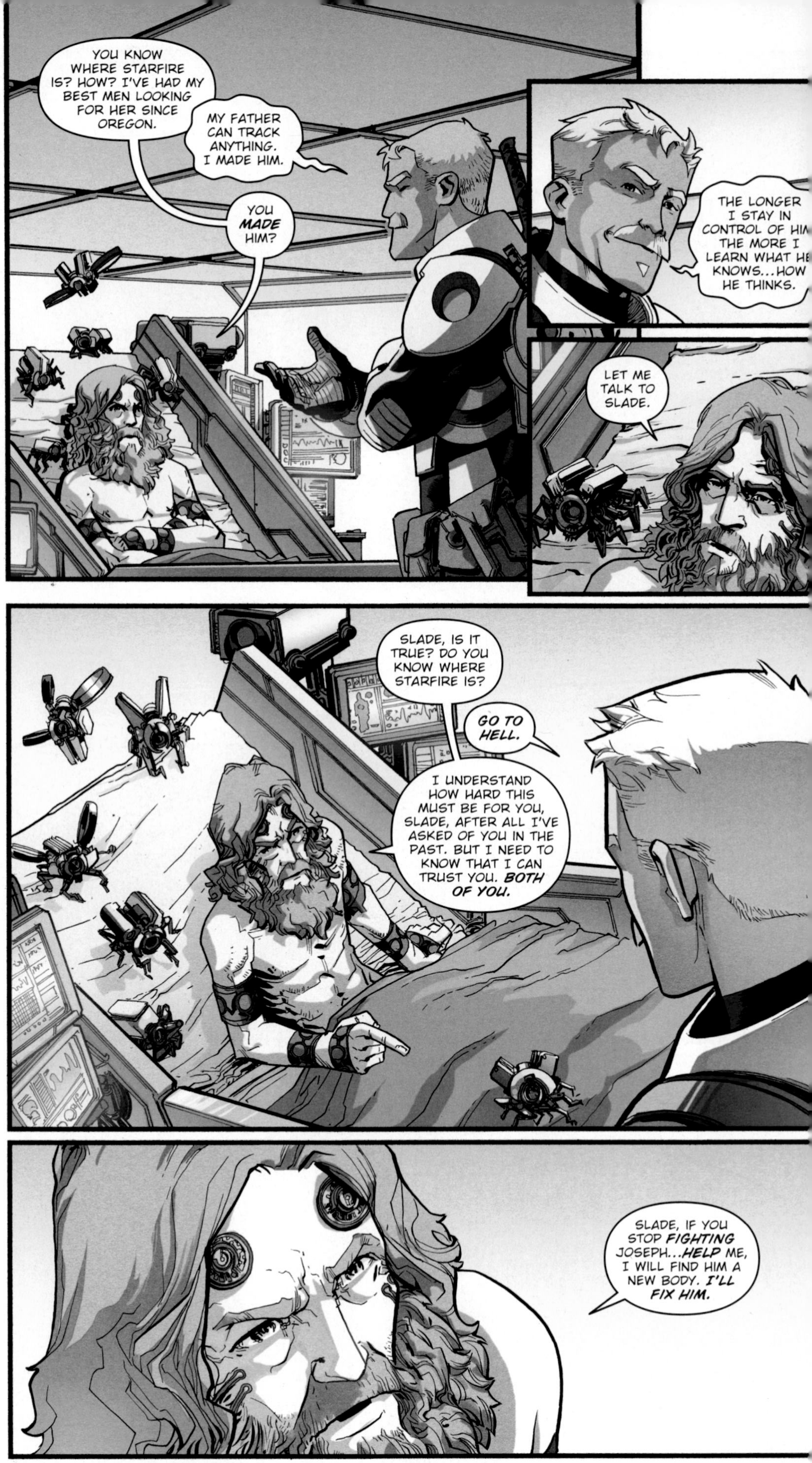
YOU KNOW WHERE STARFIRE IS? HOW? I'VE HAD MY BEST MEN LOOKING FOR HER SINCE OREGON.
MY FATHER CAN TRACK ANYTHING. I MADE HIM.
YOU ***MADE*** HIM?
THE LONGER I STAY IN CONTROL OF HIM THE MORE I LEARN WHAT HE KNOWS...HOW HE THINKS.
LET ME TALK TO SLADE.
SLADE, IS IT TRUE? DO YOU KNOW WHERE STARFIRE IS?
GO TO HELL.
I UNDERSTAND HOW HARD THIS MUST BE FOR YOU, SLADE, AFTER ALL I'VE ASKED OF YOU IN THE PAST. BUT I NEED TO KNOW THAT I CAN TRUST YOU. ***BOTH OF YOU.***
SLADE, IF YOU STOP ***FIGHTING*** JOSEPH...***HELP*** ME, I WILL FIND HIM A NEW BODY. ***I'LL FIX HIM.***

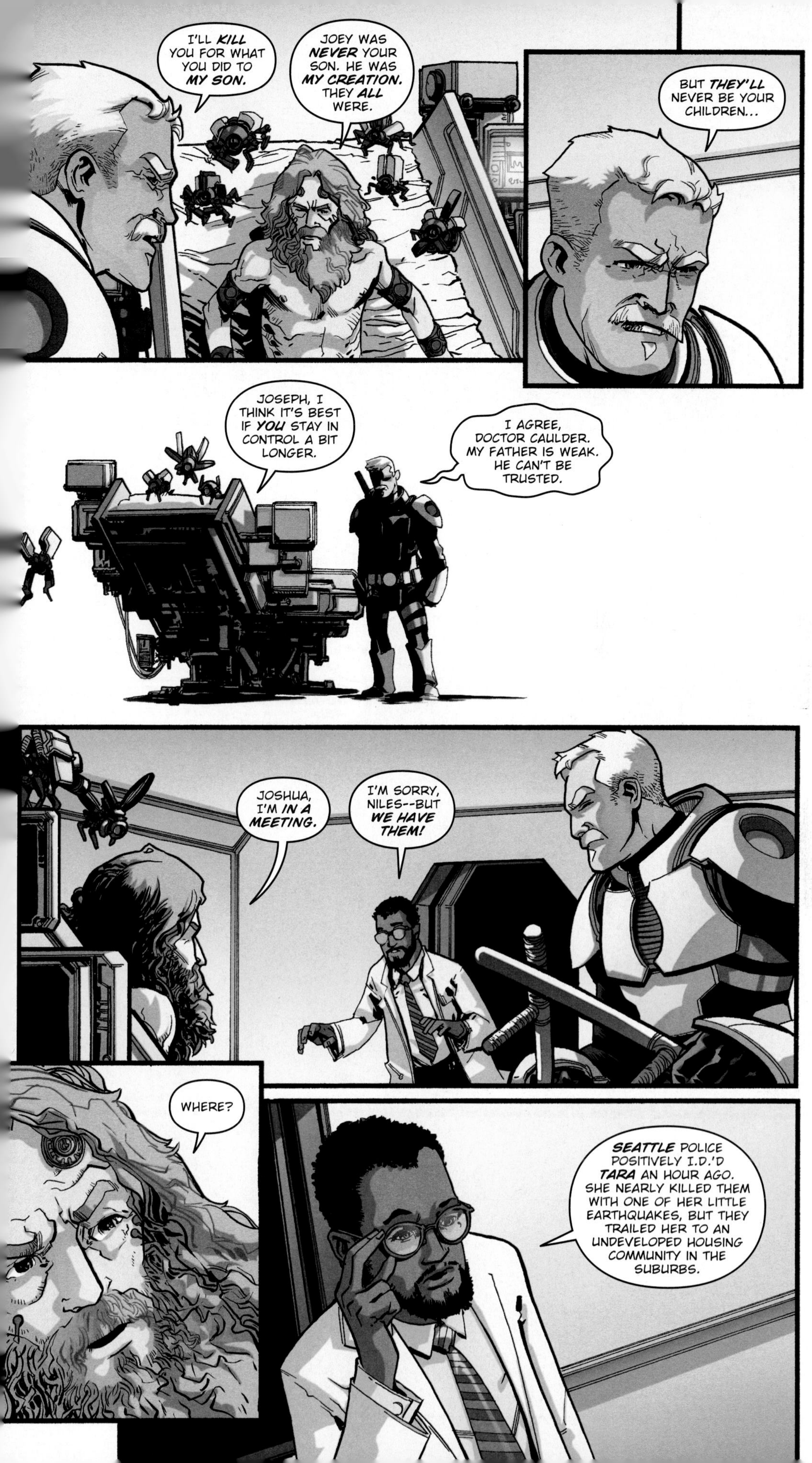
I'LL KILL YOU FOR WHAT YOU DID TO MY SON.
JOEY WAS NEVER YOUR SON. HE WAS MY CREATION. THEY ALL WERE.
BUT THEY'LL NEVER BE YOUR CHILDREN...
JOSEPH, I THINK IT'S BEST IF YOU STAY IN CONTROL A BIT LONGER.
I AGREE, DOCTOR CAULDER. MY FATHER IS WEAK. HE CAN'T BE TRUSTED.
JOSHUA, I'M IN A MEETING.
I'M SORRY, NILES--BUT WE HAVE THEM!
WHERE?
SEATTLE POLICE POSITIVELY I.D.'D TARA AN HOUR AGO. SHE NEARLY KILLED THEM WITH ONE OF HER LITTLE EARTHQUAKES, BUT THEY TRAILED HER TO AN UNDEVELOPED HOUSING COMMUNITY IN THE SUBURBS.

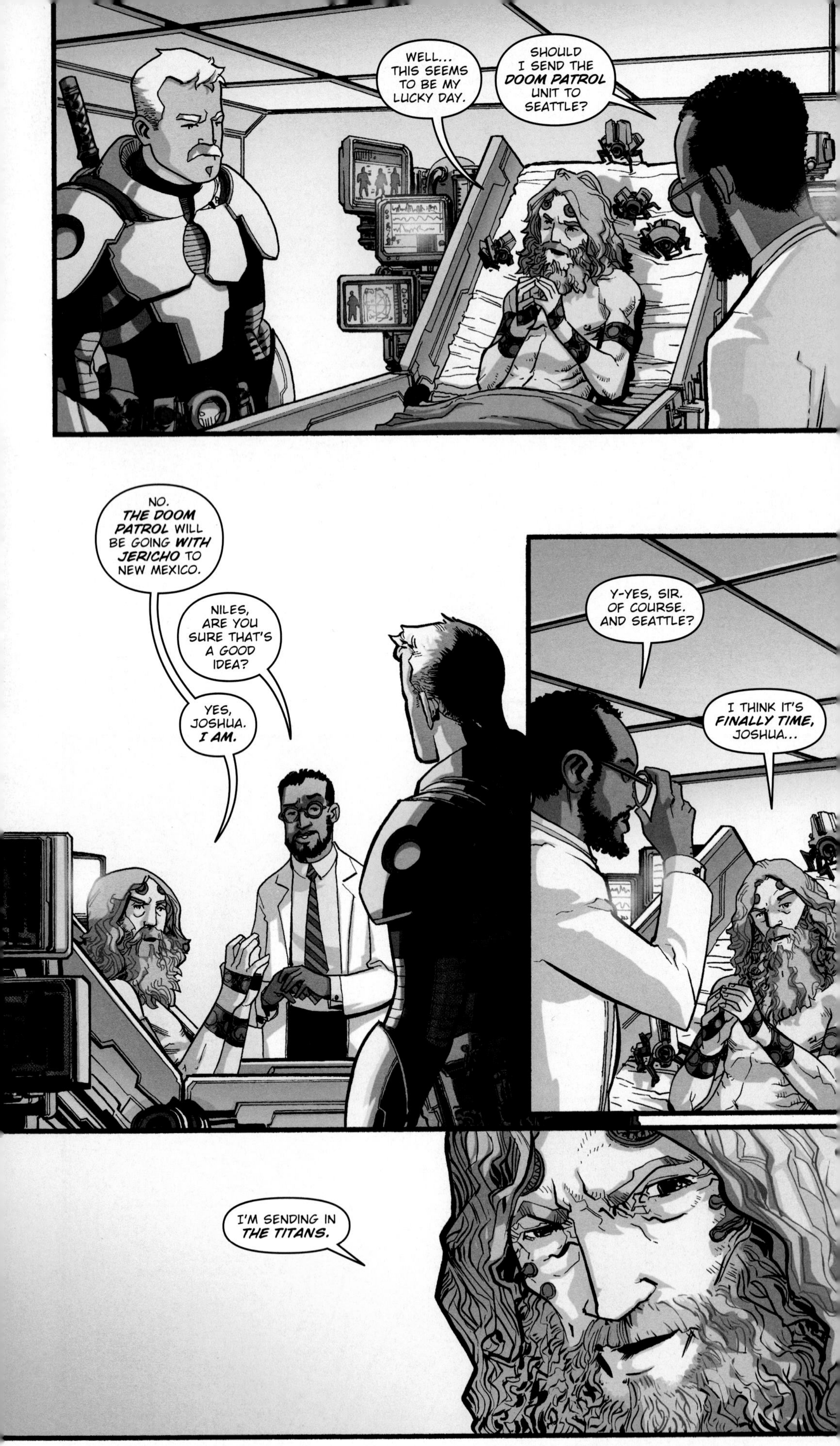
WELL... THIS SEEMS TO BE MY LUCKY DAY.
SHOULD I SEND THE *DOOM PATROL* UNIT TO SEATTLE?
NO. *THE DOOM PATROL* WILL BE GOING *WITH JERICHO* TO NEW MEXICO.
NILES, ARE YOU SURE THAT'S A GOOD IDEA?
YES, JOSHUA. *I AM.*
Y-YES, SIR. OF COURSE. AND SEATTLE?
I THINK IT'S *FINALLY TIME,* JOSHUA...
I'M SENDING IN *THE TITANS.*

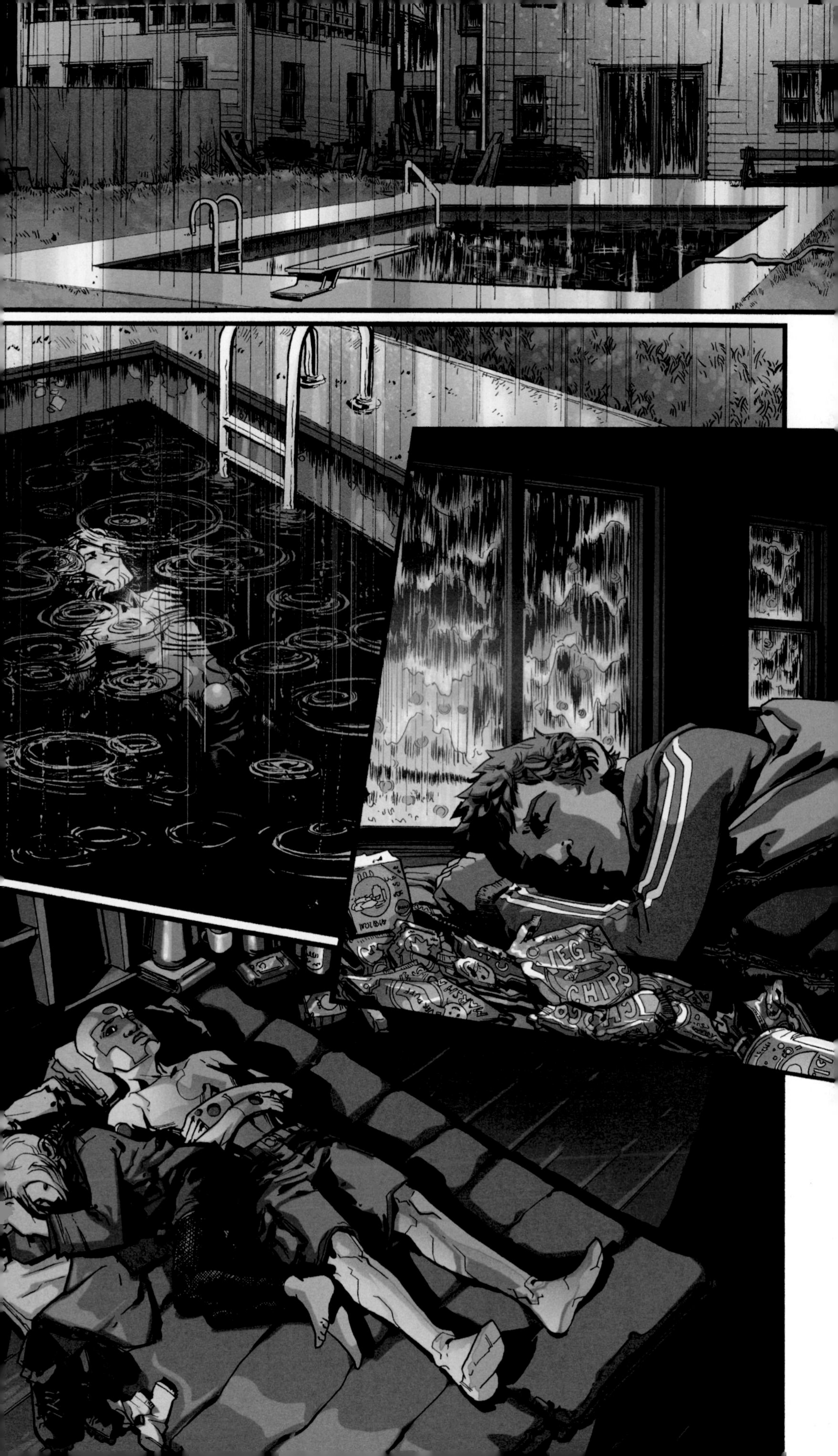
CHIPS

TARA.

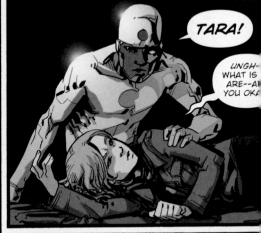

TARA!

UNGH-- WHAT IS ARE--AR YOU OKA

I--I HEAR SOMETHING!

"SOMETHING'S COMING."

WHAT IS IT? YOU'RE NOT GOING TO PUKE AGAIN, ARE YOU?

WHAT? I DON'T--

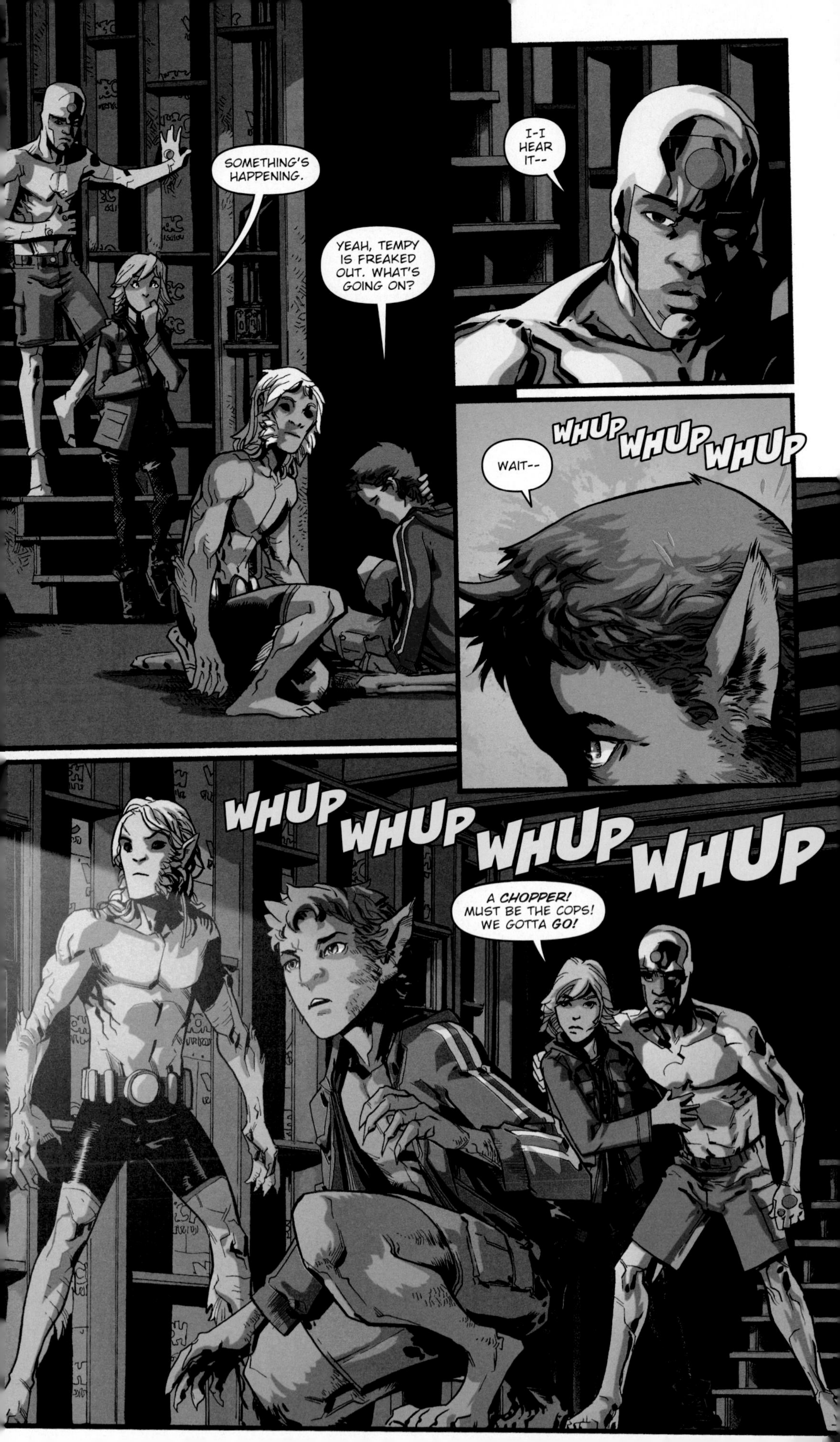
SOMETHING'S HAPPENING.
YEAH, TEMPY IS FREAKED OUT. WHAT'S GOING ON?
I-I HEAR IT--
WAIT--
WHUP WHUP WHUP
WHUP WHUP WHUP WHUP
A CHOPPER! MUST BE THE COPS! WE GOTTA GO!

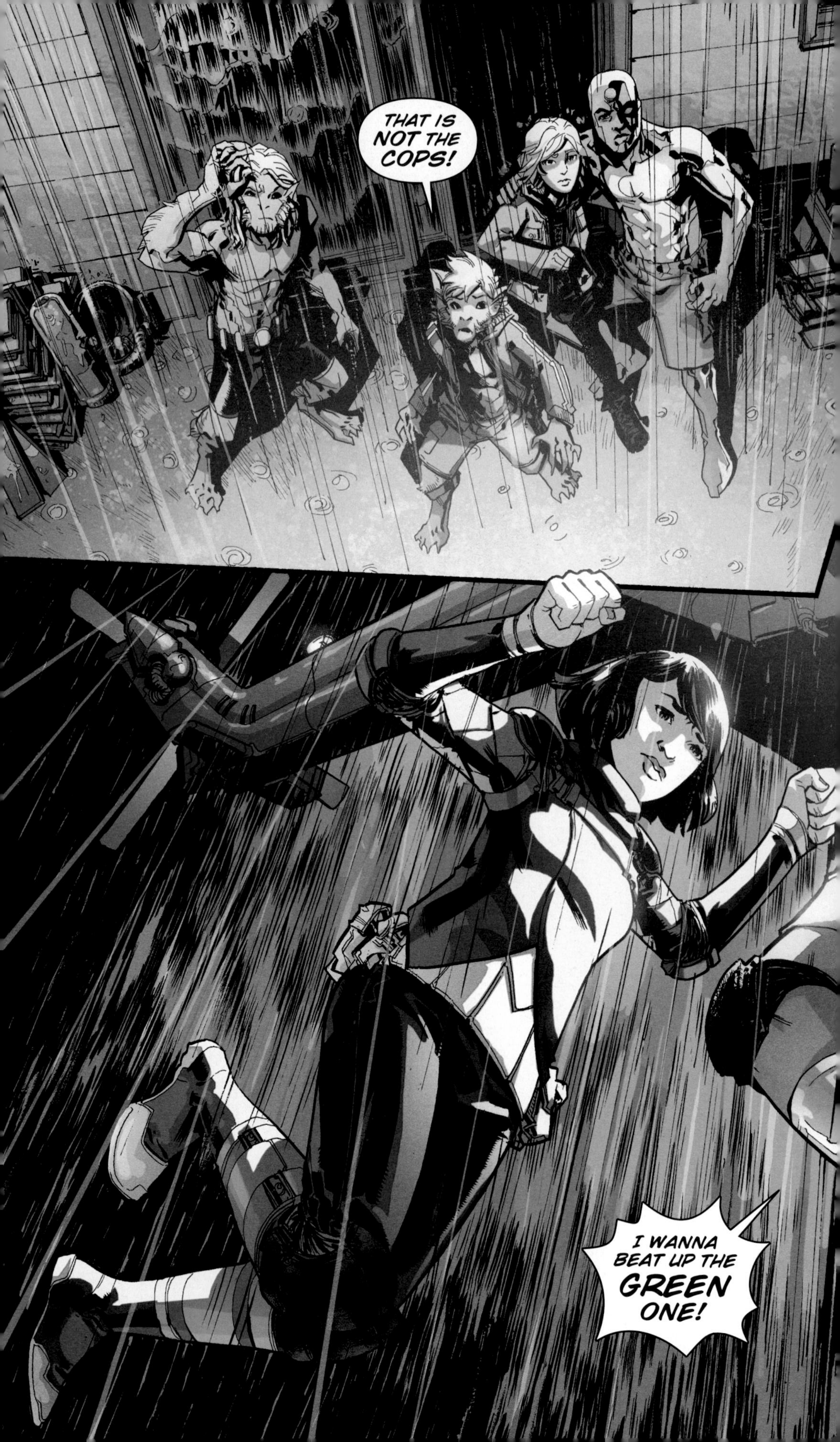
THAT IS NOT THE COPS!
I WANNA BEAT UP THE GREEN ONE!

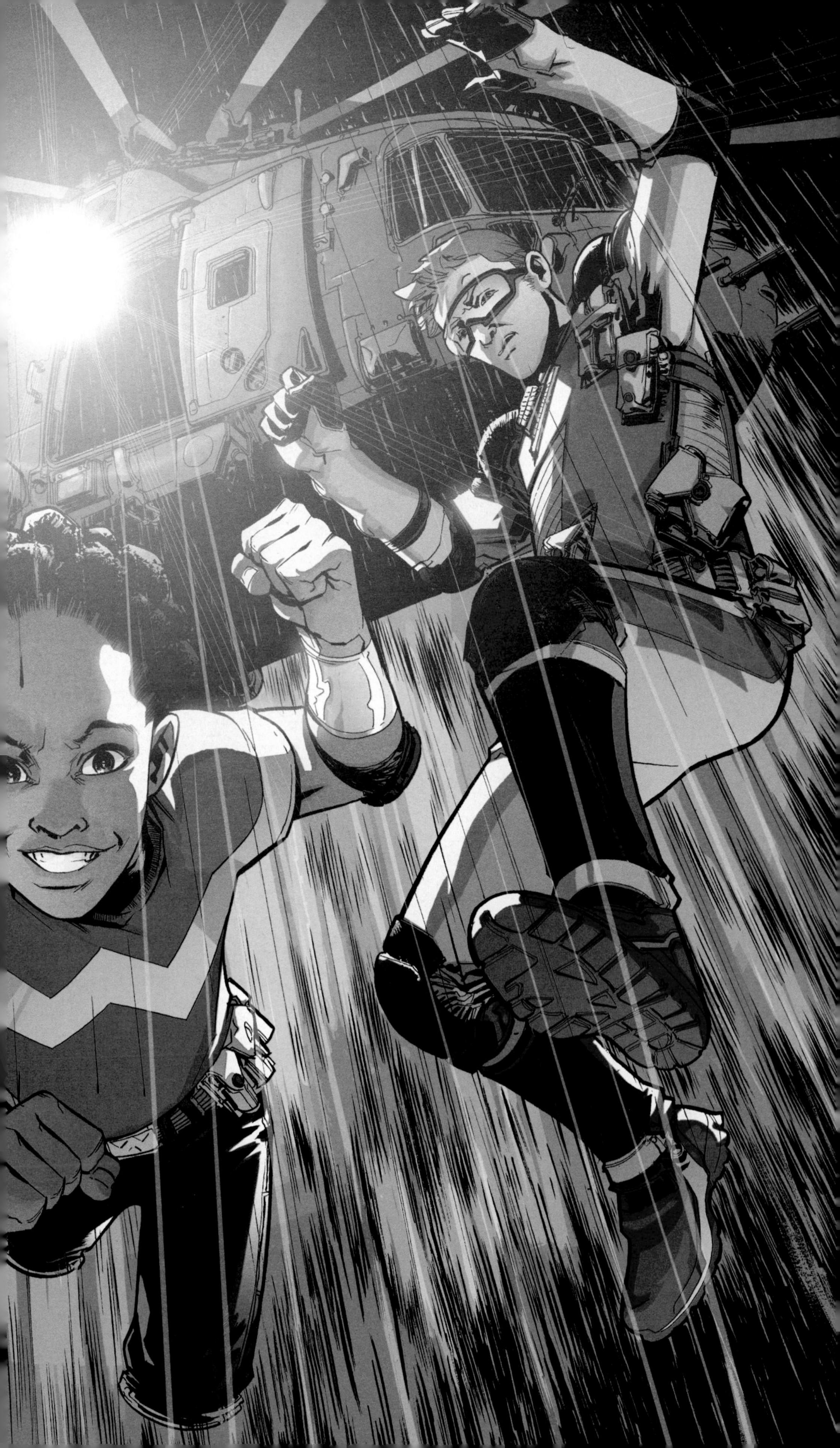

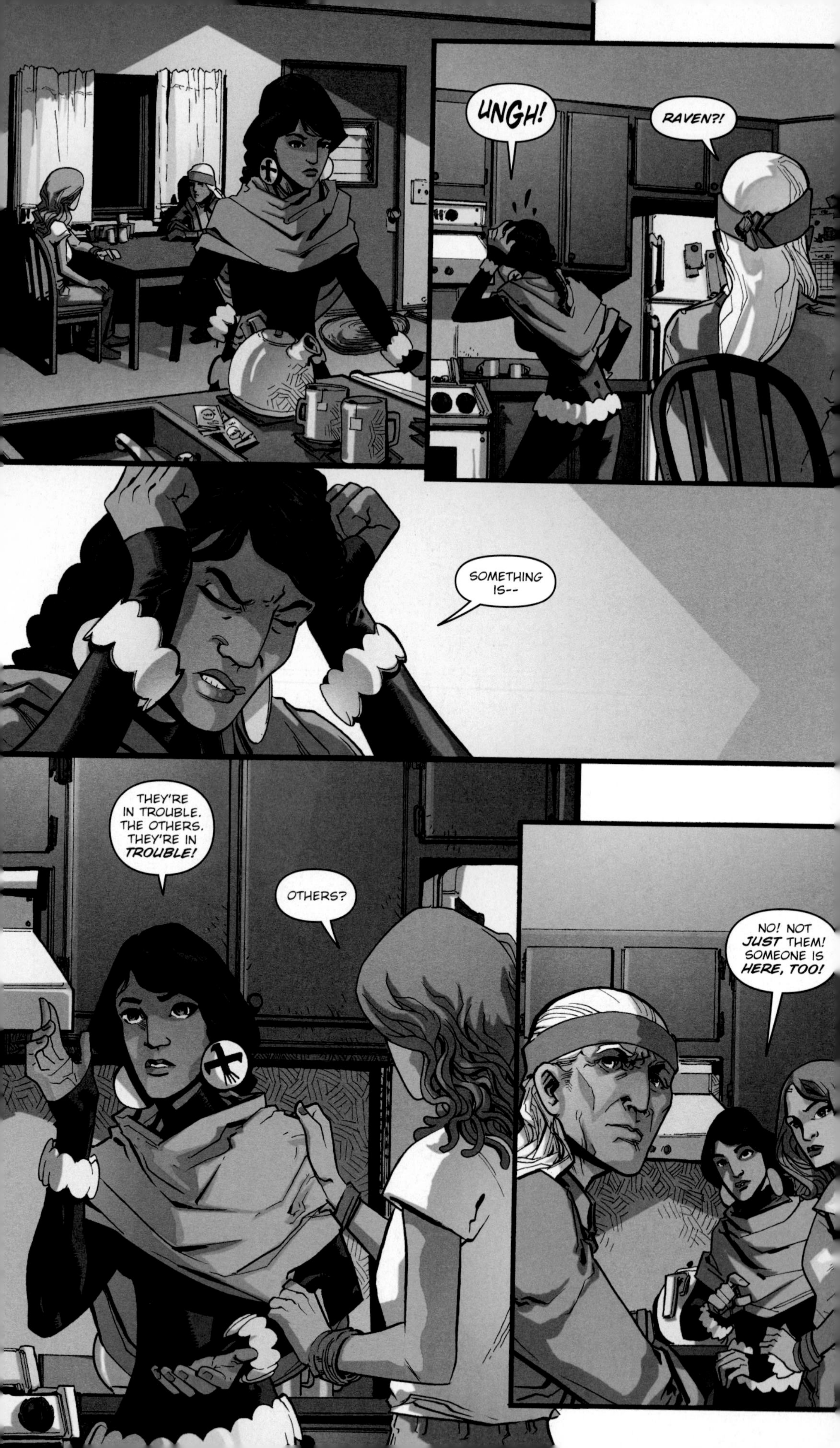
UNGH!
RAVEN?!
SOMETHING IS--
THEY'RE IN TROUBLE. THE OTHERS. THEY'RE IN *TROUBLE!*
OTHERS?
NO! NOT *JUST* THEM! SOMEONE IS *HERE, TOO!*

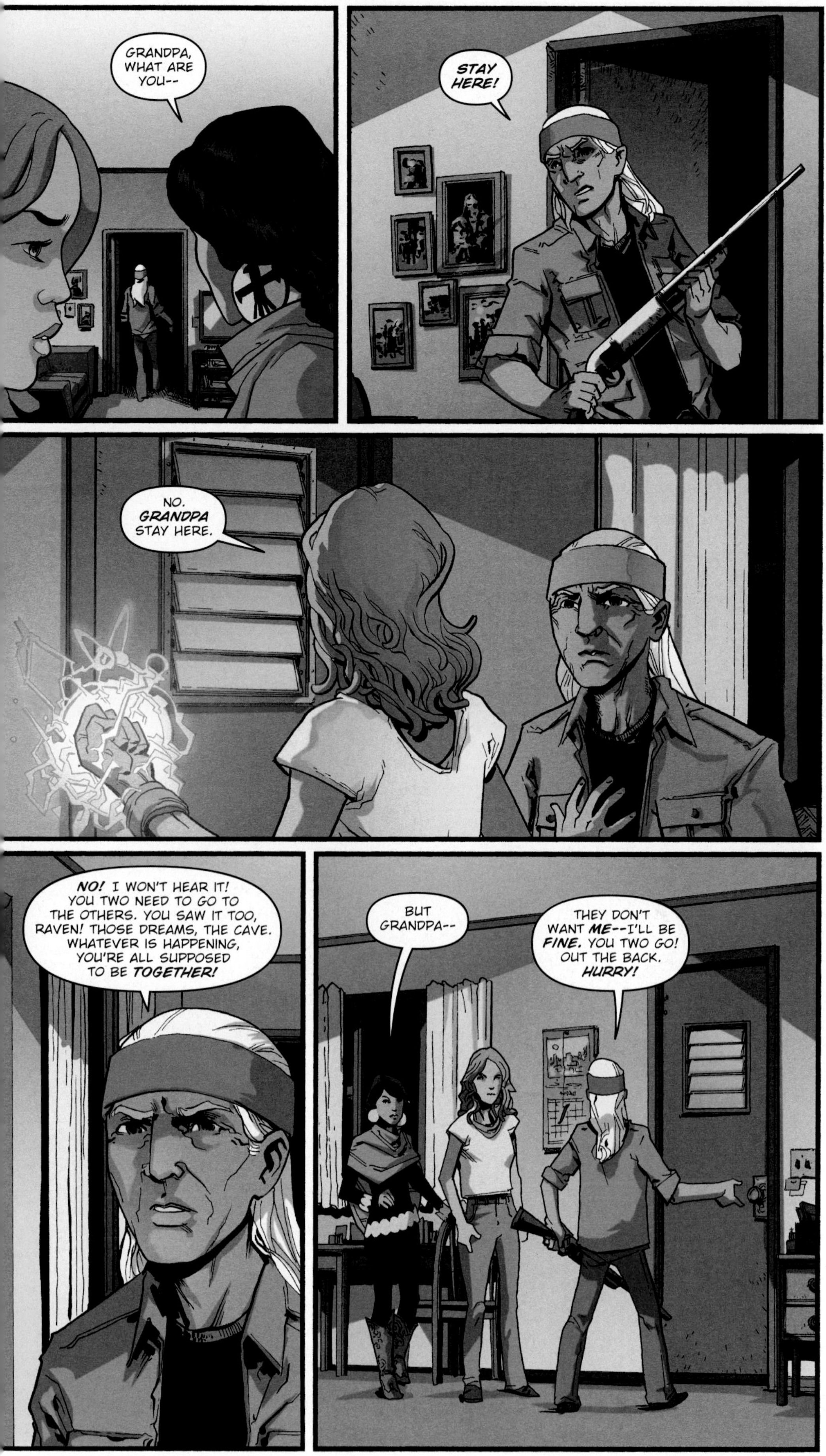
GRANDPA, WHAT ARE YOU--
STAY HERE!
NO. GRANDPA STAY HERE.
NO! I WON'T HEAR IT! YOU TWO NEED TO GO TO THE OTHERS. YOU SAW IT TOO, RAVEN! THOSE DREAMS, THE CAVE. WHATEVER IS HAPPENING, YOU'RE ALL SUPPOSED TO BE TOGETHER!
BUT GRANDPA--
THEY DON'T WANT ME--I'LL BE FINE. YOU TWO GO! OUT THE BACK. HURRY!

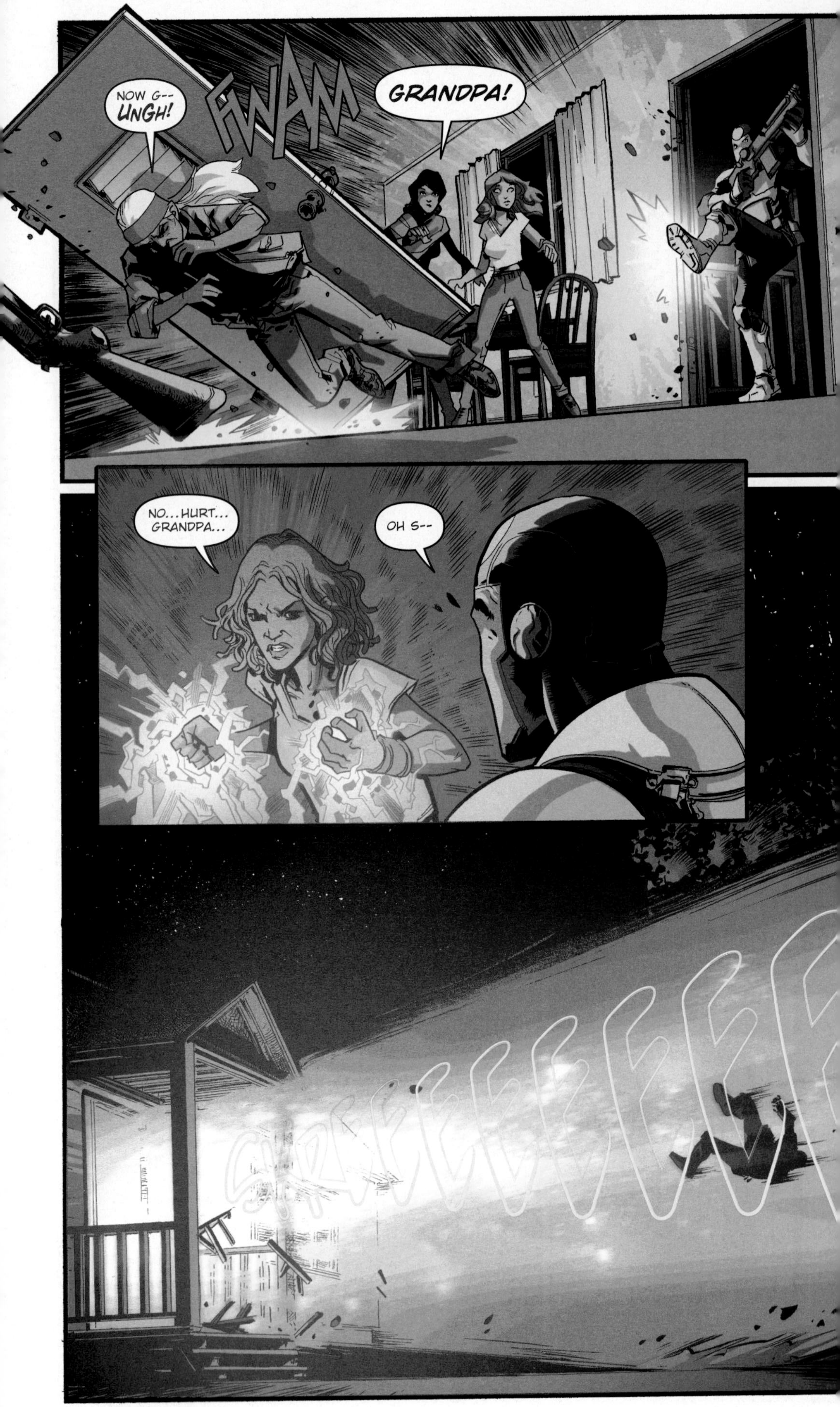
NOW G--
UNGH!
FWAM
GRANDPA!
NO...HURT...
GRANDPA...
OH S--

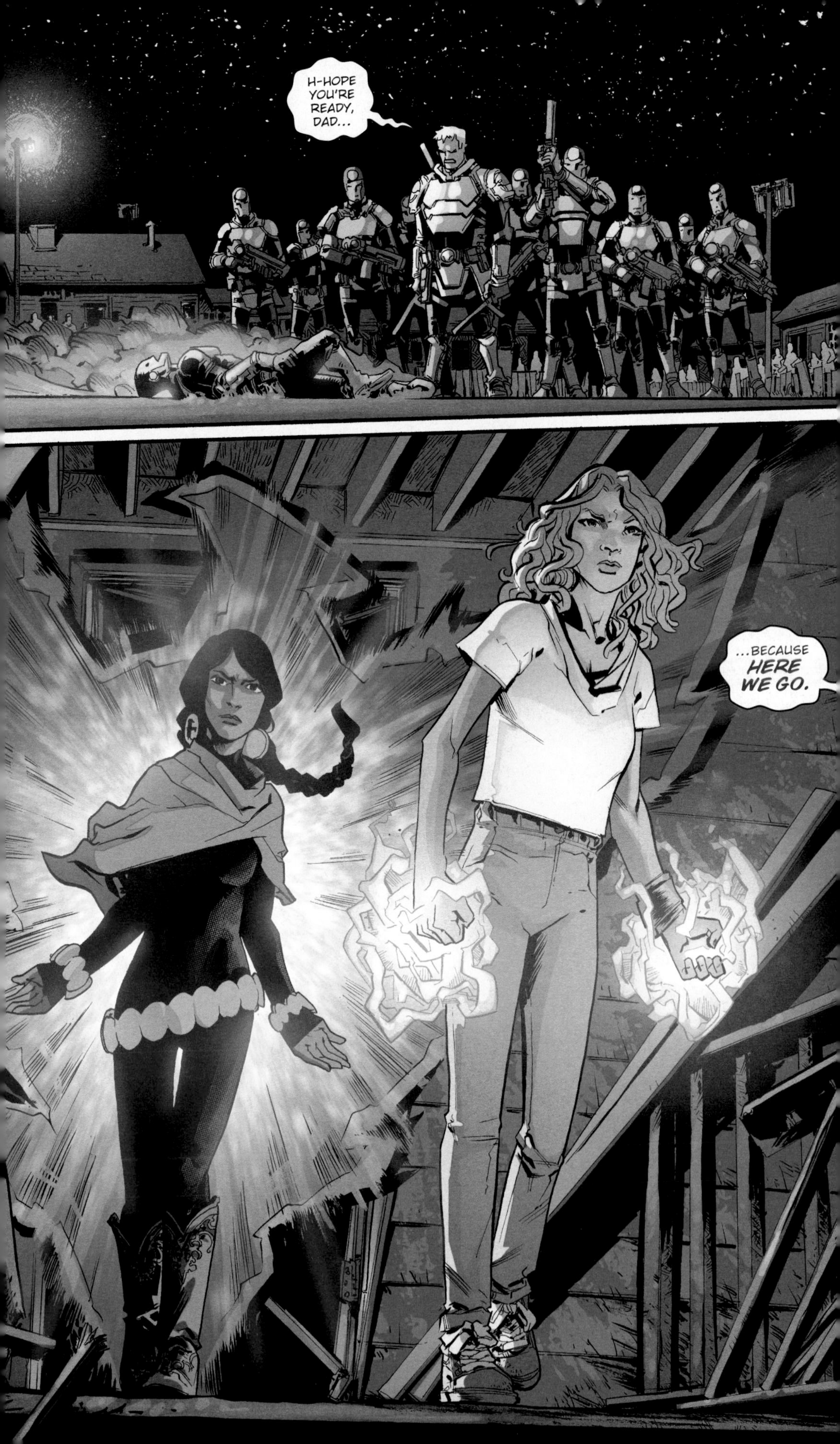

H-HOPE YOU'RE READY, DAD...
...BECAUSE HERE WE GO.

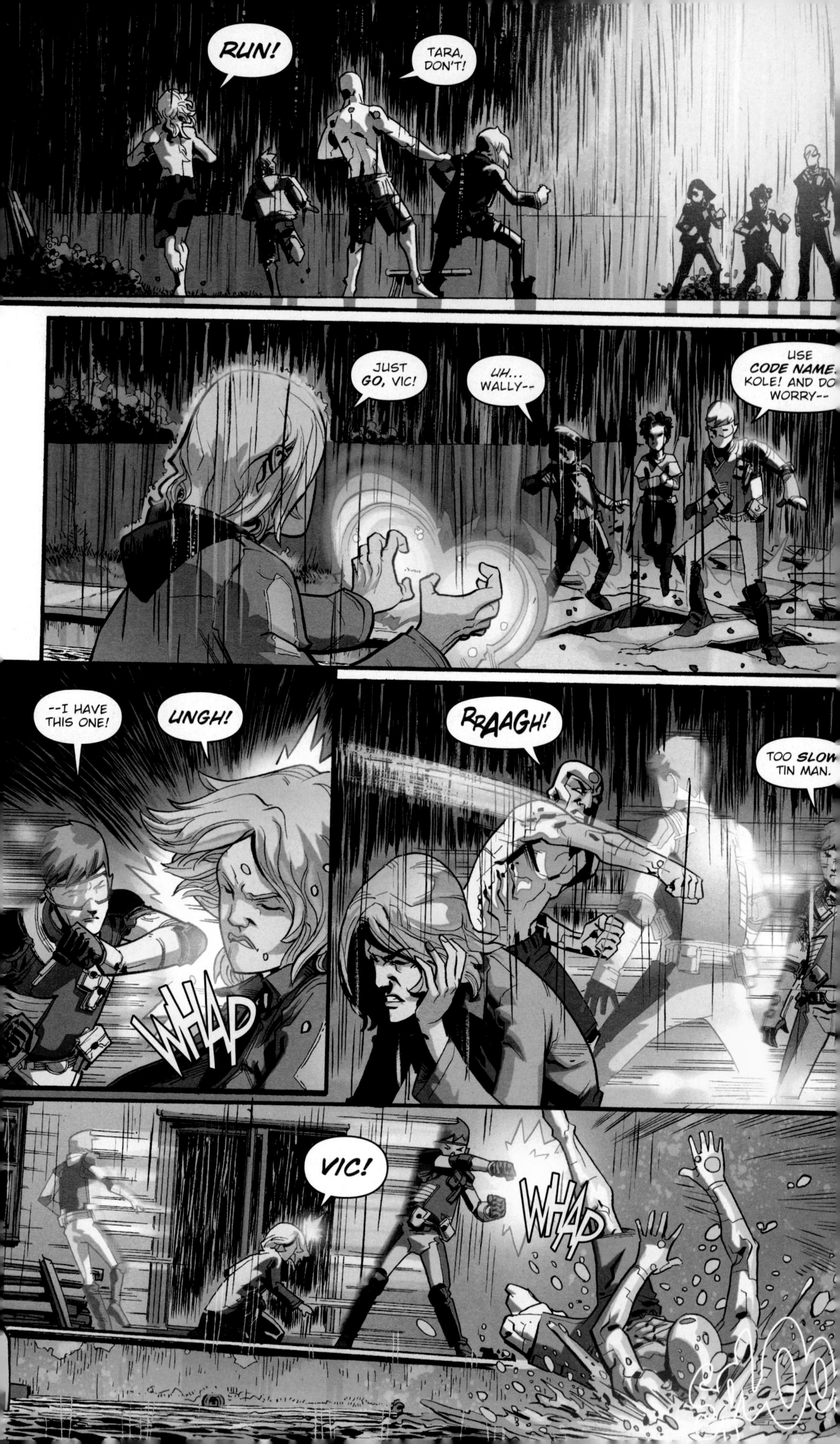
RUN!
TARA, DON'T!
JUST GO, VIC!
UH... WALLY--
USE CODE NAME. KOLE! AND DO WORRY--
--I HAVE THIS ONE!
UNGH!
WHAP
RRAAGH!
TOO SLOW TIN MAN.
VIC!
WHAP

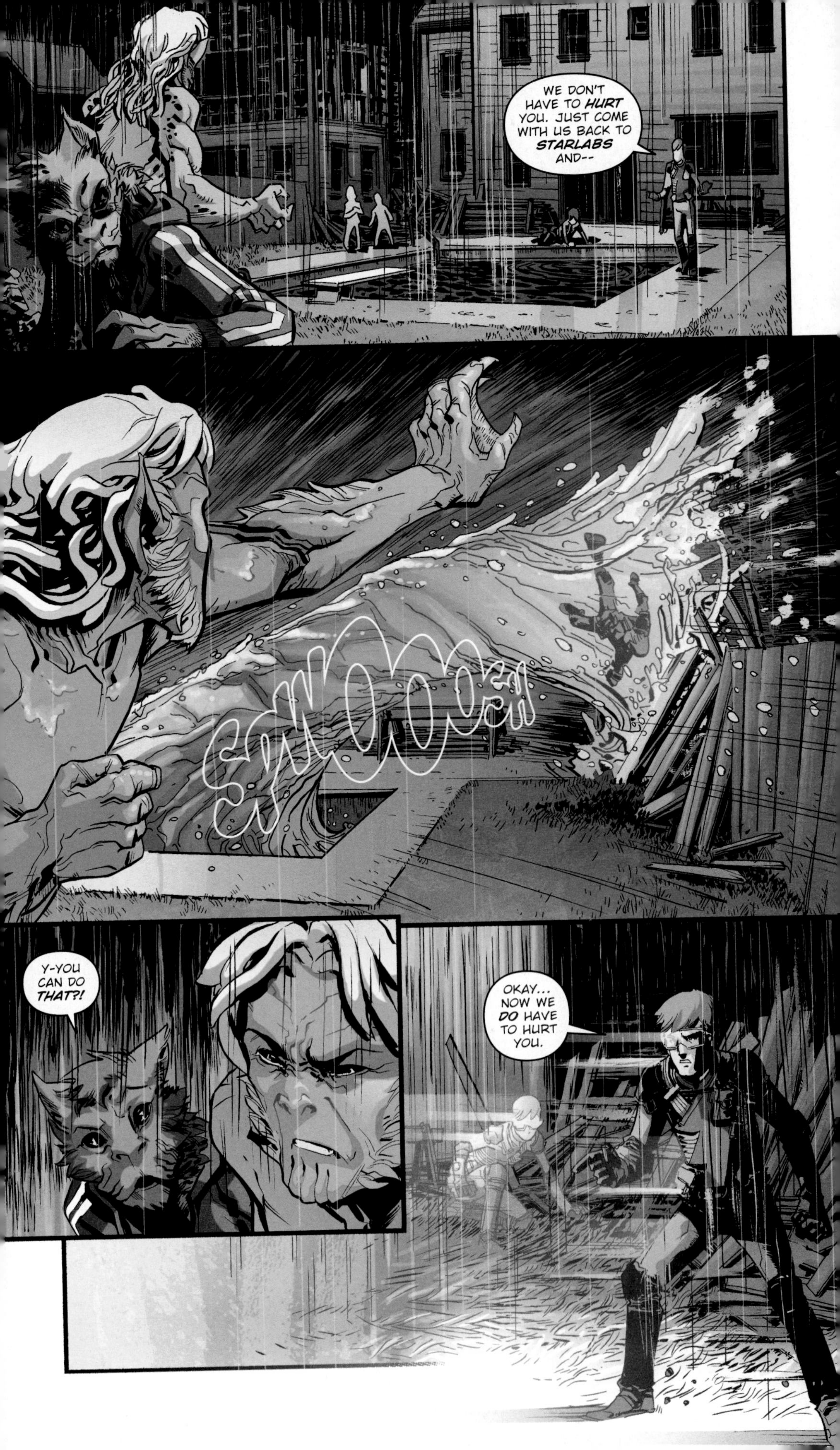
WE DON'T HAVE TO HURT YOU. JUST COME WITH US BACK TO STARLABS AND--
Y-YOU CAN DO THAT?!
OKAY... NOW WE DO HAVE TO HURT YOU.

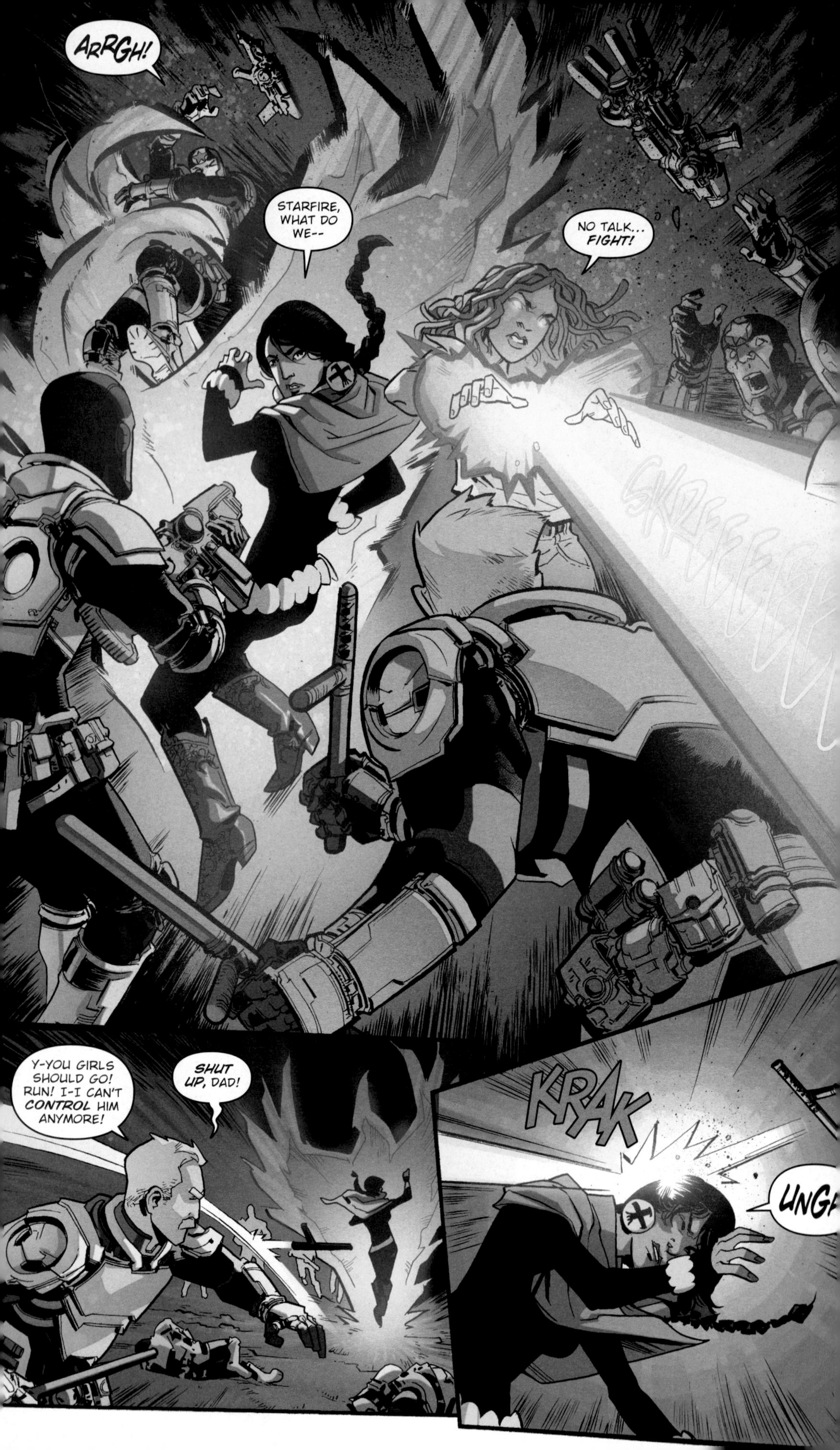
ARRGH!
STARFIRE, WHAT DO WE--
NO TALK... FIGHT!
SKREEEEE
Y-YOU GIRLS SHOULD GO! RUN! I-I CAN'T CONTROL HIM ANYMORE!
SHUT UP, DAD!
KRAK
UNG

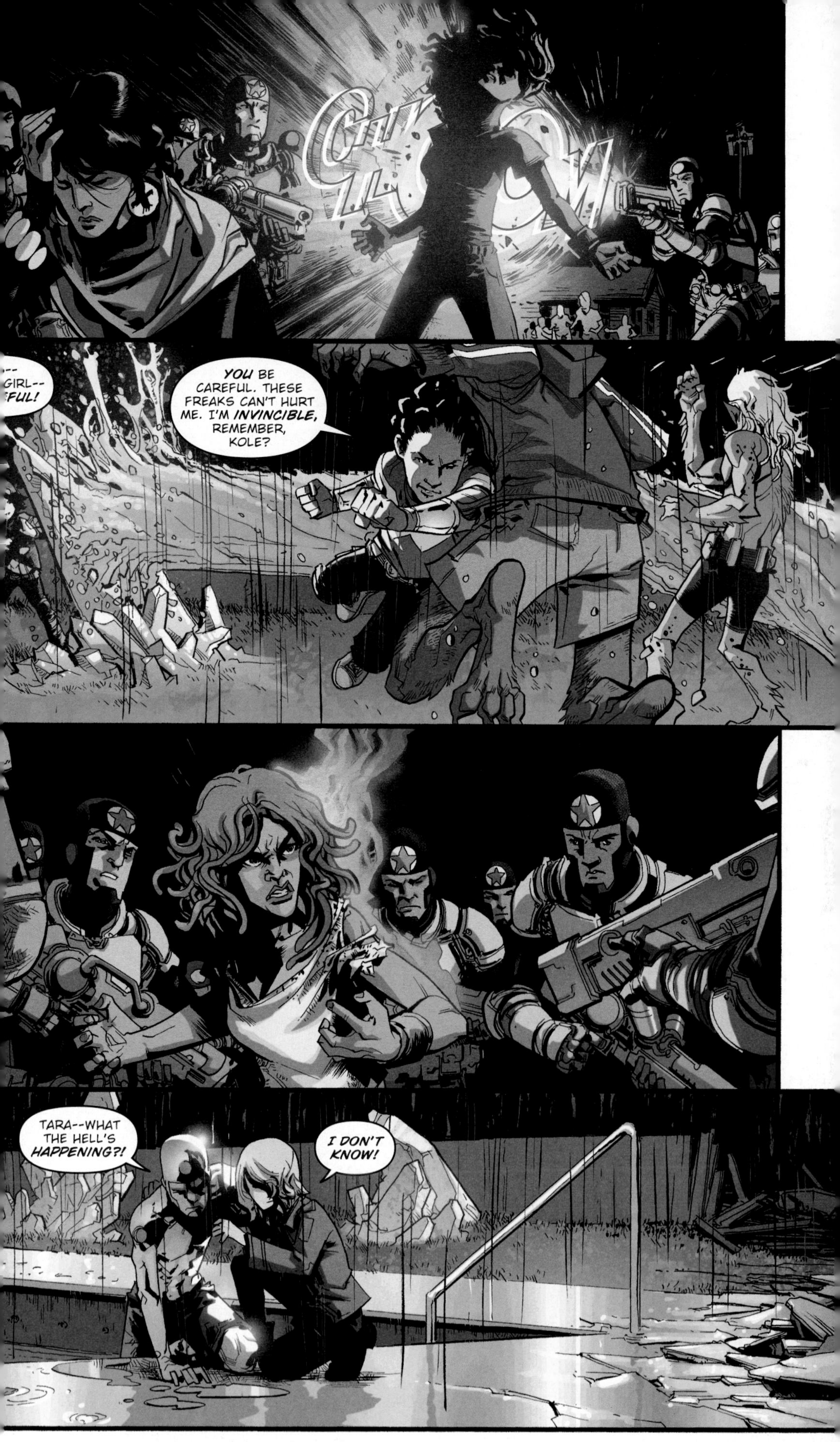
GIRL--
YOU BE CAREFUL. THESE FREAKS CAN'T HURT ME. I'M INVINCIBLE, REMEMBER, KOLE?
TARA--WHAT THE HELL'S HAPPENING?!
I DON'T KNOW!

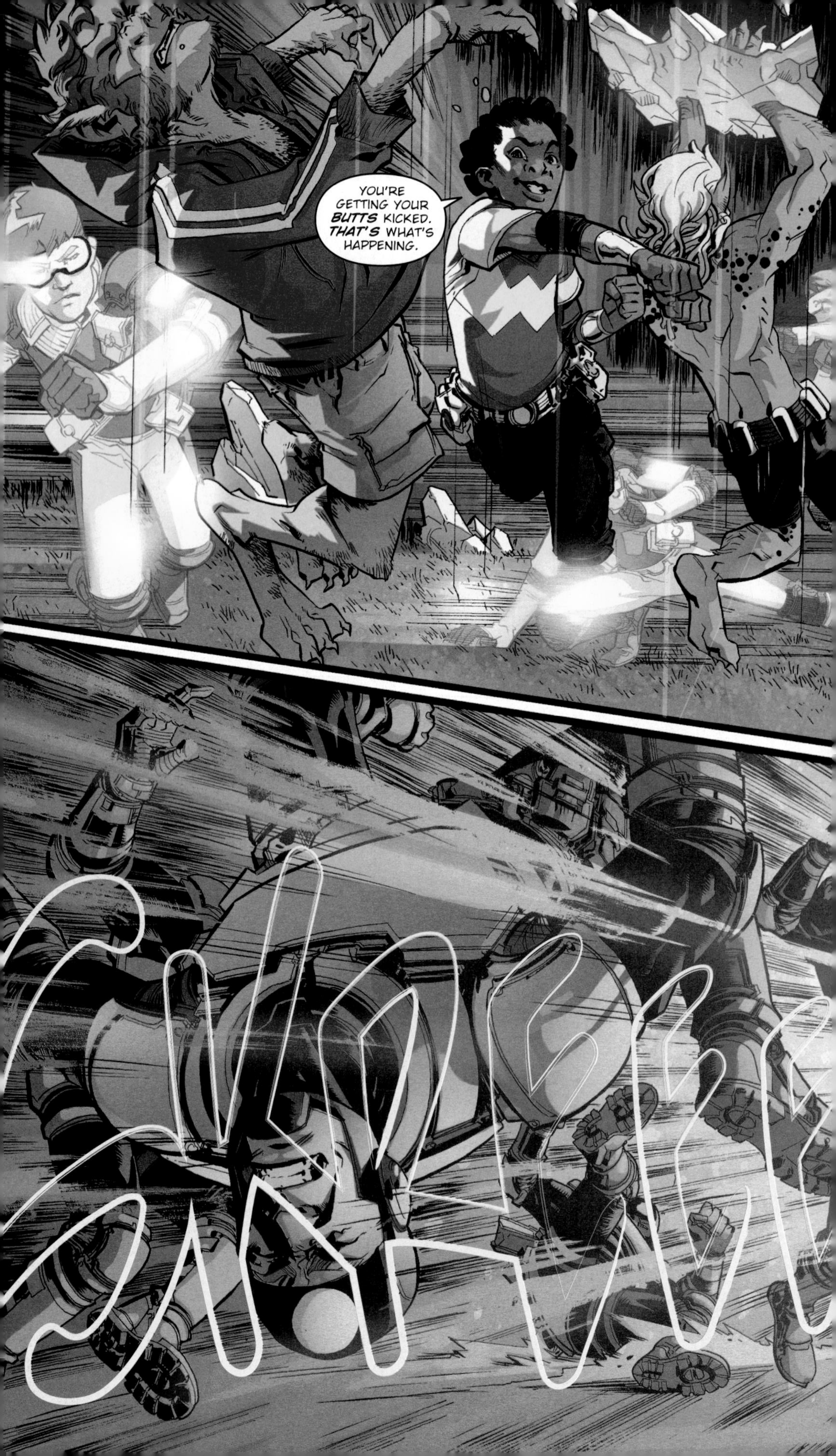
YOU'RE GETTING YOUR BUTTS KICKED. THAT'S WHAT'S HAPPENING.

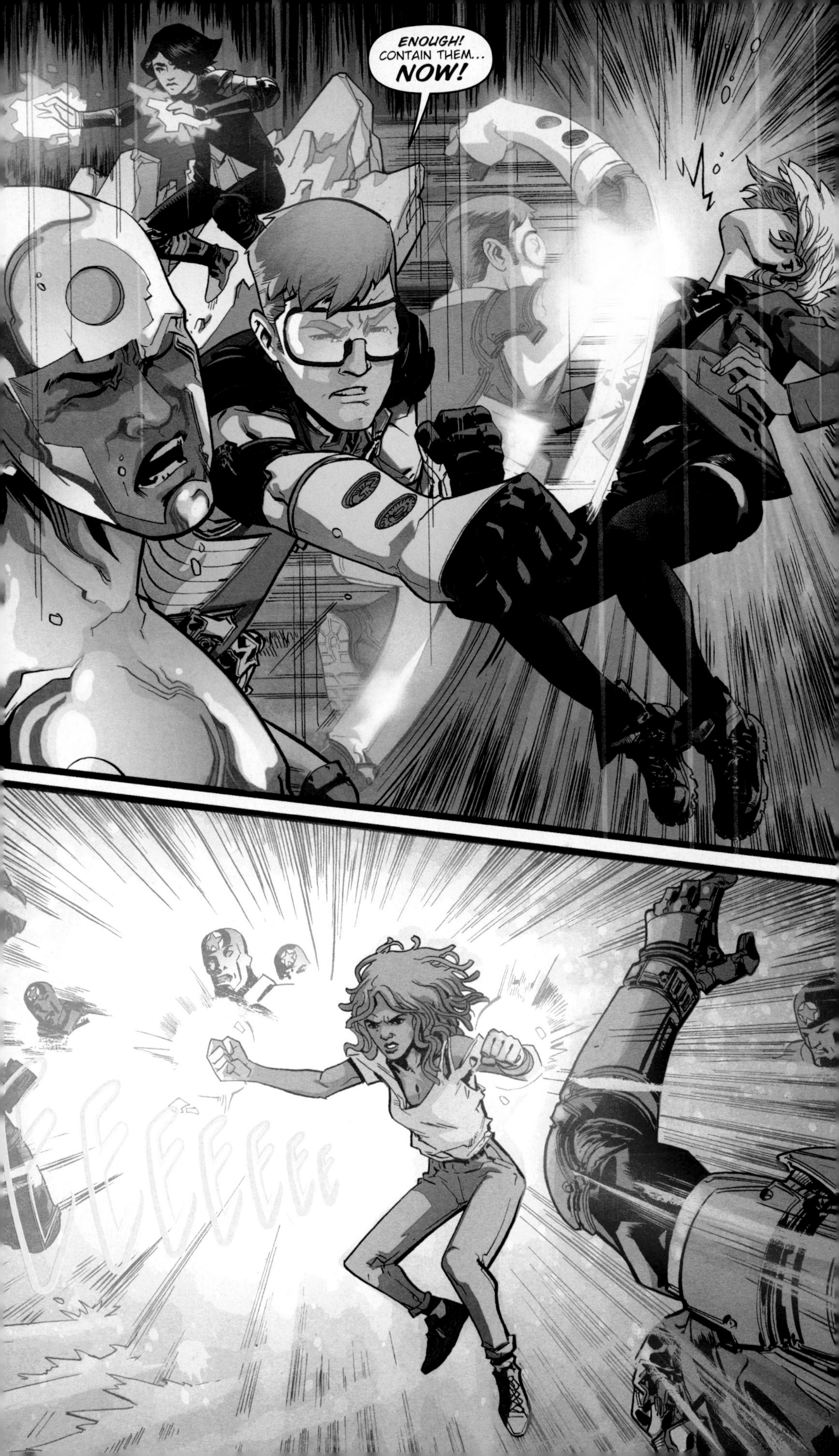
ENOUGH! CONTAIN THEM... NOW!
EEEEEEE

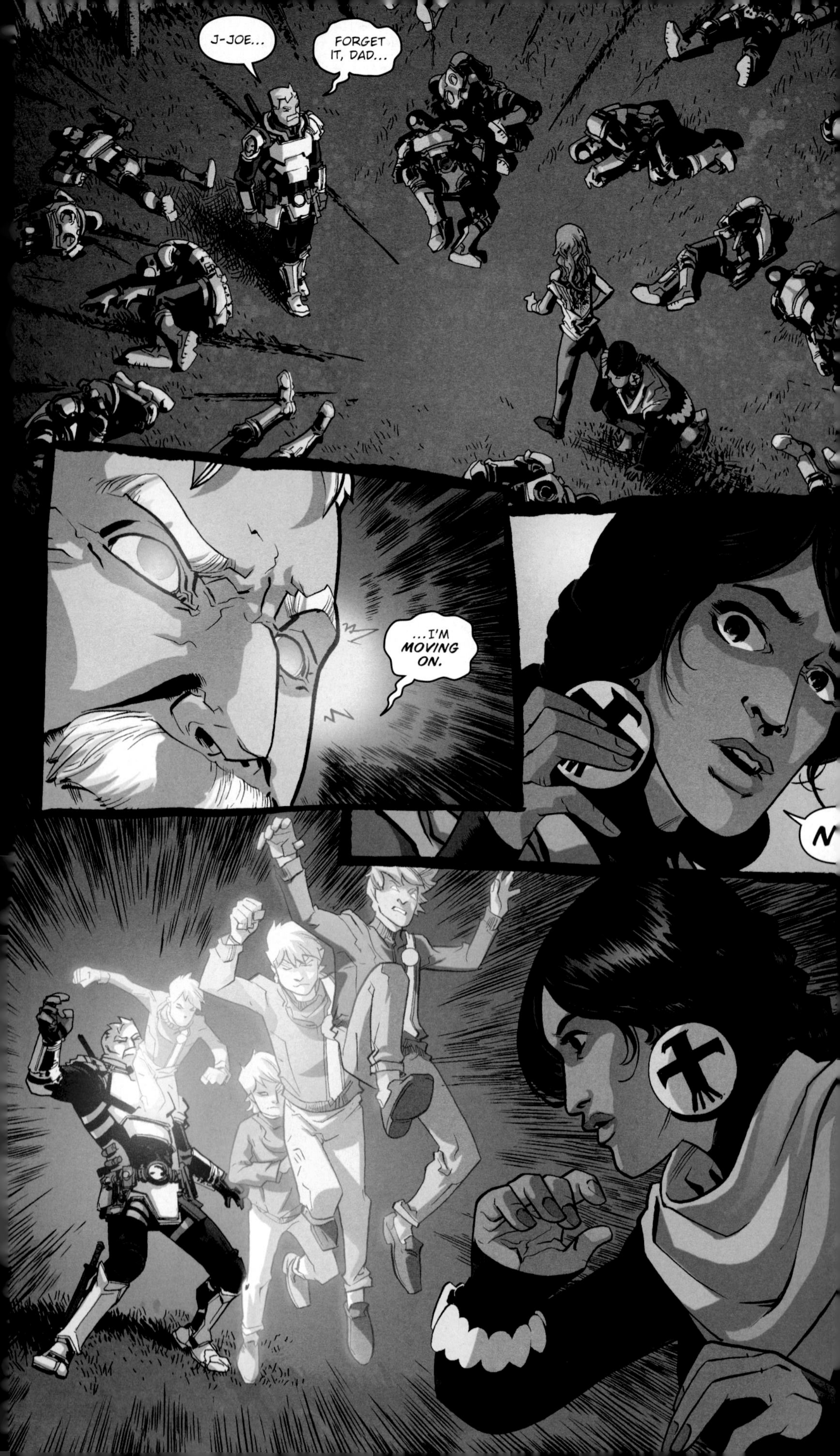
J-JOE...
FORGET IT, DAD...
...I'M MOVING ON.
N

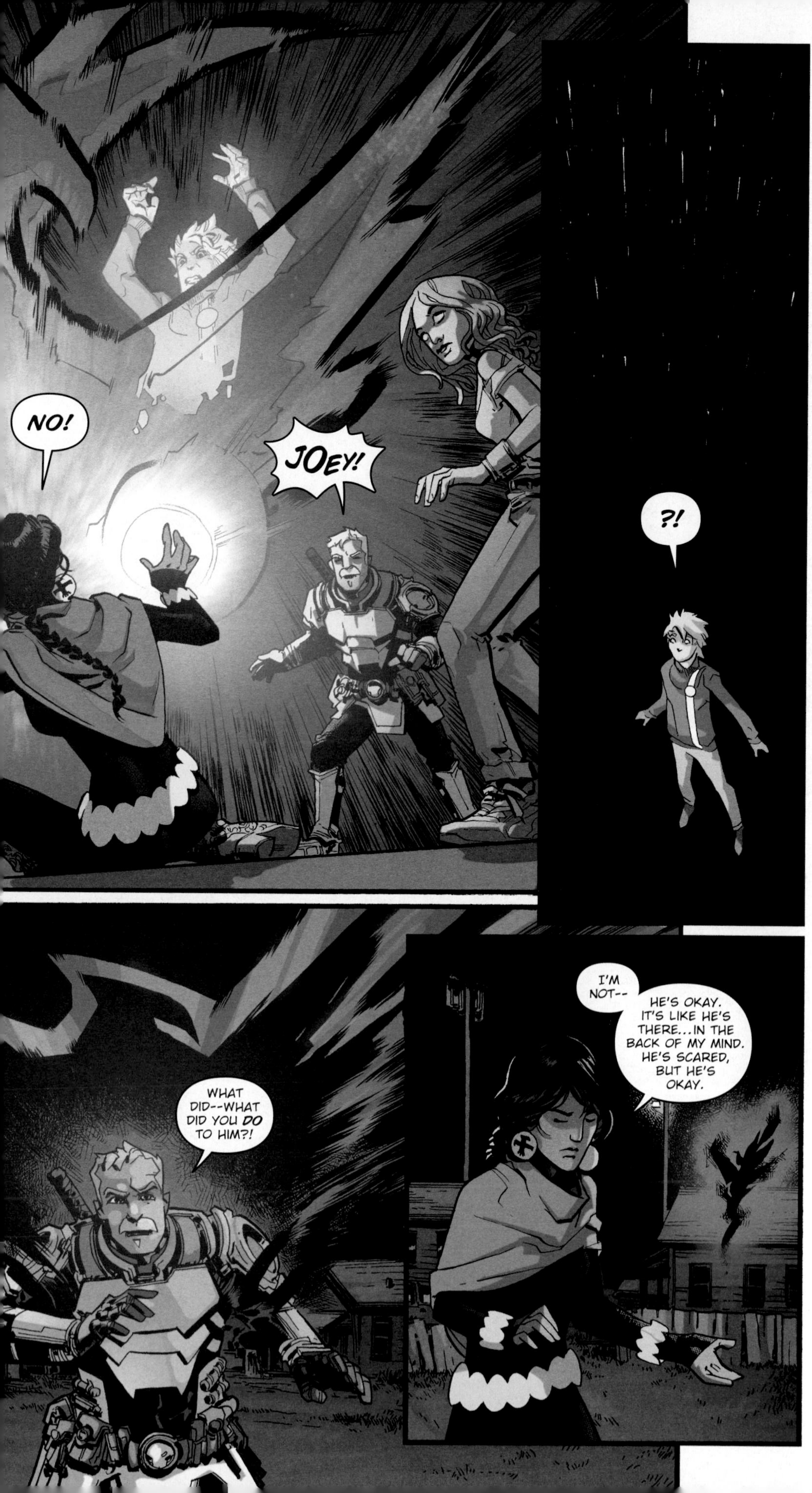
NO!
JOEY!
?!
WHAT DID--WHAT DID YOU DO TO HIM?!
I'M NOT--
HE'S OKAY. IT'S LIKE HE'S THERE...IN THE BACK OF MY MIND. HE'S SCARED, BUT HE'S OKAY.

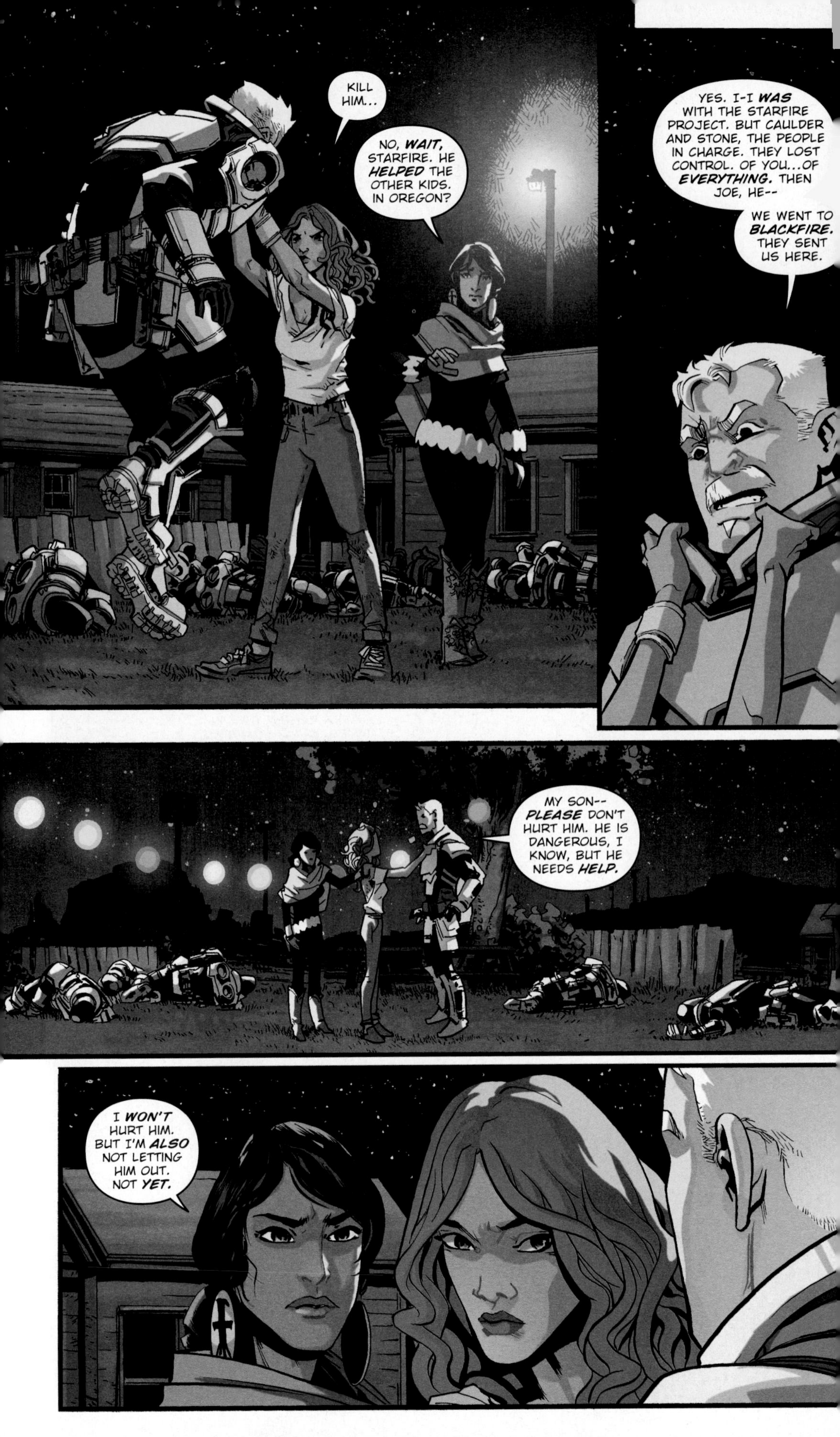
KILL HIM...
NO, WAIT, STARFIRE. HE HELPED THE OTHER KIDS. IN OREGON?
YES. I-I WAS WITH THE STARFIRE PROJECT. BUT CAULDER AND STONE, THE PEOPLE IN CHARGE. THEY LOST CONTROL. OF YOU...OF EVERYTHING. THEN JOE, HE--
WE WENT TO BLACKFIRE. THEY SENT US HERE.
MY SON-- PLEASE DON'T HURT HIM. HE IS DANGEROUS, I KNOW, BUT HE NEEDS HELP.
I WON'T HURT HIM. BUT I'M ALSO NOT LETTING HIM OUT. NOT YET.

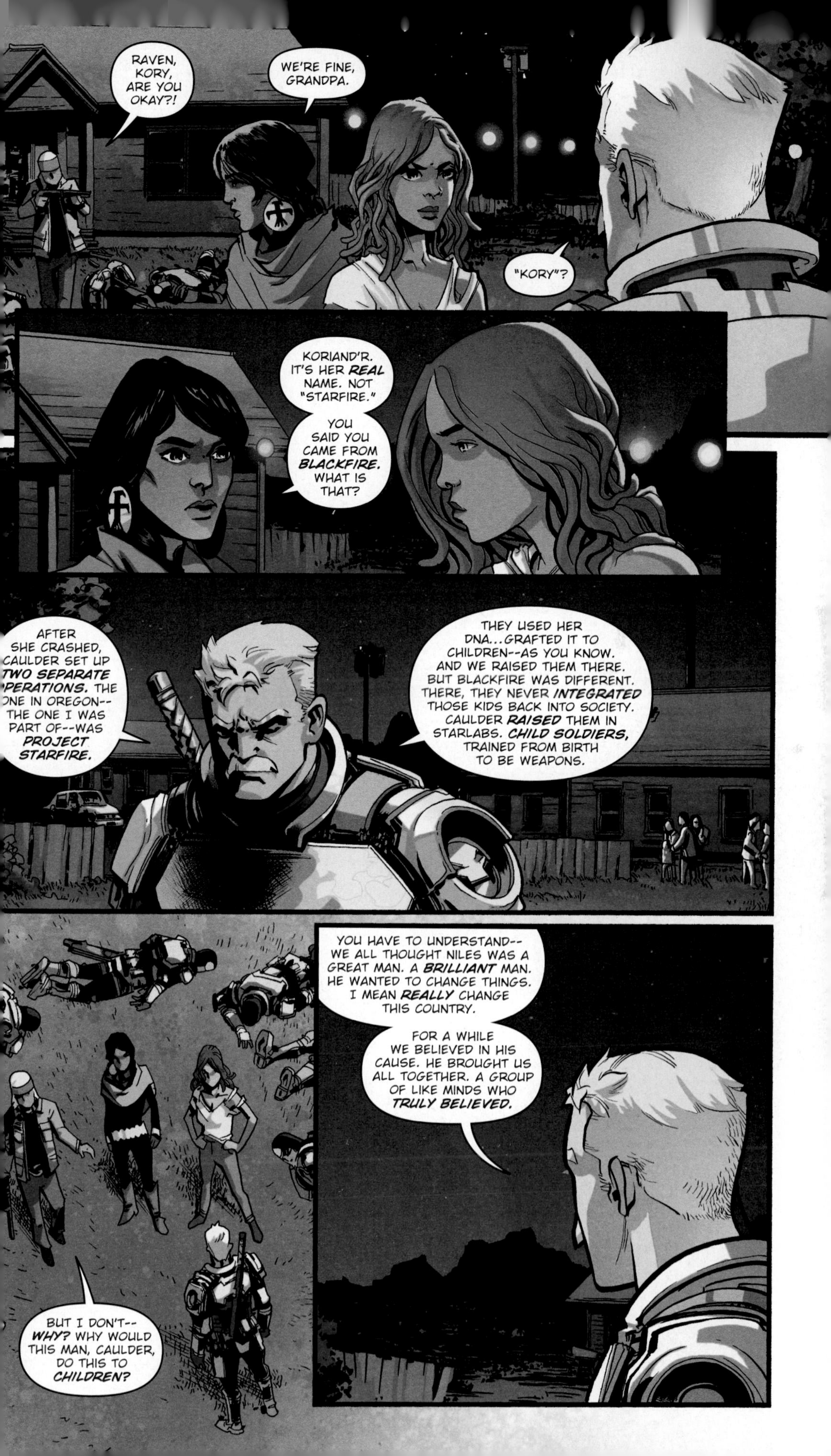
RAVEN, KORY, ARE YOU OKAY?!
WE'RE FINE, GRANDPA.
"KORY"?
KORIAND'R. IT'S HER REAL NAME. NOT "STARFIRE."
YOU SAID YOU CAME FROM BLACKFIRE. WHAT IS THAT?
AFTER SHE CRASHED, CAULDER SET UP TWO SEPARATE OPERATIONS. THE ONE IN OREGON--THE ONE I WAS PART OF--WAS PROJECT STARFIRE.
THEY USED HER DNA...GRAFTED IT TO CHILDREN--AS YOU KNOW. AND WE RAISED THEM THERE. BUT BLACKFIRE WAS DIFFERENT. THERE, THEY NEVER INTEGRATED THOSE KIDS BACK INTO SOCIETY. CAULDER RAISED THEM IN STARLABS. CHILD SOLDIERS, TRAINED FROM BIRTH TO BE WEAPONS.
BUT I DON'T--WHY? WHY WOULD THIS MAN, CAULDER, DO THIS TO CHILDREN?
YOU HAVE TO UNDERSTAND--WE ALL THOUGHT NILES WAS A GREAT MAN. A BRILLIANT MAN. HE WANTED TO CHANGE THINGS. I MEAN REALLY CHANGE THIS COUNTRY.
FOR A WHILE WE BELIEVED IN HIS CAUSE. HE BROUGHT US ALL TOGETHER. A GROUP OF LIKE MINDS WHO TRULY BELIEVED.

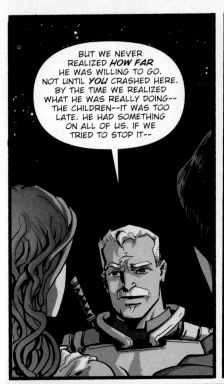

BUT WE NEVER REALIZED *HOW FAR* HE WAS WILLING TO GO. NOT UNTIL *YOU* CRASHED HERE. BY THE TIME WE REALIZED WHAT HE WAS REALLY DOING--THE CHILDREN--IT WAS TOO LATE. HE HAD SOMETHING ON ALL OF US. IF WE TRIED TO STOP IT--

DON'T EXPECT US TO FEEL *SORRY* FOR YOU. YOU WERE COWARDS. *ALL* OF YOU.

YES, I--YES. BUT I WANT TO HELP. I WANT TO HELP *JOEY*. I WANT TO HELP *YOU*.

THE OTHER KIDS--THE ONES FROM OREGON. THEY'RE IN TROUBLE. I SENSED IT RIGHT BEFORE YOU ATTACKED.

YES. CAULDER FOUND THEM. HE SENT HIS *"TITANS"* AFTER THEM.

THEY HELP STARFIRE. THEY HELP ME. WE NEED HELP THEM.

YOU DON'T UNDERSTAND. THESE AREN'T JUST KIDS--*THEY ARE WEAPONS...*

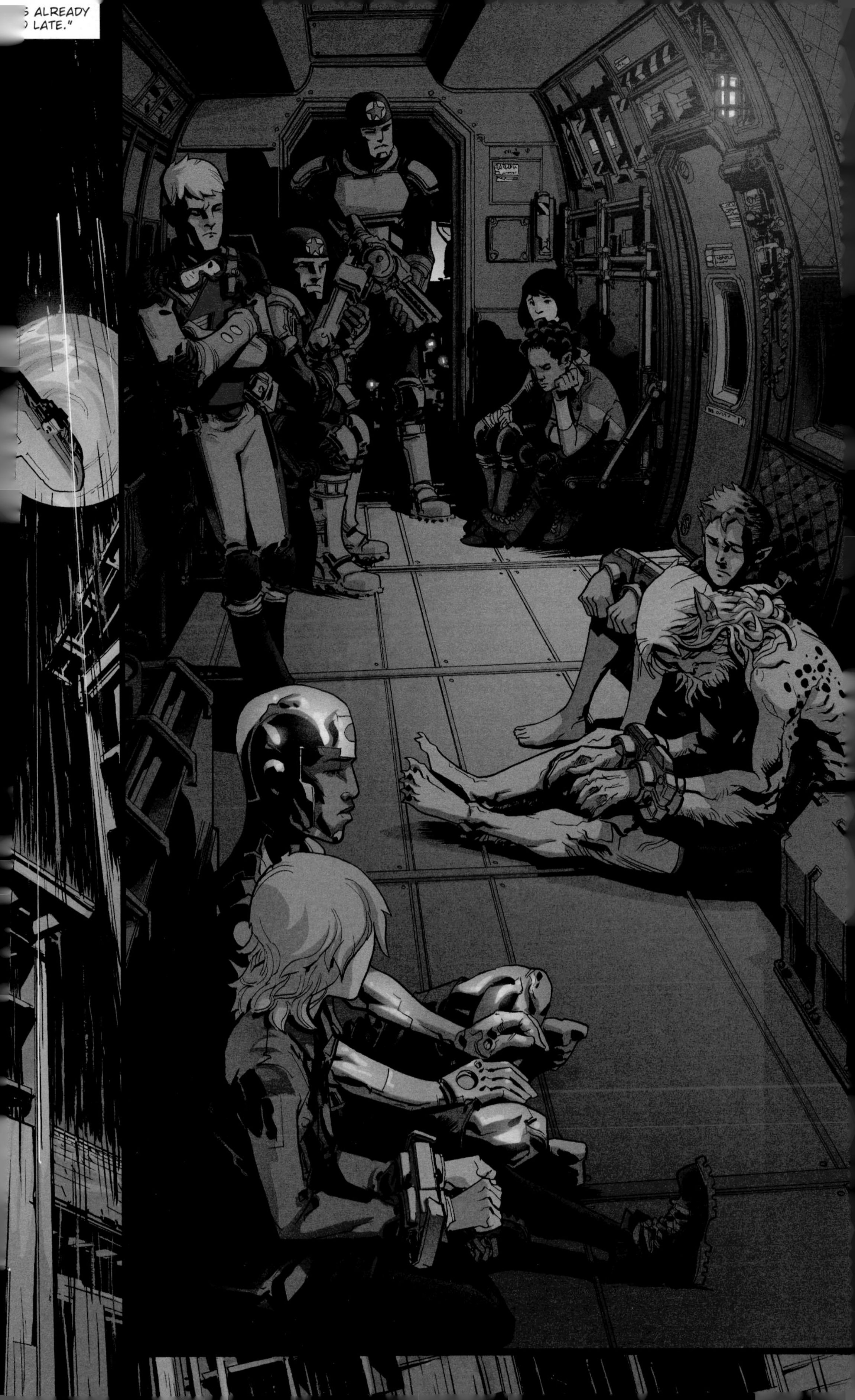
ALREADY
LATE."

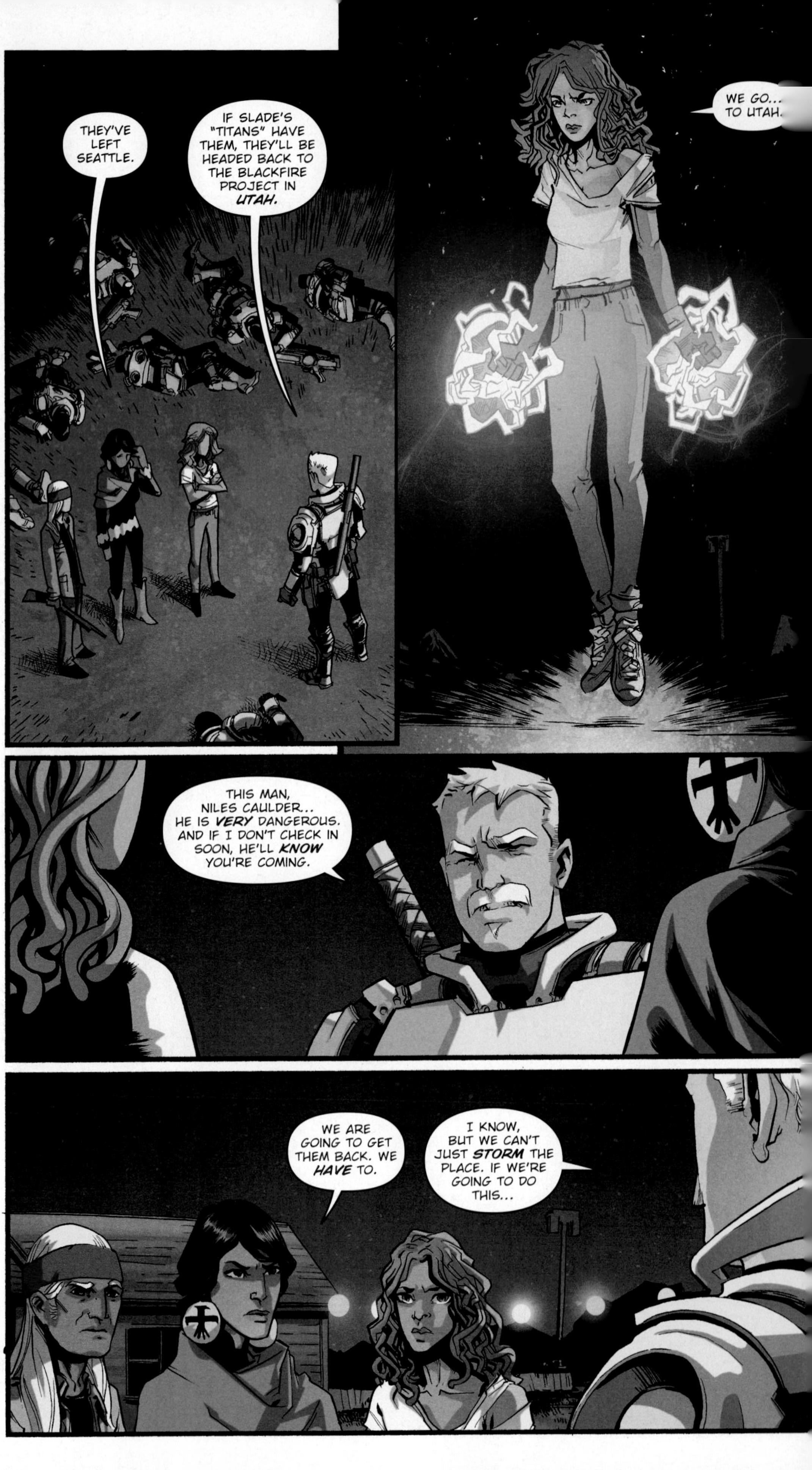
THEY'VE LEFT SEATTLE.
IF SLADE'S "TITANS" HAVE THEM, THEY'LL BE HEADED BACK TO THE BLACKFIRE PROJECT IN UTAH.
WE GO... TO UTAH.
THIS MAN, NILES CAULDER... HE IS VERY DANGEROUS. AND IF I DON'T CHECK IN SOON, HE'LL KNOW YOU'RE COMING.
WE ARE GOING TO GET THEM BACK. WE HAVE TO.
I KNOW, BUT WE CAN'T JUST STORM THE PLACE. IF WE'RE GOING TO DO THIS...

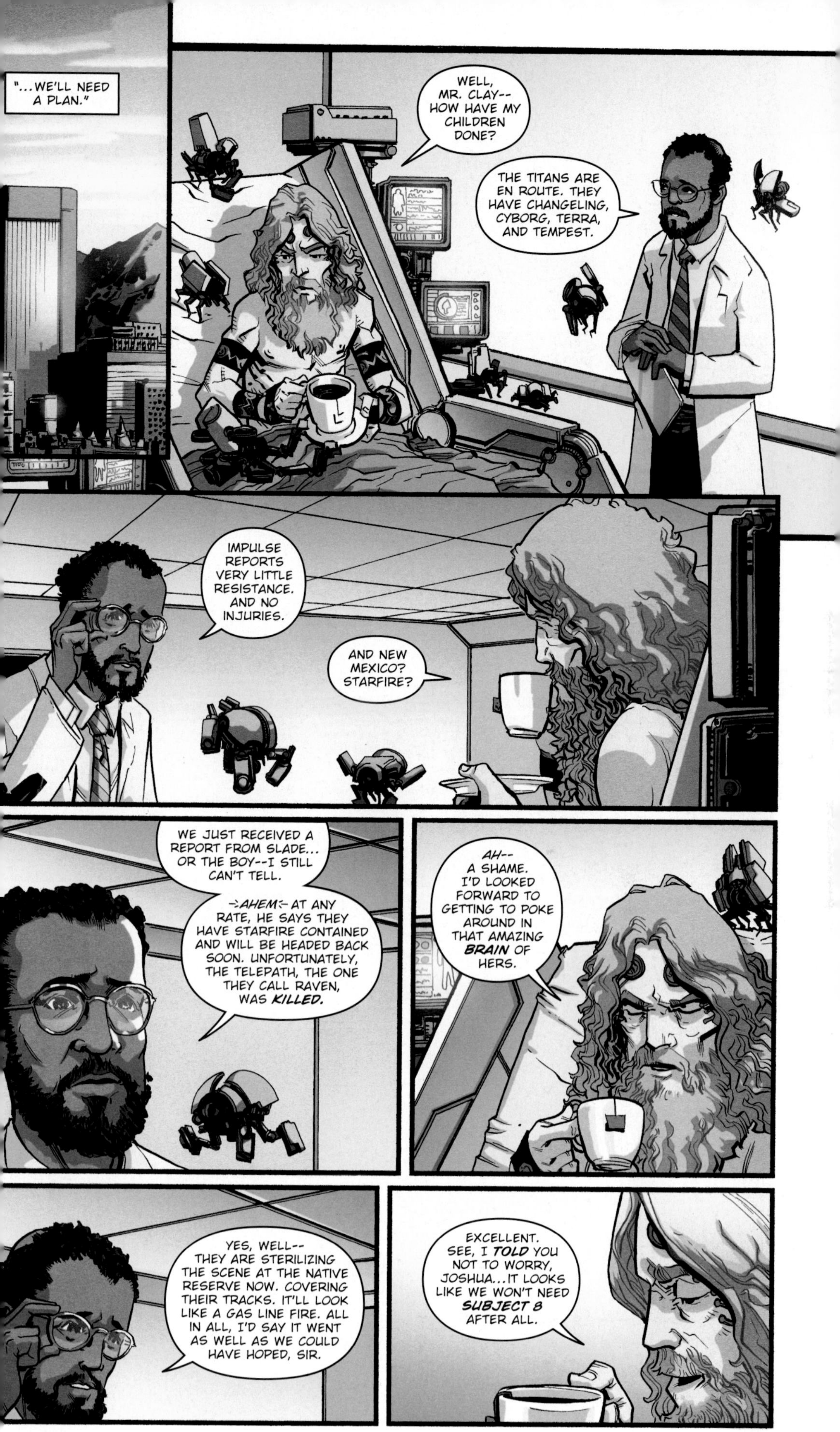

"...WE'LL NEED A PLAN."
WELL, MR. CLAY-- HOW HAVE MY CHILDREN DONE?
THE TITANS ARE EN ROUTE. THEY HAVE CHANGELING, CYBORG, TERRA, AND TEMPEST.
IMPULSE REPORTS VERY LITTLE RESISTANCE. AND NO INJURIES.
AND NEW MEXICO? STARFIRE?
WE JUST RECEIVED A REPORT FROM SLADE... OR THE BOY--I STILL CAN'T TELL.
-AHEM- AT ANY RATE, HE SAYS THEY HAVE STARFIRE CONTAINED AND WILL BE HEADED BACK SOON. UNFORTUNATELY, THE TELEPATH, THE ONE THEY CALL RAVEN, WAS KILLED.
AH-- A SHAME. I'D LOOKED FORWARD TO GETTING TO POKE AROUND IN THAT AMAZING BRAIN OF HERS.
YES, WELL-- THEY ARE STERILIZING THE SCENE AT THE NATIVE RESERVE NOW. COVERING THEIR TRACKS. IT'LL LOOK LIKE A GAS LINE FIRE. ALL IN ALL, I'D SAY IT WENT AS WELL AS WE COULD HAVE HOPED, SIR.
EXCELLENT. SEE, I TOLD YOU NOT TO WORRY, JOSHUA...IT LOOKS LIKE WE WON'T NEED SUBJECT 8 AFTER ALL.

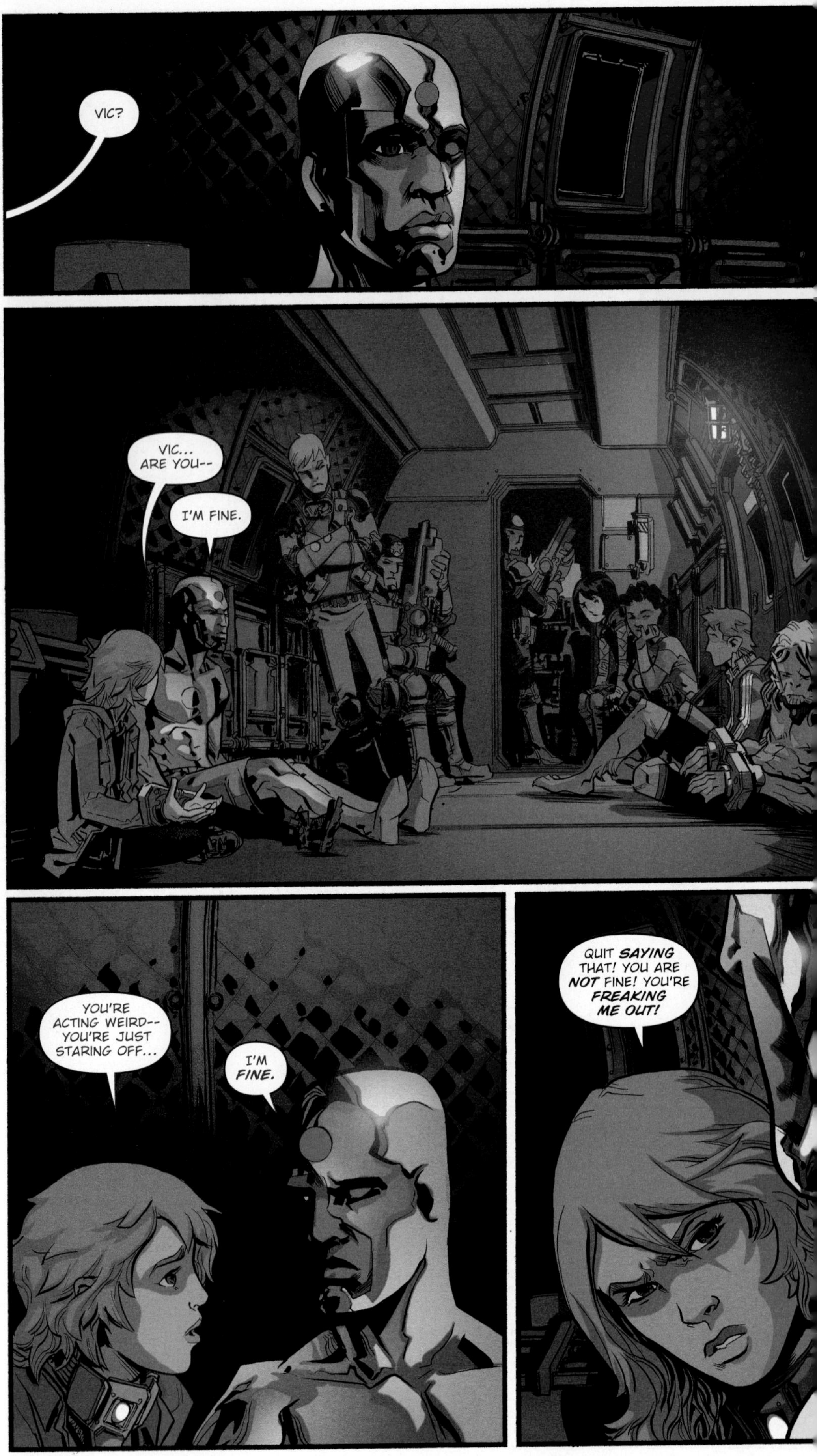

VIC?
VIC... ARE YOU--
I'M FINE.
YOU'RE ACTING WEIRD-- YOU'RE JUST STARING OFF...
I'M FINE.
QUIT SAYING THAT! YOU ARE NOT FINE! YOU'RE FREAKING ME OUT!

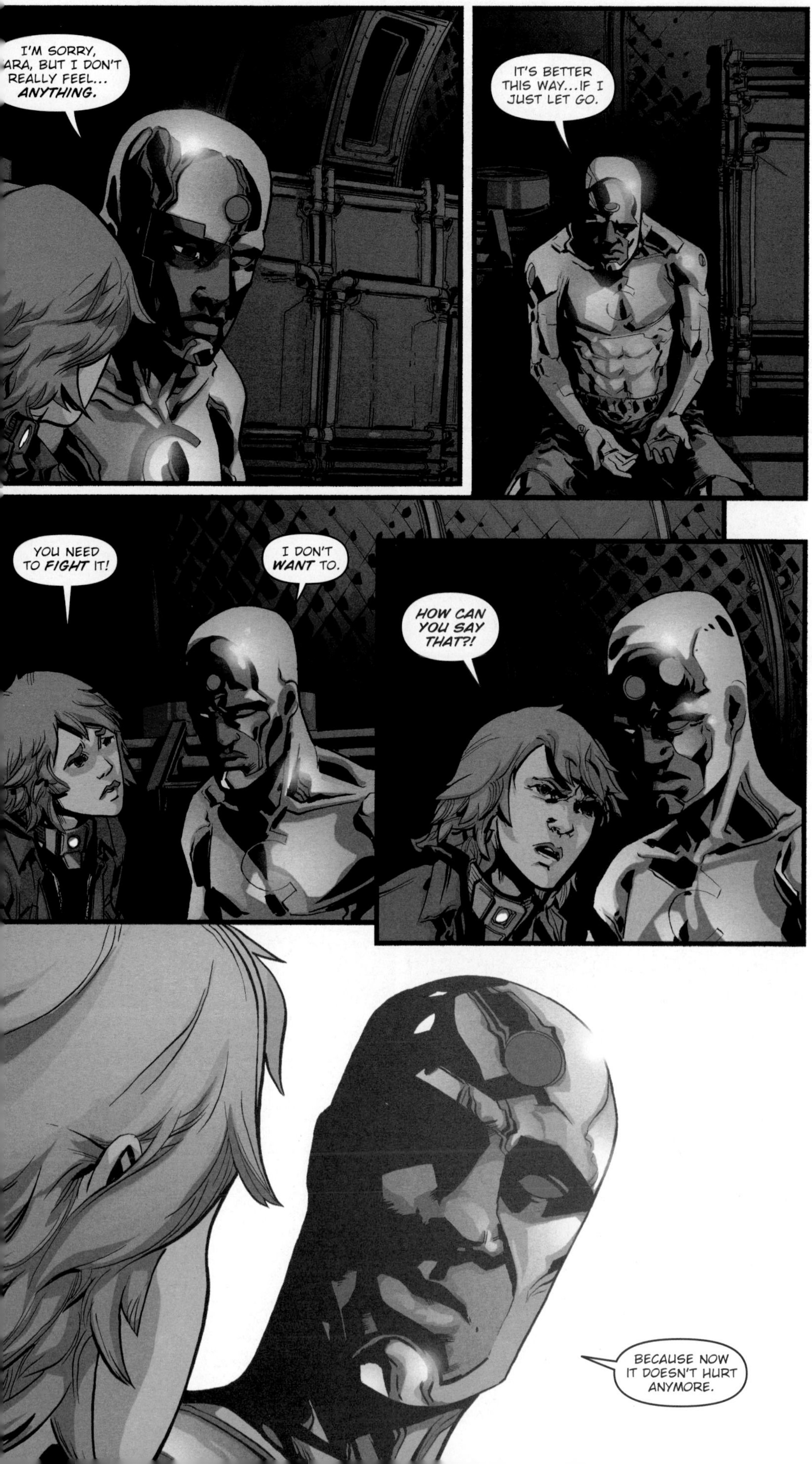
I'M SORRY, ARA, BUT I DON'T REALLY FEEL... ANYTHING.
IT'S BETTER THIS WAY...IF I JUST LET GO.
YOU NEED TO FIGHT IT!
I DON'T WANT TO.
HOW CAN YOU SAY THAT?!
BECAUSE NOW IT DOESN'T HURT ANYMORE.

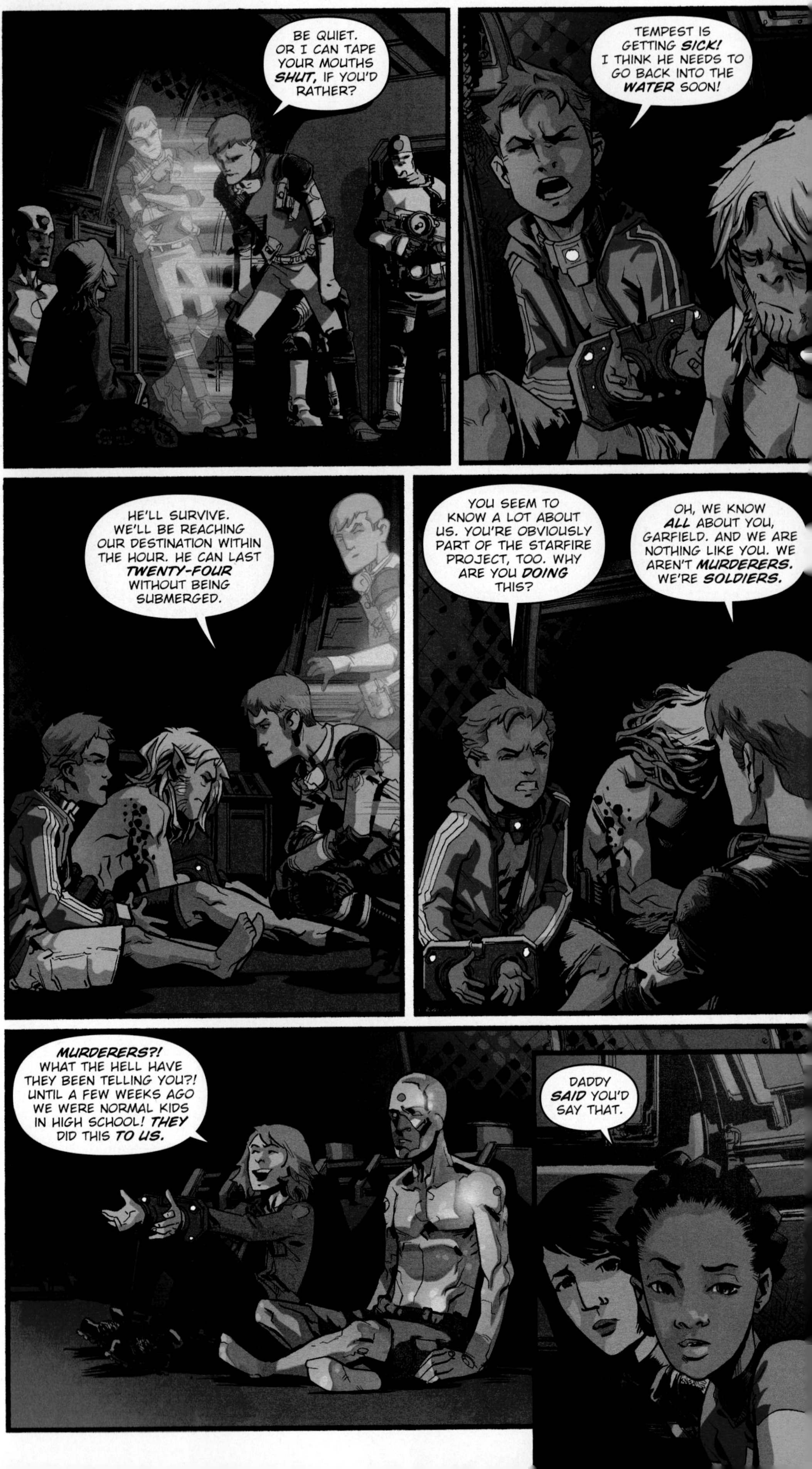
BE QUIET. OR I CAN TAPE YOUR MOUTHS SHUT, IF YOU'D RATHER?
TEMPEST IS GETTING SICK! I THINK HE NEEDS TO GO BACK INTO THE WATER SOON!
HE'LL SURVIVE. WE'LL BE REACHING OUR DESTINATION WITHIN THE HOUR. HE CAN LAST TWENTY-FOUR WITHOUT BEING SUBMERGED.
YOU SEEM TO KNOW A LOT ABOUT US. YOU'RE OBVIOUSLY PART OF THE STARFIRE PROJECT, TOO. WHY ARE YOU DOING THIS?
OH, WE KNOW ALL ABOUT YOU, GARFIELD. AND WE ARE NOTHING LIKE YOU. WE AREN'T MURDERERS. WE'RE SOLDIERS.
MURDERERS?! WHAT THE HELL HAVE THEY BEEN TELLING YOU?! UNTIL A FEW WEEKS AGO WE WERE NORMAL KIDS IN HIGH SCHOOL! THEY DID THIS TO US.
DADDY SAID YOU'D SAY THAT.

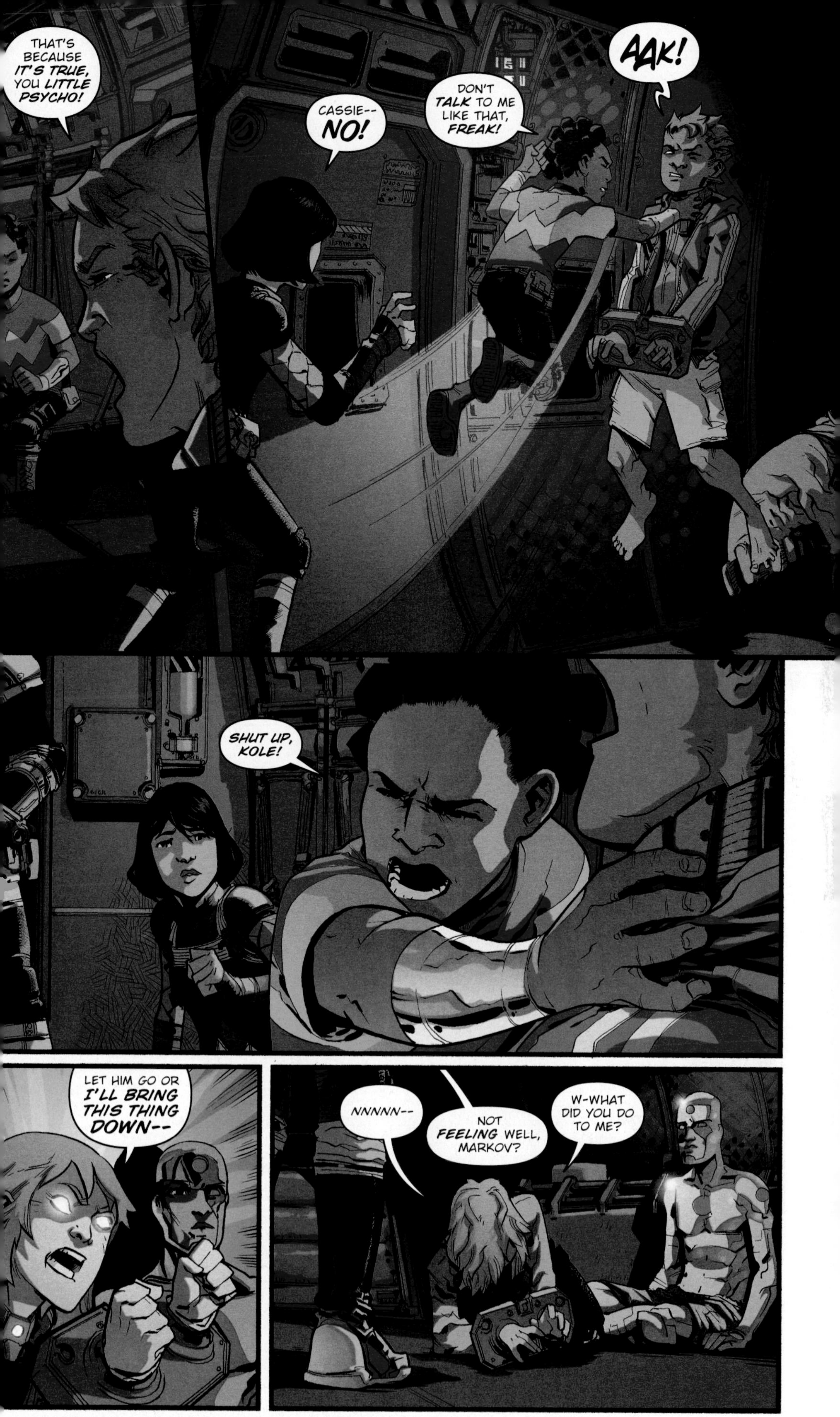
THAT'S BECAUSE IT'S TRUE, YOU LITTLE PSYCHO!
CASSIE-- NO!
DON'T TALK TO ME LIKE THAT, FREAK!
AAK!
SHUT UP, KOLE!
LET HIM GO OR I'LL BRING THIS THING DOWN--
NNNNN--
NOT FEELING WELL, MARKOV?
W-WHAT DID YOU DO TO ME?

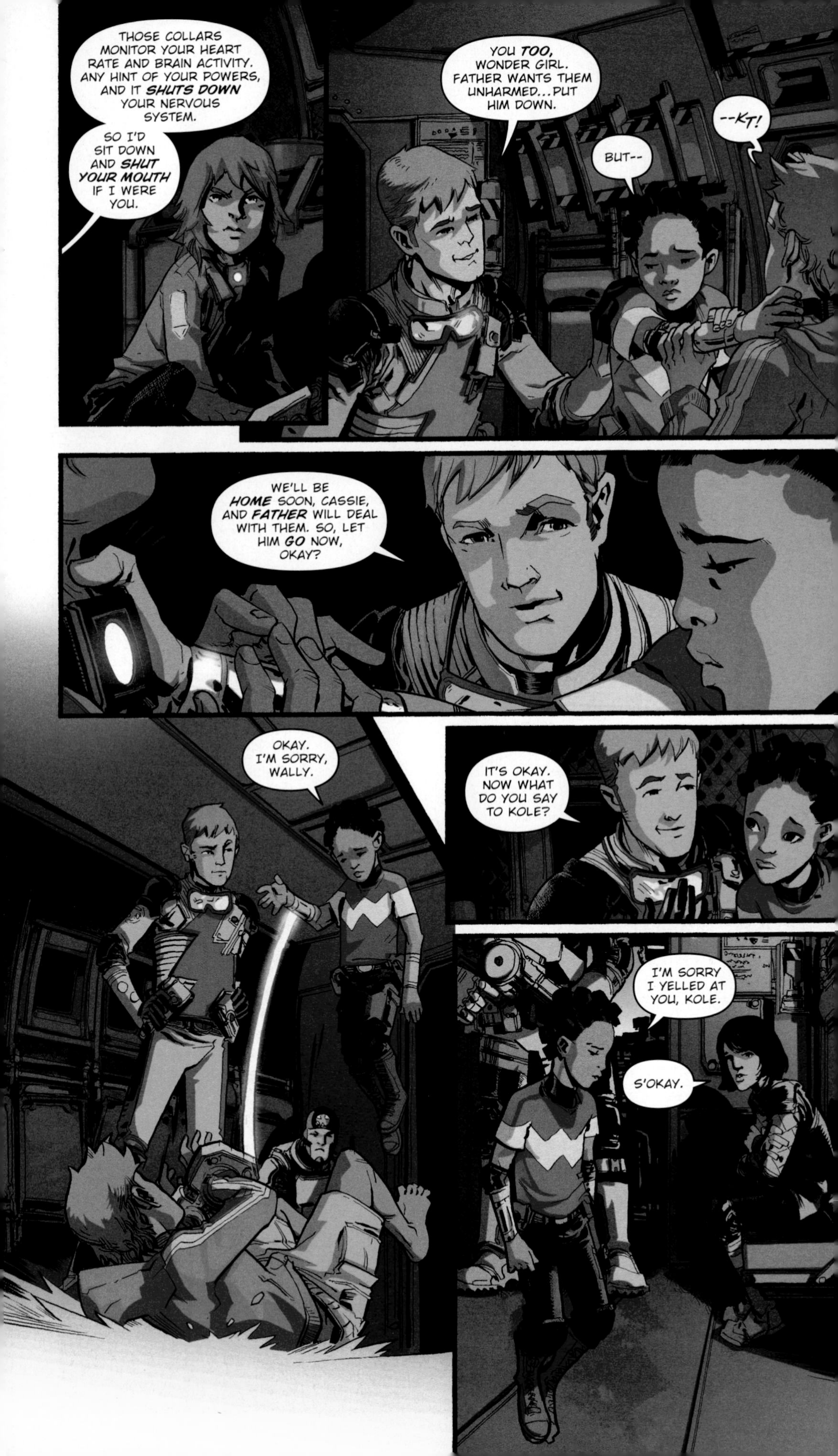
THOSE COLLARS MONITOR YOUR HEART RATE AND BRAIN ACTIVITY. ANY HINT OF YOUR POWERS, AND IT SHUTS DOWN YOUR NERVOUS SYSTEM.
SO I'D SIT DOWN AND SHUT YOUR MOUTH IF I WERE YOU.
YOU TOO, WONDER GIRL. FATHER WANTS THEM UNHARMED...PUT HIM DOWN.
BUT--
--KT!
WE'LL BE HOME SOON, CASSIE, AND FATHER WILL DEAL WITH THEM. SO, LET HIM GO NOW, OKAY?
OKAY. I'M SORRY, WALLY.
IT'S OKAY. NOW WHAT DO YOU SAY TO KOLE?
I'M SORRY I YELLED AT YOU, KOLE.
S'OKAY.

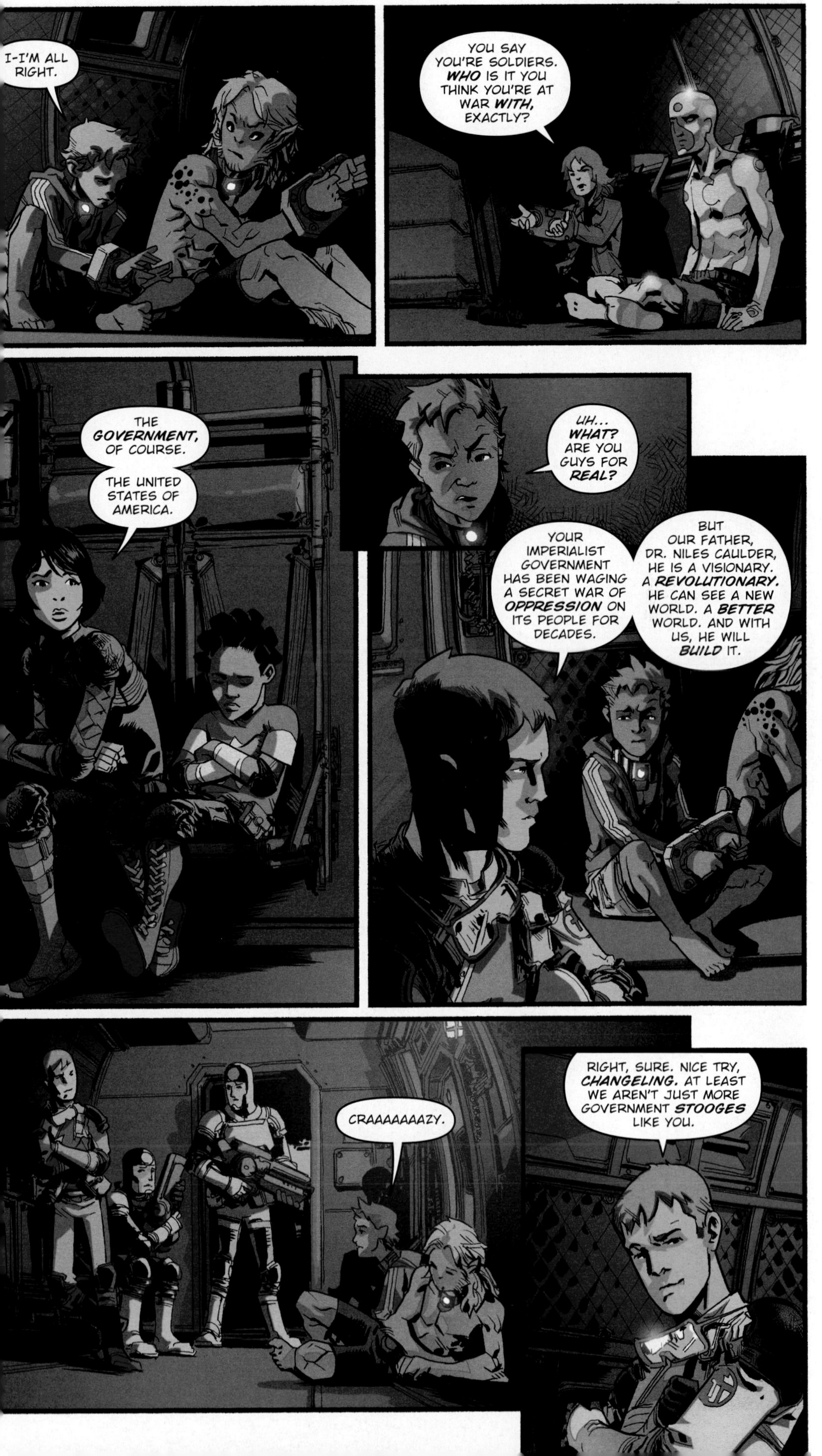
I-I'M ALL RIGHT.
YOU SAY YOU'RE SOLDIERS. WHO IS IT YOU THINK YOU'RE AT WAR WITH, EXACTLY?
THE GOVERNMENT, OF COURSE.
THE UNITED STATES OF AMERICA.
UH... WHAT? ARE YOU GUYS FOR REAL?
YOUR IMPERIALIST GOVERNMENT HAS BEEN WAGING A SECRET WAR OF OPPRESSION ON ITS PEOPLE FOR DECADES.
BUT OUR FATHER, DR. NILES CAULDER, HE IS A VISIONARY. A REVOLUTIONARY. HE CAN SEE A NEW WORLD. A BETTER WORLD. AND WITH US, HE WILL BUILD IT.
CRAAAAAAAAZY.
RIGHT, SURE. NICE TRY, CHANGELING. AT LEAST WE AREN'T JUST MORE GOVERNMENT STOOGES LIKE YOU.

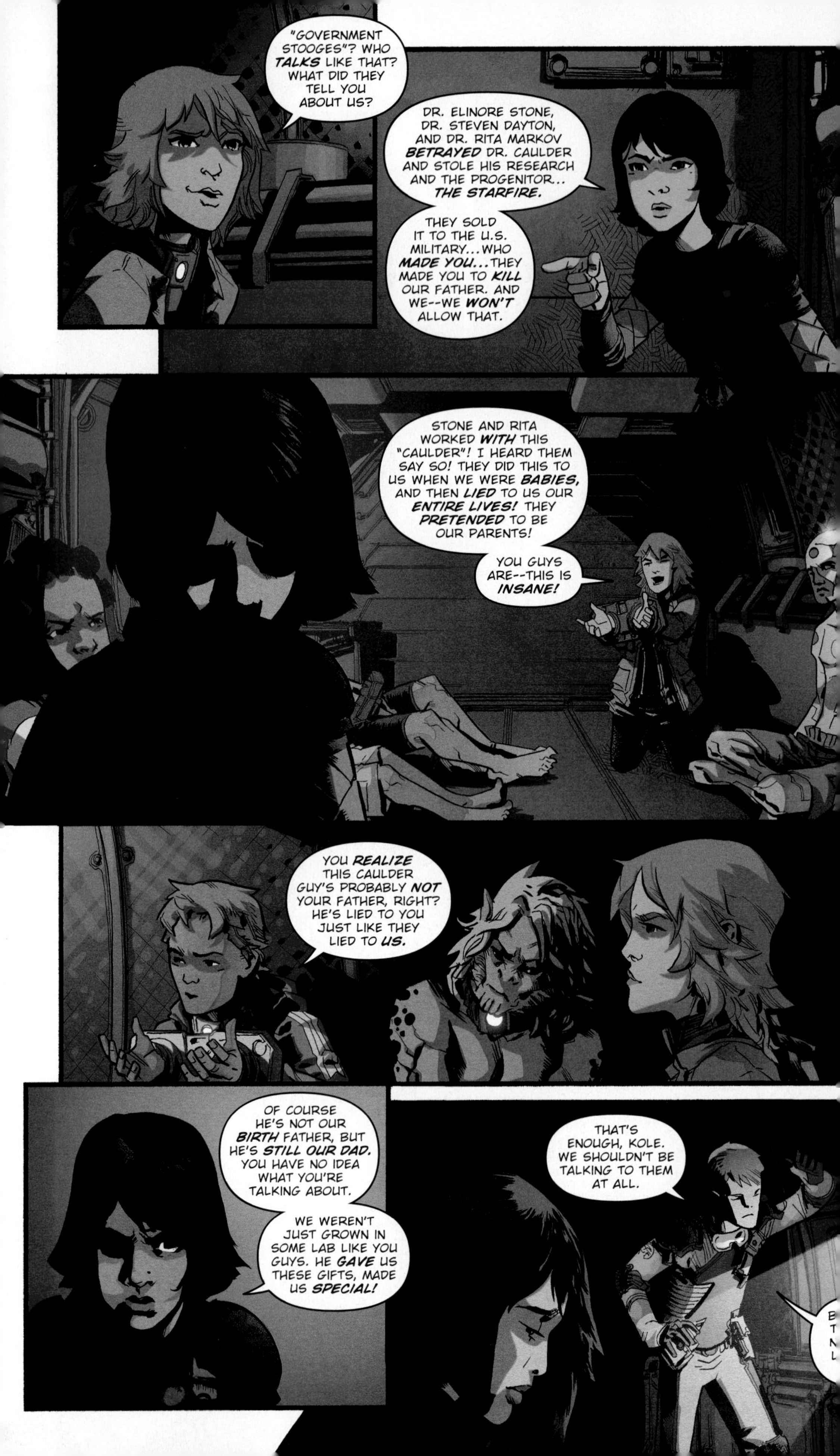
"GOVERNMENT STOOGES"? WHO TALKS LIKE THAT? WHAT DID THEY TELL YOU ABOUT US?
DR. ELINORE STONE, DR. STEVEN DAYTON, AND DR. RITA MARKOV BETRAYED DR. CAULDER AND STOLE HIS RESEARCH AND THE PROGENITOR... THE STARFIRE.
THEY SOLD IT TO THE U.S. MILITARY...WHO MADE YOU...THEY MADE YOU TO KILL OUR FATHER. AND WE--WE WON'T ALLOW THAT.
STONE AND RITA WORKED WITH THIS "CAULDER"! I HEARD THEM SAY SO! THEY DID THIS TO US WHEN WE WERE BABIES, AND THEN LIED TO US OUR ENTIRE LIVES! THEY PRETENDED TO BE OUR PARENTS!
YOU GUYS ARE--THIS IS INSANE!
YOU REALIZE THIS CAULDER GUY'S PROBABLY NOT YOUR FATHER, RIGHT? HE'S LIED TO YOU JUST LIKE THEY LIED TO US.
OF COURSE HE'S NOT OUR BIRTH FATHER, BUT HE'S STILL OUR DAD. YOU HAVE NO IDEA WHAT YOU'RE TALKING ABOUT.
WE WEREN'T JUST GROWN IN SOME LAB LIKE YOU GUYS. HE GAVE US THESE GIFTS, MADE US SPECIAL!
THAT'S ENOUGH, KOLE. WE SHOULDN'T BE TALKING TO THEM AT ALL.

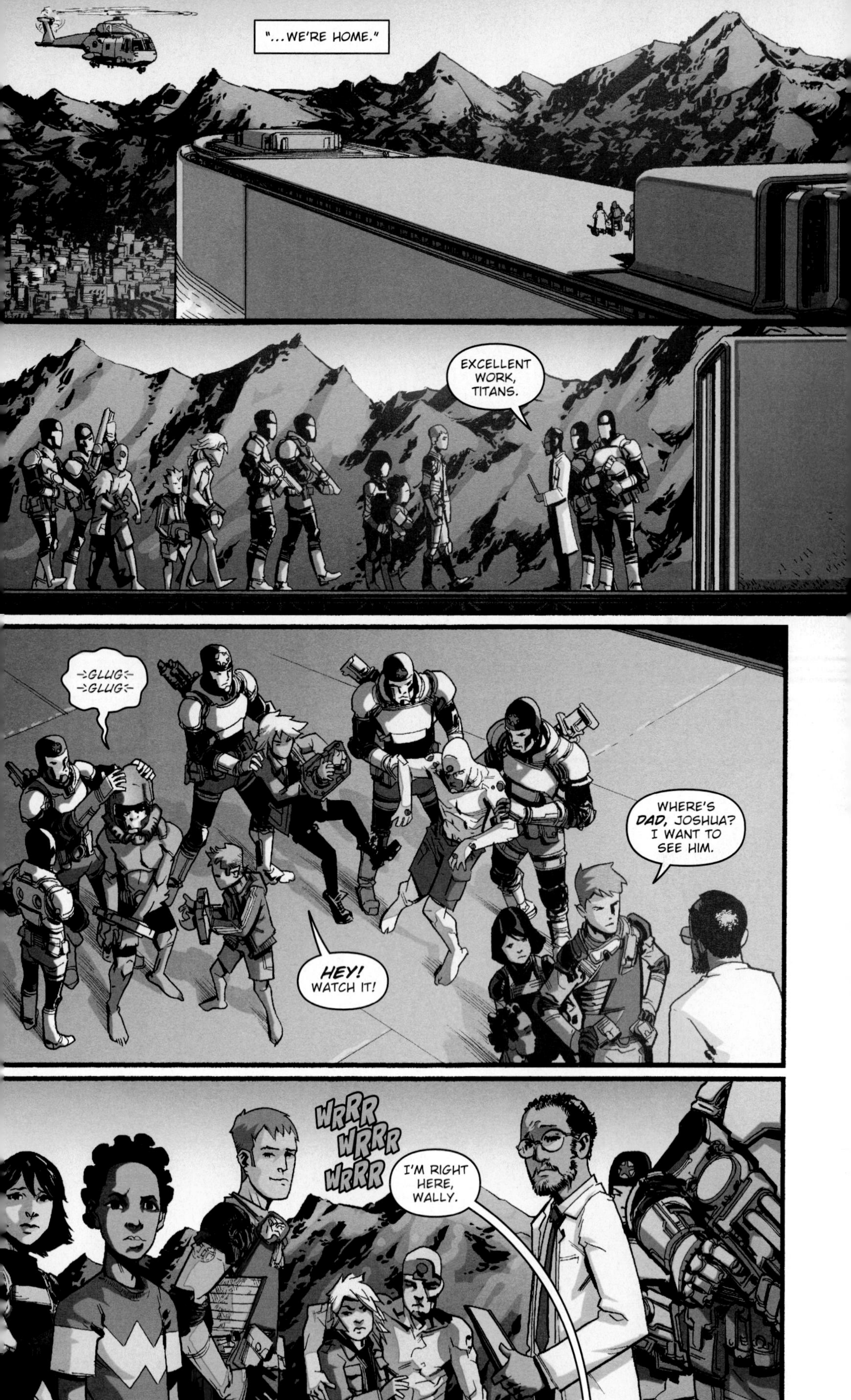
"...WE'RE HOME."
EXCELLENT WORK, TITANS.
-GLUG- -GLUG-
WHERE'S DAD, JOSHUA? I WANT TO SEE HIM.
HEY! WATCH IT!
WRRR WRRR WRRR
I'M RIGHT HERE, WALLY.

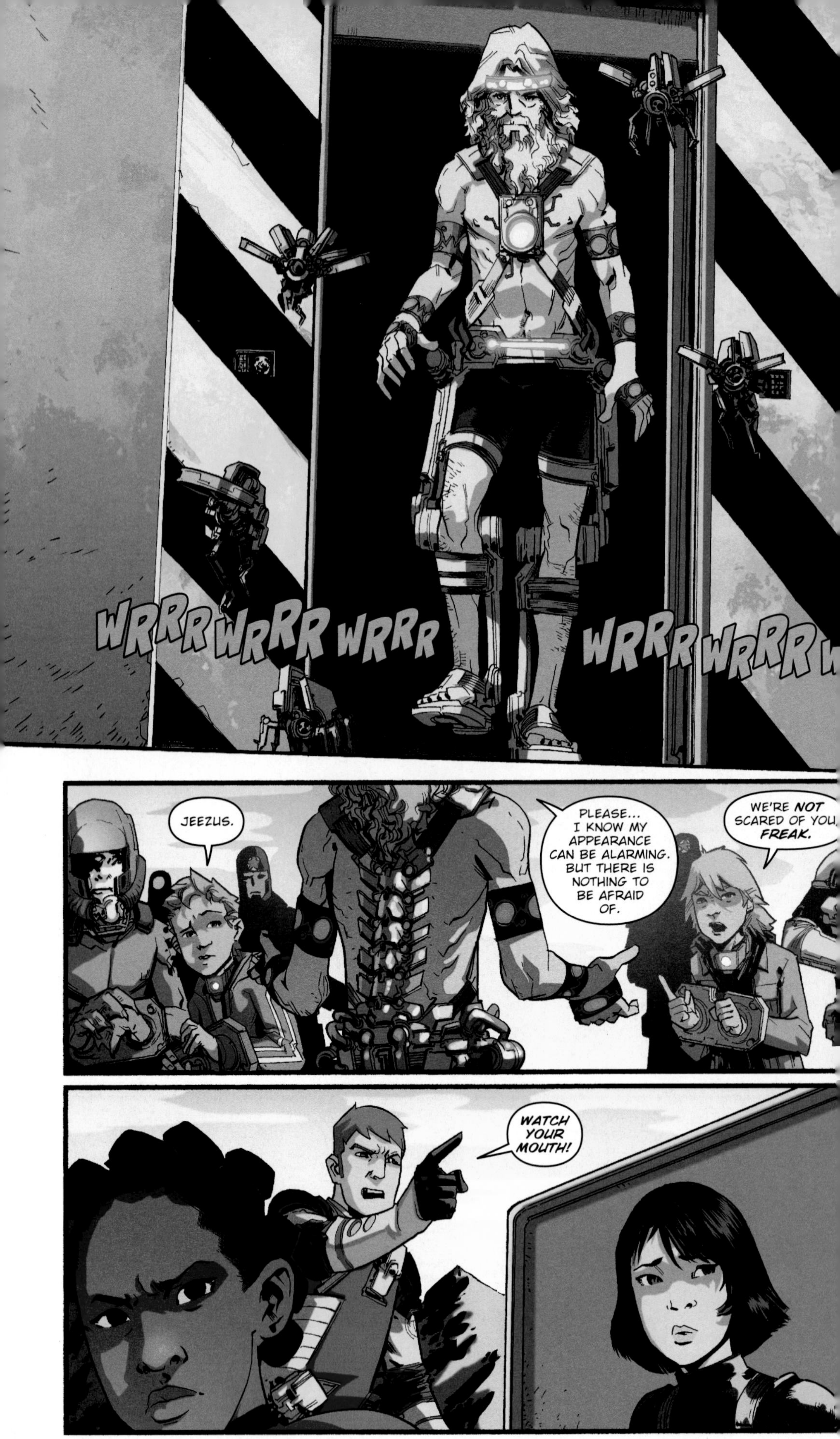
WRRR WRRR WRRR
WRRR WRRRR W
JEEZUS.
PLEASE... I KNOW MY APPEARANCE CAN BE ALARMING. BUT THERE IS NOTHING TO BE AFRAID OF.
WE'RE *NOT* SCARED OF YOU, *FREAK.*
WATCH YOUR MOUTH!

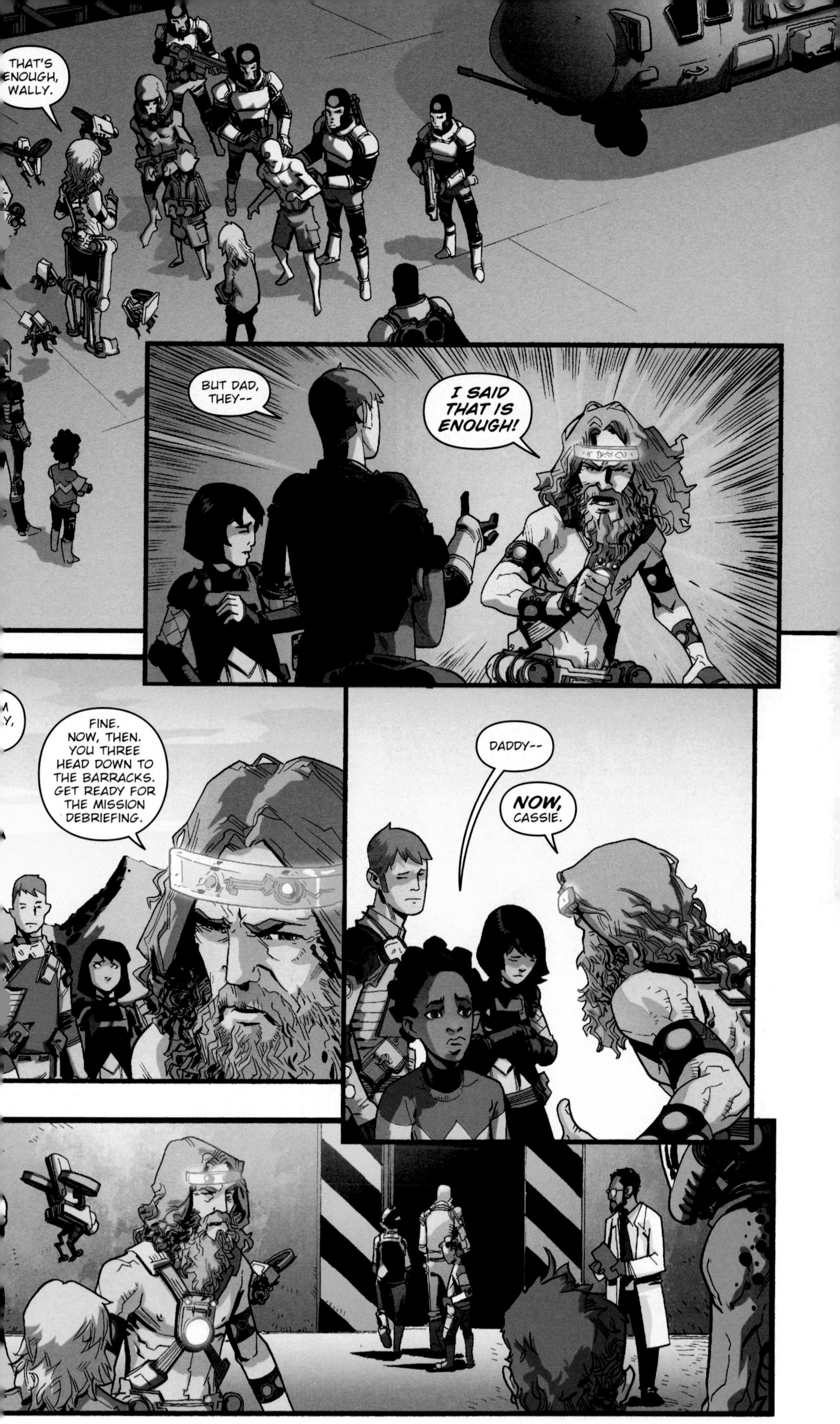
THAT'S ENOUGH, WALLY.
BUT DAD, THEY--
I SAID THAT IS ENOUGH!
FINE. NOW, THEN. YOU THREE HEAD DOWN TO THE BARRACKS. GET READY FOR THE MISSION DEBRIEFING.
DADDY--
NOW, CASSIE.

MY GOD! *LOOK* AT YOU, VICTOR. WE NEVER *ANTICIPATED* THIS!

JOSHUA, TAKE VICTOR TO THE *GARAGE* IMMEDIATELY. I WANT TO START RECORDING EVERYTHING WE CAN ABOUT THE METAMORPHOSIS.

VIC! *NO!*

I *DO* APOLOGIZE FOR THE COLLARS. A NECESSARY PRECAUTION, GIVEN WHAT YOU ALL DID IN OREGON. ALL I ASK IS THAT YOU HEAR ME OUT...

WHY, SO YOU CAN BRAINWASH *US* INTO BEING YOUR GOOD LITTLE PSYCHO-SOLDIERS, *TOO?*

NO. NOT SOLDIERS, *HEROES.*

HEROES? FOR TAKING DOWN THE GOVERNMENT? DON'T YOU MEAN *TERRORISTS?*

YOU WILL HELP TO FINALLY *FREE* THIS COUNTRY FROM THE PIGS WHO CONTROL IT. YOU WILL GO DOWN IN HISTORY AS THE GREATEST HEROES THIS COUNTRY *HAS EVER KNOWN.*

YOU'LL BE RICH AND FAMOUS BEYOND YOUR WILDEST DREAMS. YOU'LL BE *GODS.*

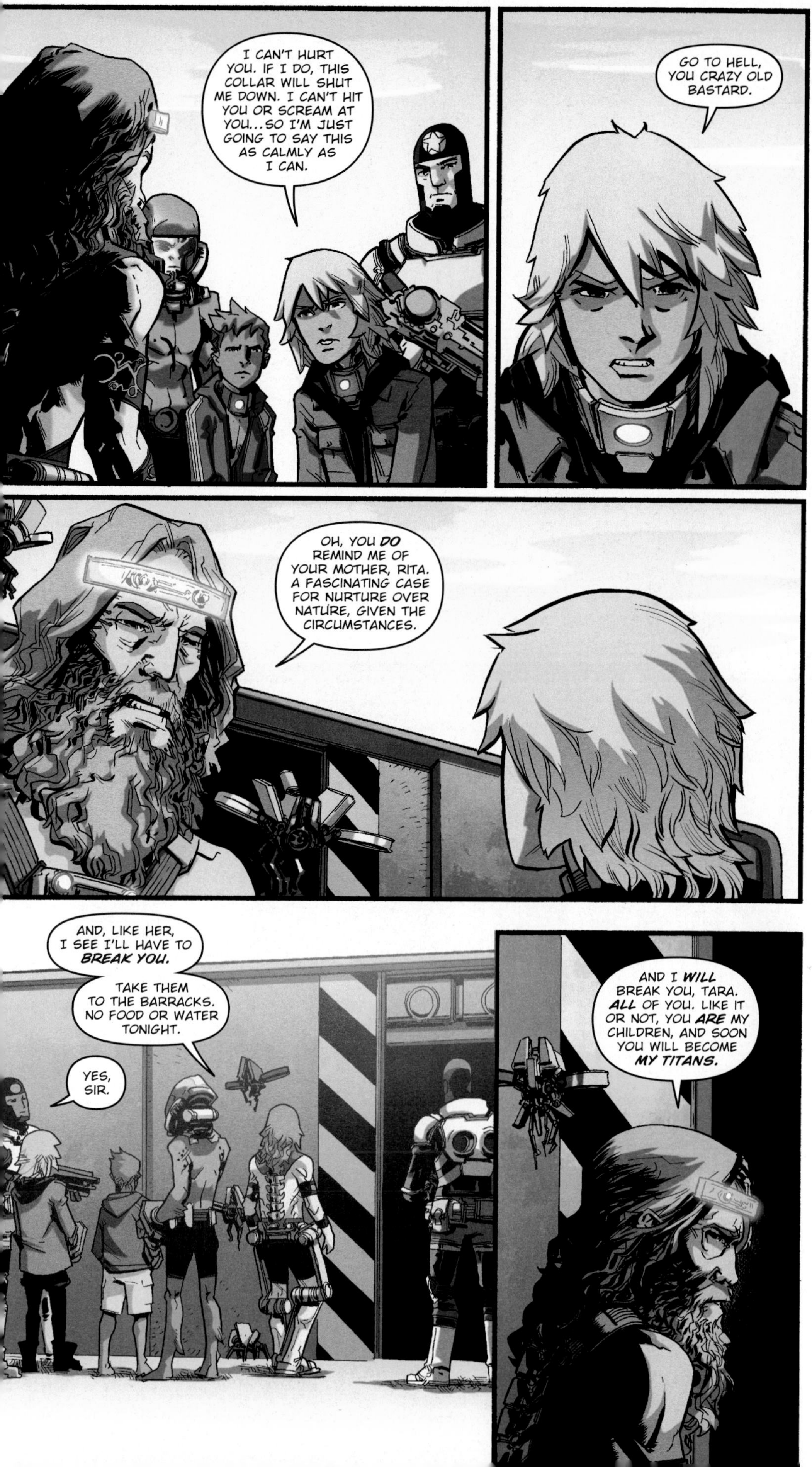
I CAN'T HURT YOU. IF I DO, THIS COLLAR WILL SHUT ME DOWN. I CAN'T HIT YOU OR SCREAM AT YOU...SO I'M JUST GOING TO SAY THIS AS CALMLY AS I CAN.
GO TO HELL, YOU CRAZY OLD BASTARD.
OH, YOU ***DO*** REMIND ME OF YOUR MOTHER, RITA. A FASCINATING CASE FOR NURTURE OVER NATURE, GIVEN THE CIRCUMSTANCES.
AND, LIKE HER, I SEE I'LL HAVE TO ***BREAK YOU.***
TAKE THEM TO THE BARRACKS. NO FOOD OR WATER TONIGHT.
YES, SIR.
AND I ***WILL*** BREAK YOU, TARA. ***ALL*** OF YOU. LIKE IT OR NOT, YOU ***ARE*** MY CHILDREN, AND SOON YOU WILL BECOME ***MY TITANS.***

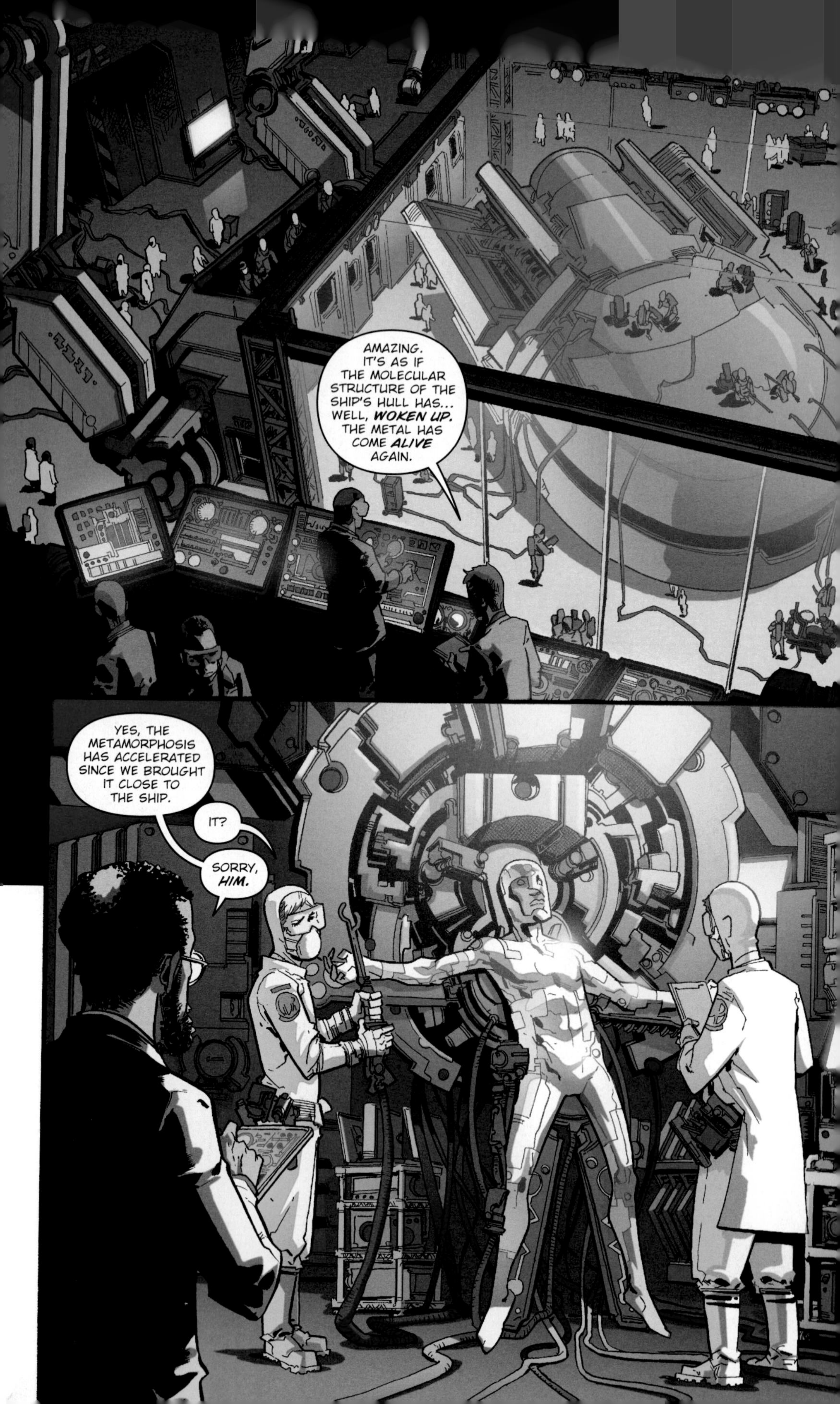
AMAZING. IT'S AS IF THE MOLECULAR STRUCTURE OF THE SHIP'S HULL HAS... WELL, **WOKEN UP.** THE METAL HAS COME **ALIVE** AGAIN.
YES, THE METAMORPHOSIS HAS ACCELERATED SINCE WE BROUGHT IT CLOSE TO THE SHIP.
IT?
SORRY, **HIM.**

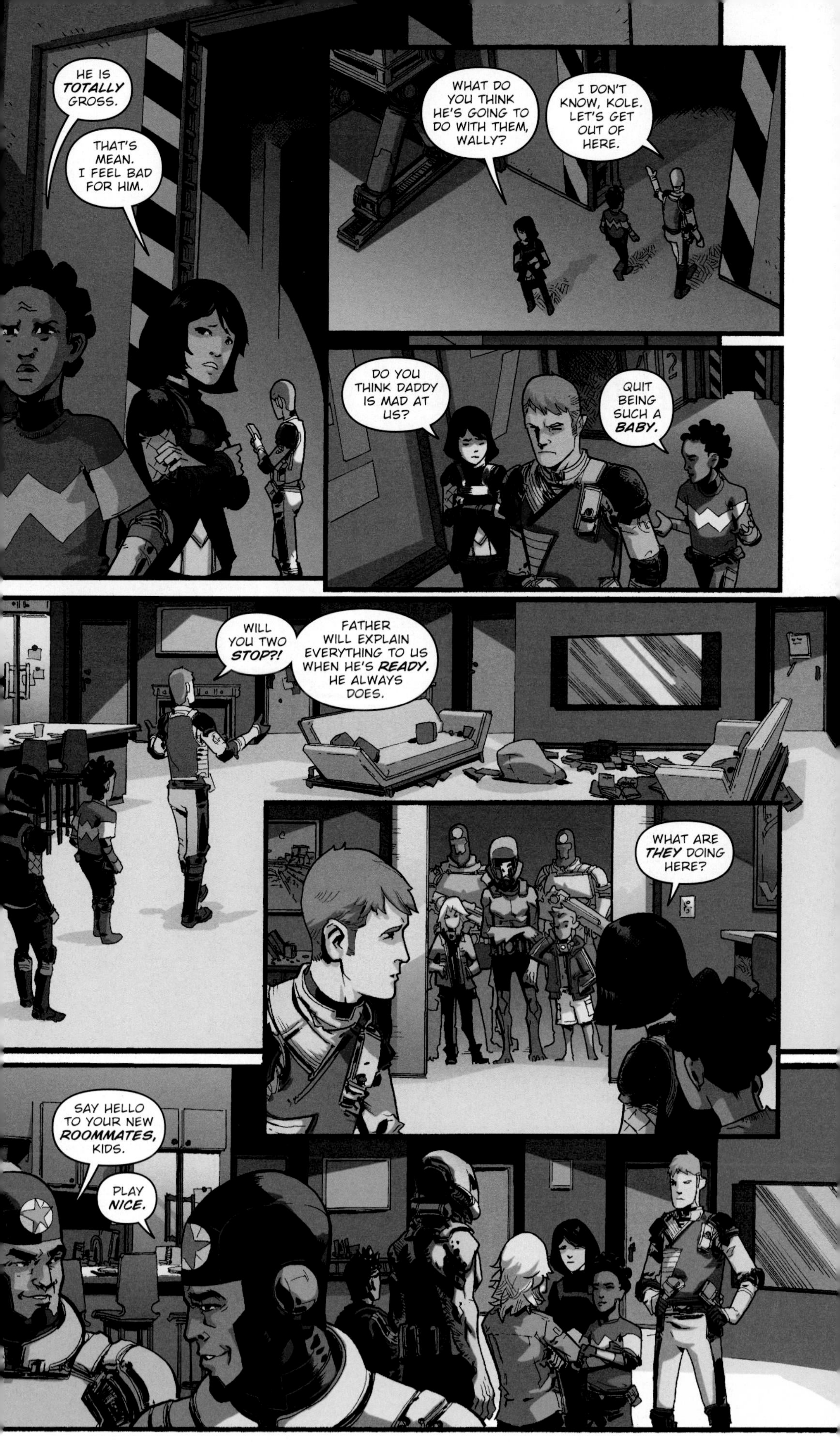

HE IS TOTALLY GROSS.
THAT'S MEAN. I FEEL BAD FOR HIM.
WHAT DO YOU THINK HE'S GOING TO DO WITH THEM, WALLY?
I DON'T KNOW, KOLE. LET'S GET OUT OF HERE.
DO YOU THINK DADDY IS MAD AT US?
QUIT BEING SUCH A BABY.
WILL YOU TWO STOP?!
FATHER WILL EXPLAIN EVERYTHING TO US WHEN HE'S READY. HE ALWAYS DOES.
WHAT ARE THEY DOING HERE?
SAY HELLO TO YOUR NEW ROOMMATES, KIDS.
PLAY NICE.

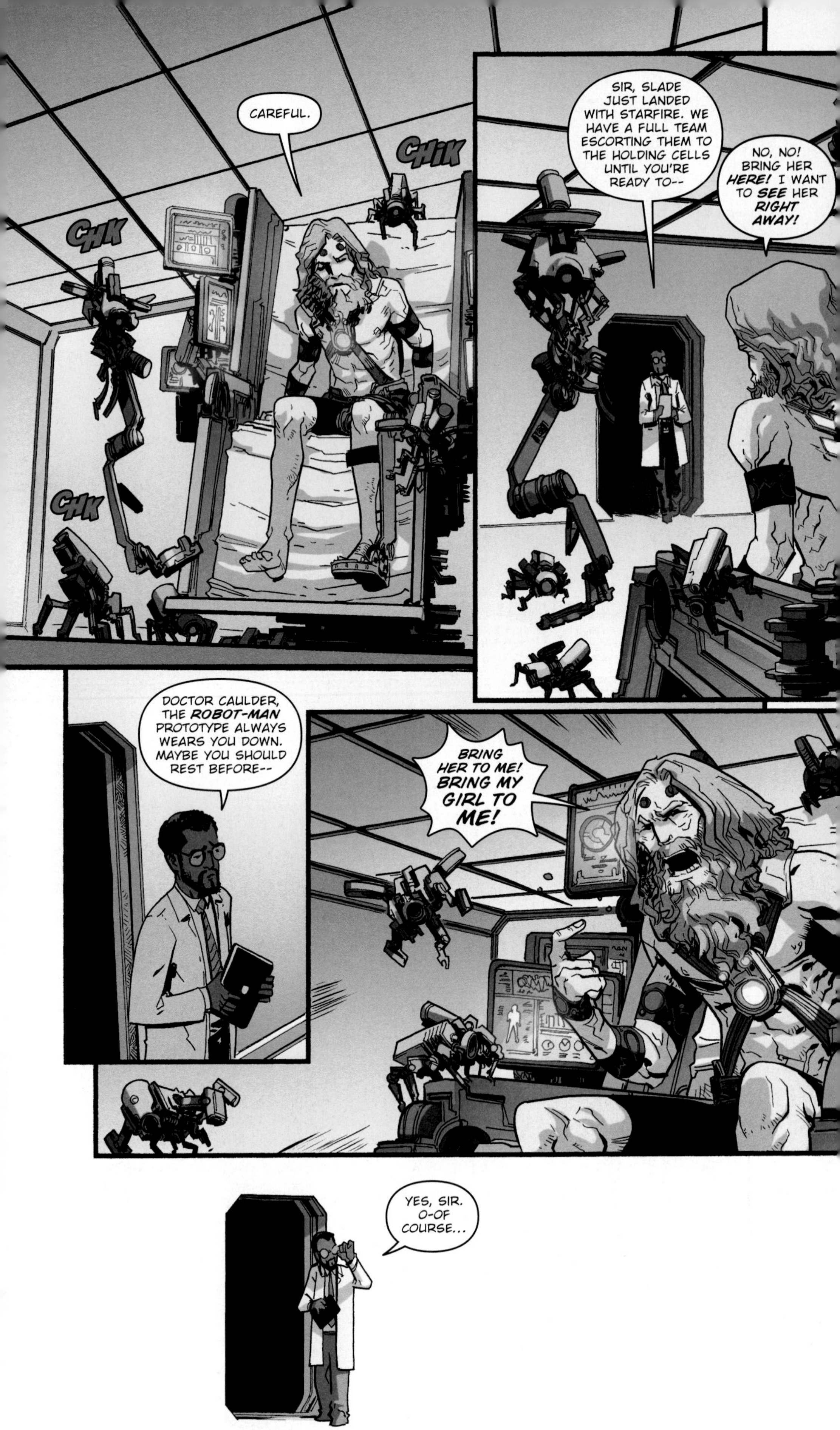
CAREFUL.
CHIK
CHK
CHK
SIR, SLADE JUST LANDED WITH STARFIRE. WE HAVE A FULL TEAM ESCORTING THEM TO THE HOLDING CELLS UNTIL YOU'RE READY TO--
NO, NO! BRING HER HERE! I WANT TO SEE HER RIGHT AWAY!
DOCTOR CAULDER, THE ROBOT-MAN PROTOTYPE ALWAYS WEARS YOU DOWN. MAYBE YOU SHOULD REST BEFORE--
BRING HER TO ME! BRING MY GIRL TO ME!
YES, SIR. O-OF COURSE...

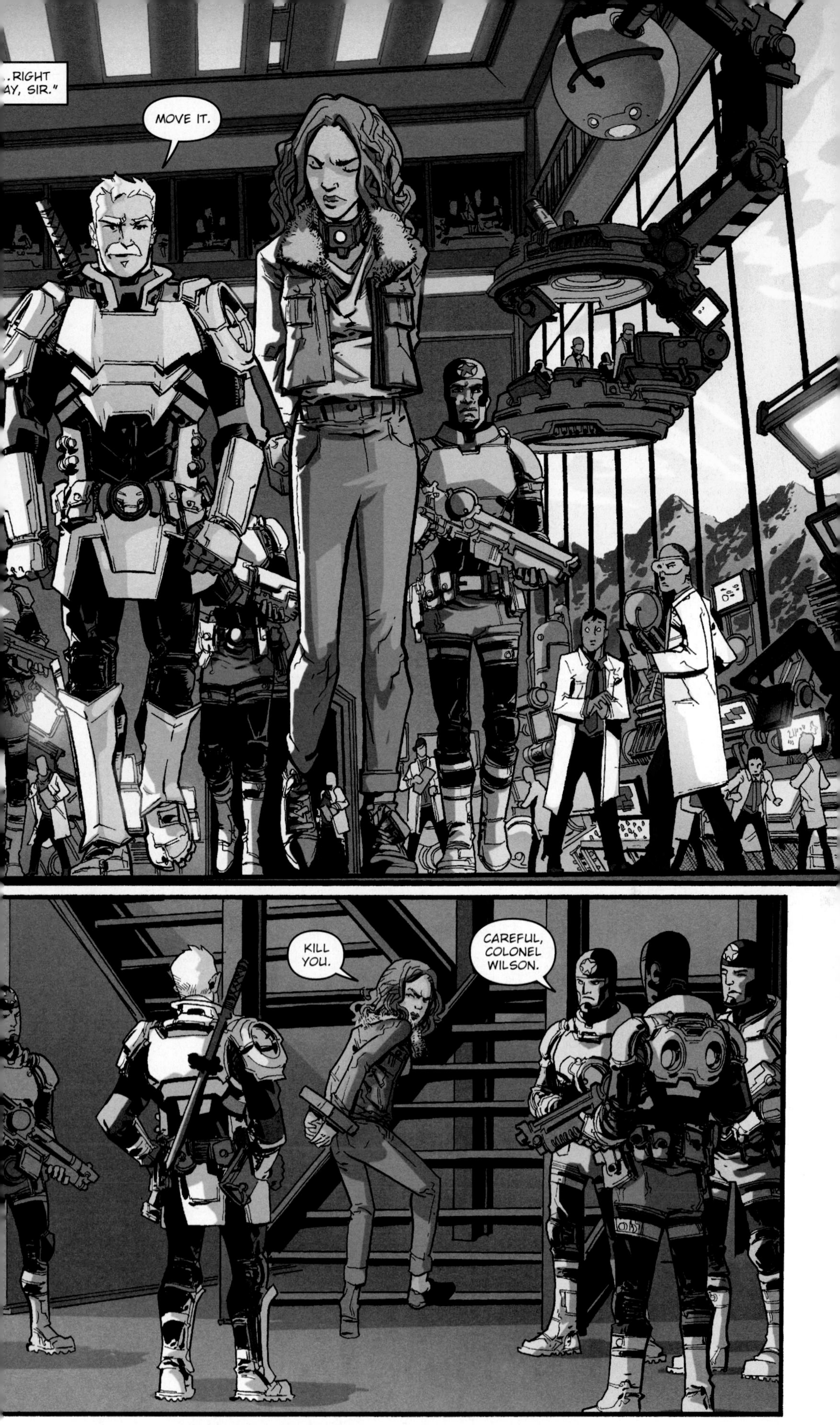
...RIGHT
AY, SIR."
MOVE IT.
KILL YOU.
CAREFUL, COLONEL WILSON.

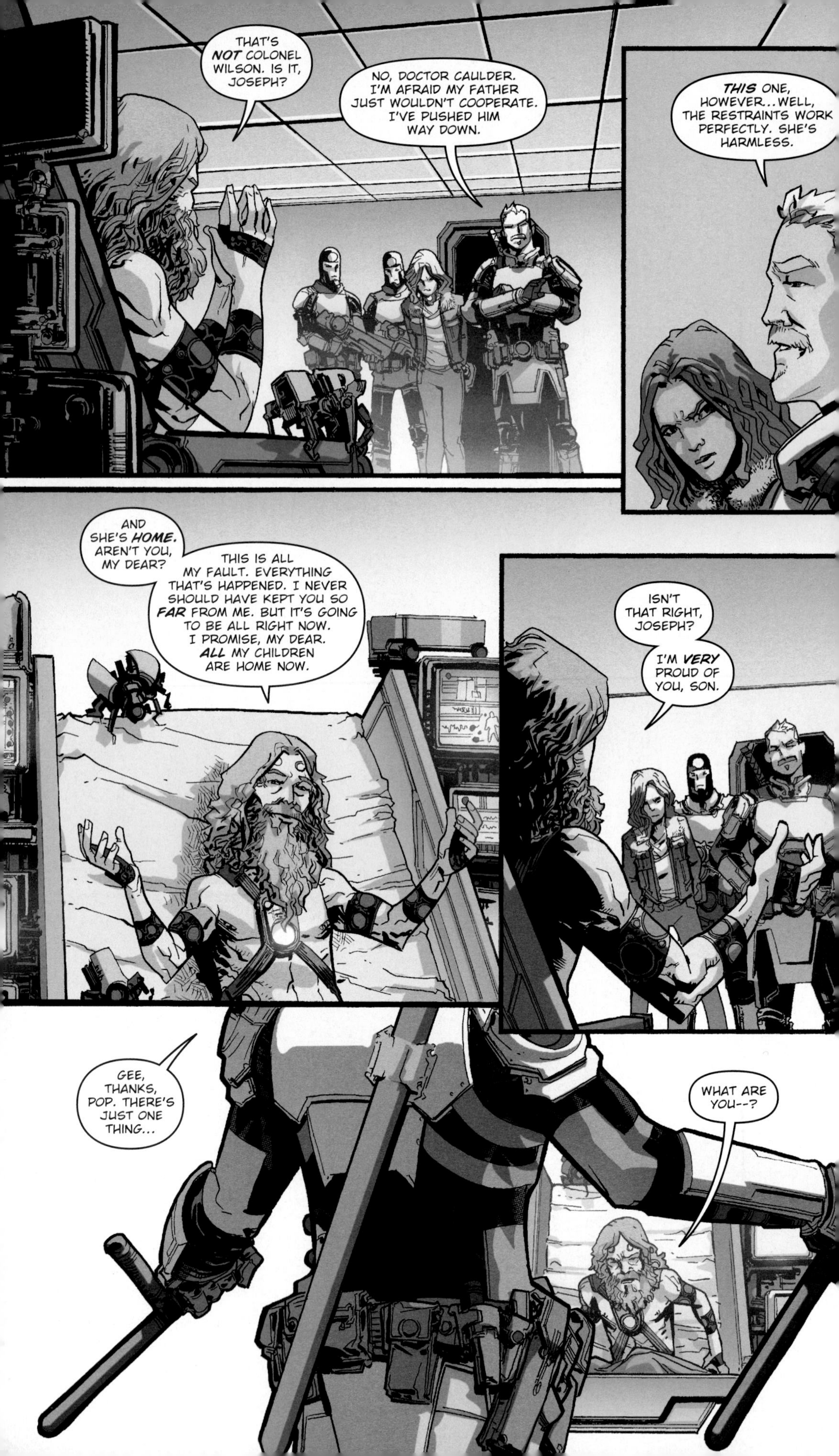
THAT'S NOT COLONEL WILSON. IS IT, JOSEPH?
NO, DOCTOR CAULDER. I'M AFRAID MY FATHER JUST WOULDN'T COOPERATE. I'VE PUSHED HIM WAY DOWN.
THIS ONE, HOWEVER...WELL, THE RESTRAINTS WORK PERFECTLY. SHE'S HARMLESS.
AND SHE'S HOME. AREN'T YOU, MY DEAR?
THIS IS ALL MY FAULT. EVERYTHING THAT'S HAPPENED. I NEVER SHOULD HAVE KEPT YOU SO FAR FROM ME. BUT IT'S GOING TO BE ALL RIGHT NOW. I PROMISE, MY DEAR. ALL MY CHILDREN ARE HOME NOW.
ISN'T THAT RIGHT, JOSEPH?
I'M VERY PROUD OF YOU, SON.
GEE, THANKS, POP. THERE'S JUST ONE THING...
WHAT ARE YOU--?

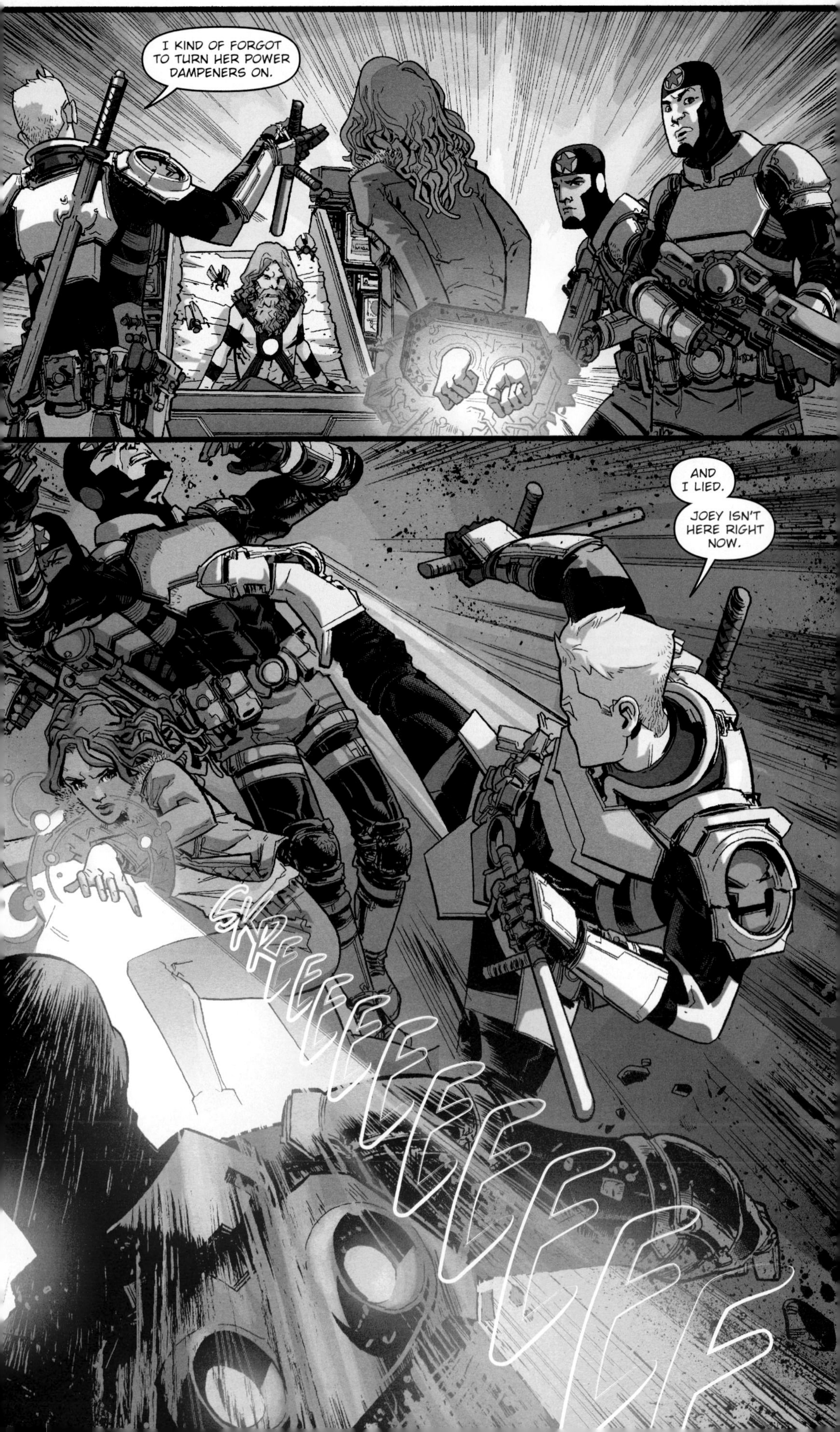
I KIND OF FORGOT TO TURN HER POWER DAMPENERS ON.
AND I LIED.
JOEY ISN'T HERE RIGHT NOW.
SKREEEEEEEEEEE

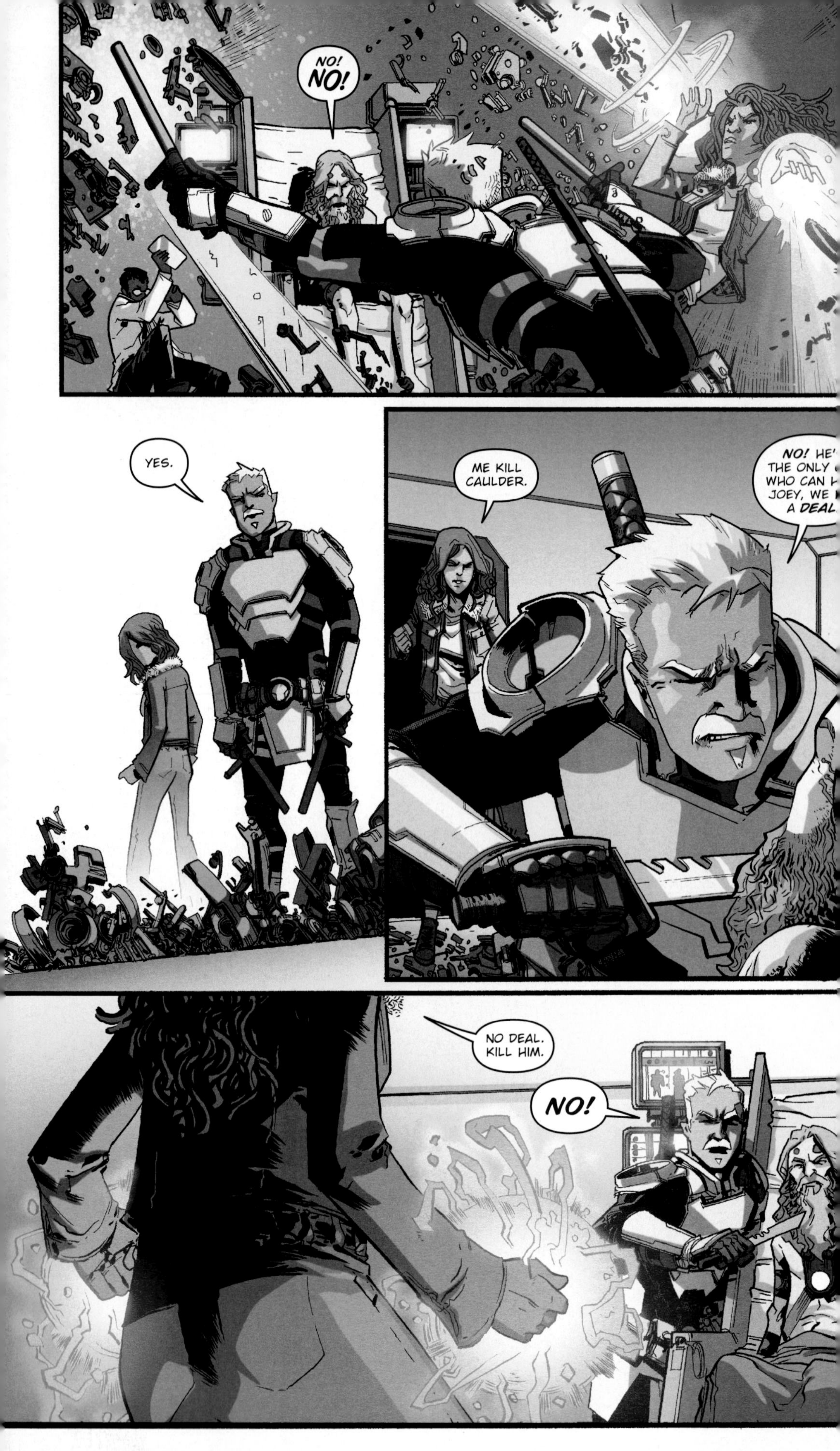
NO! NO!
YES.
ME KILL CAULDER.
NO! HE' THE ONLY WHO CAN JOEY, WE A DEAL
NO DEAL. KILL HIM.
NO!

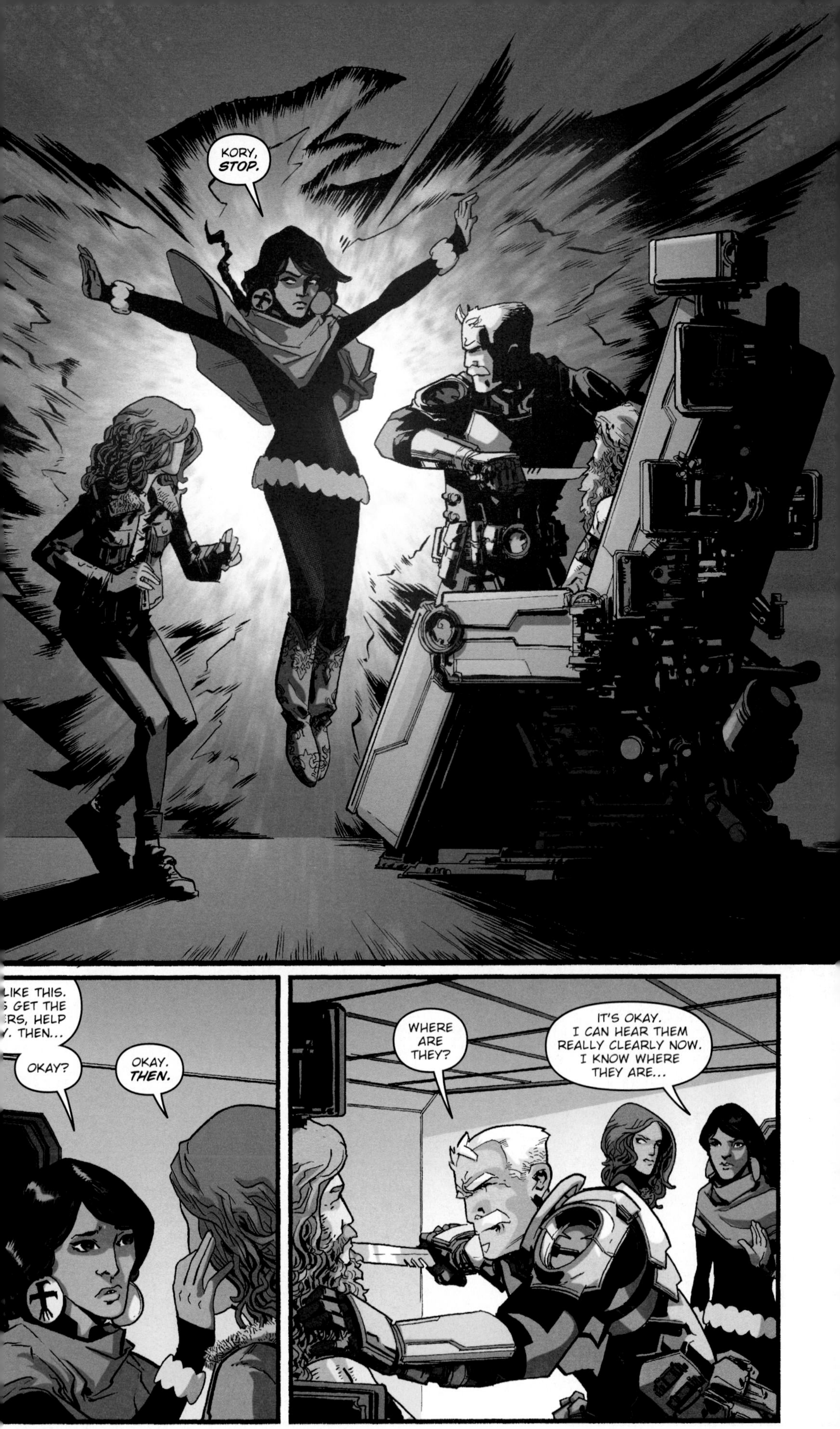
KORY, STOP.
LIKE THIS.
S GET THE
ERS, HELP
Y. THEN...
OKAY?
OKAY. THEN.
WHERE ARE THEY?
IT'S OKAY. I CAN HEAR THEM REALLY CLEARLY NOW. I KNOW WHERE THEY ARE...

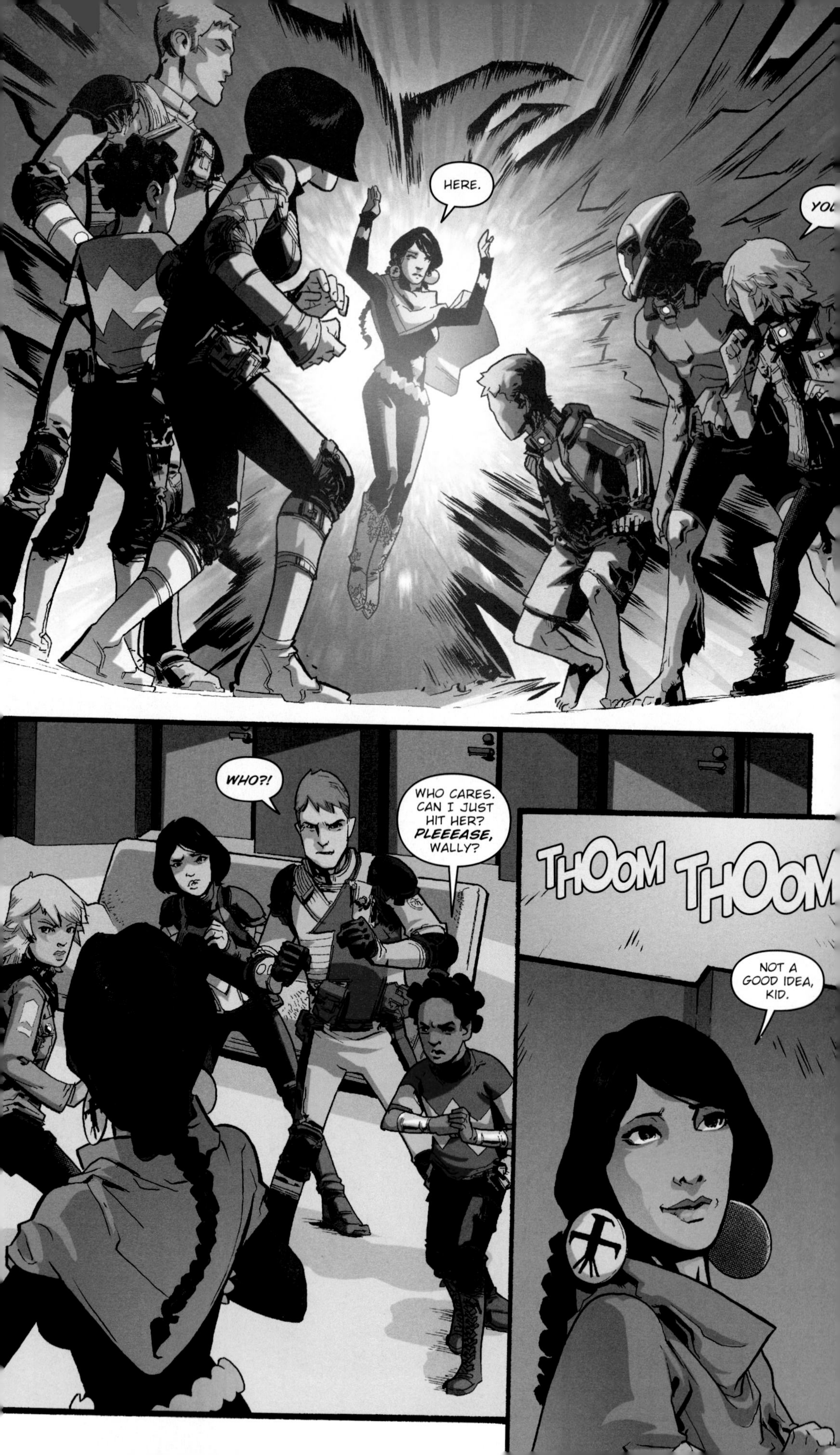
HERE.
WHO?!
WHO CARES. CAN I JUST HIT HER? **PLEEEASE,** WALLY?
THOOM THOOM
NOT A GOOD IDEA, KID.

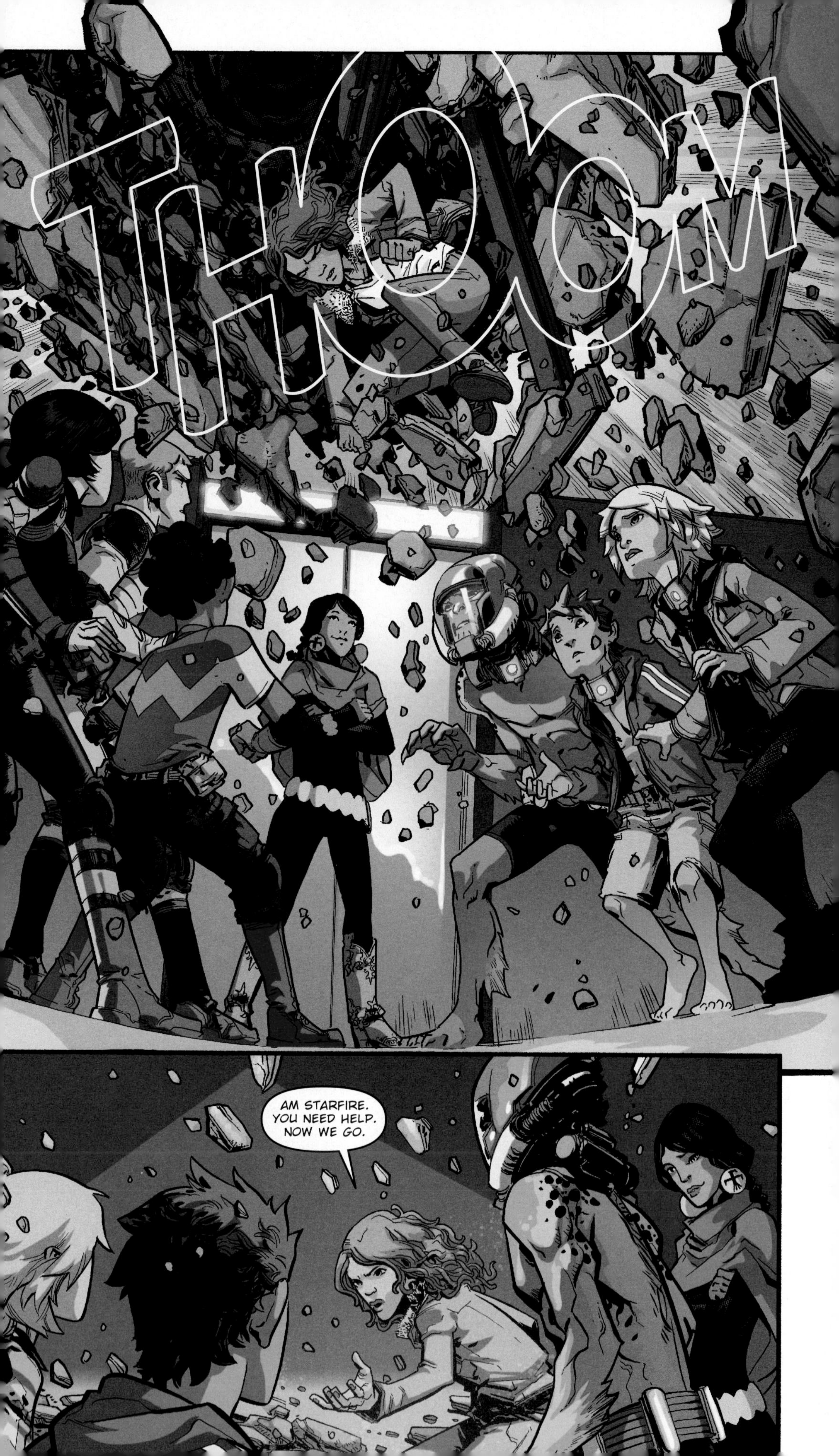
THOOM
AM STARFIRE. YOU NEED HELP. NOW WE GO.

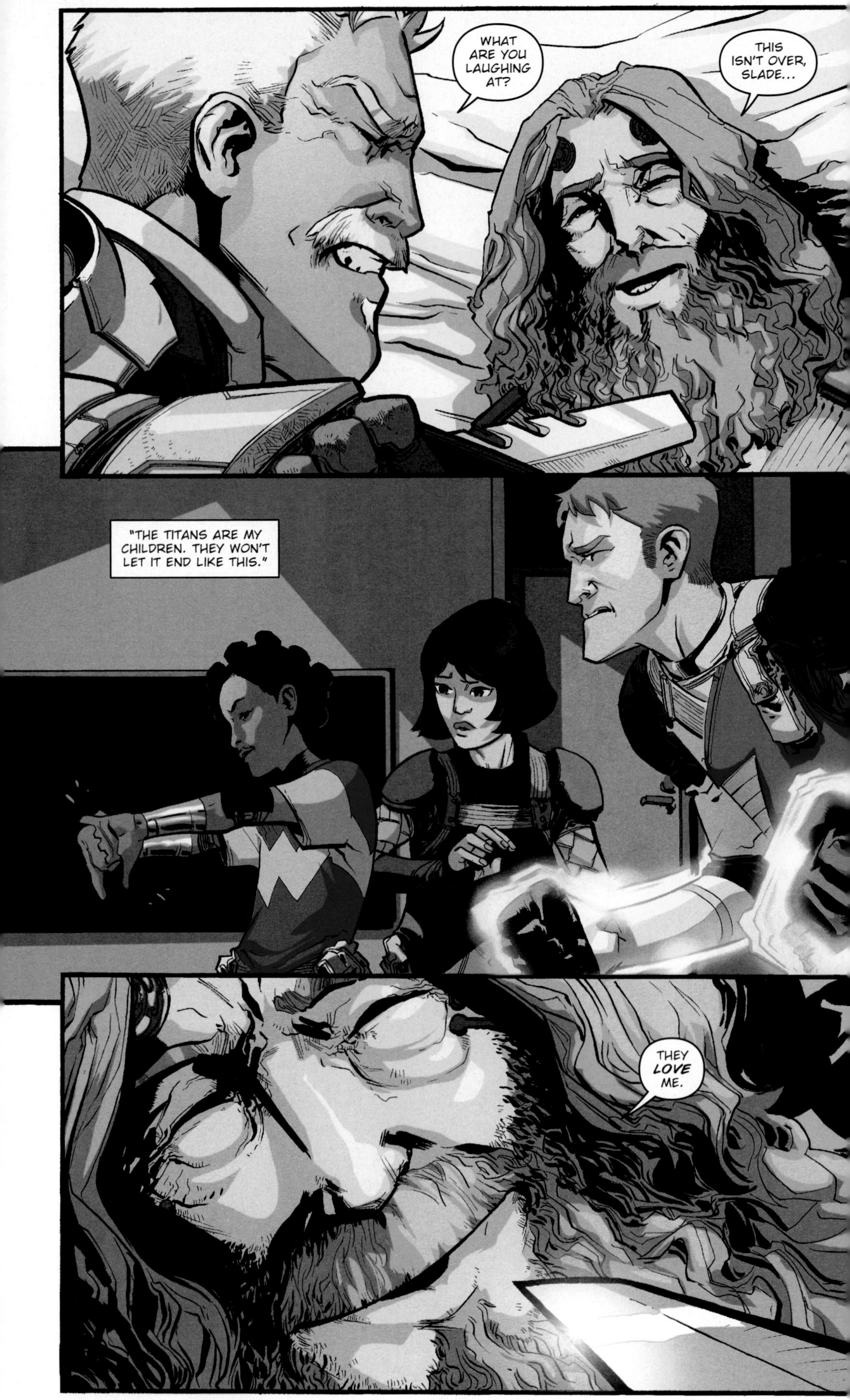
WHAT ARE YOU LAUGHING AT?
THIS ISN'T OVER, SLADE...
"THE TITANS ARE MY CHILDREN. THEY WON'T LET IT END LIKE THIS."
THEY *LOVE* ME.

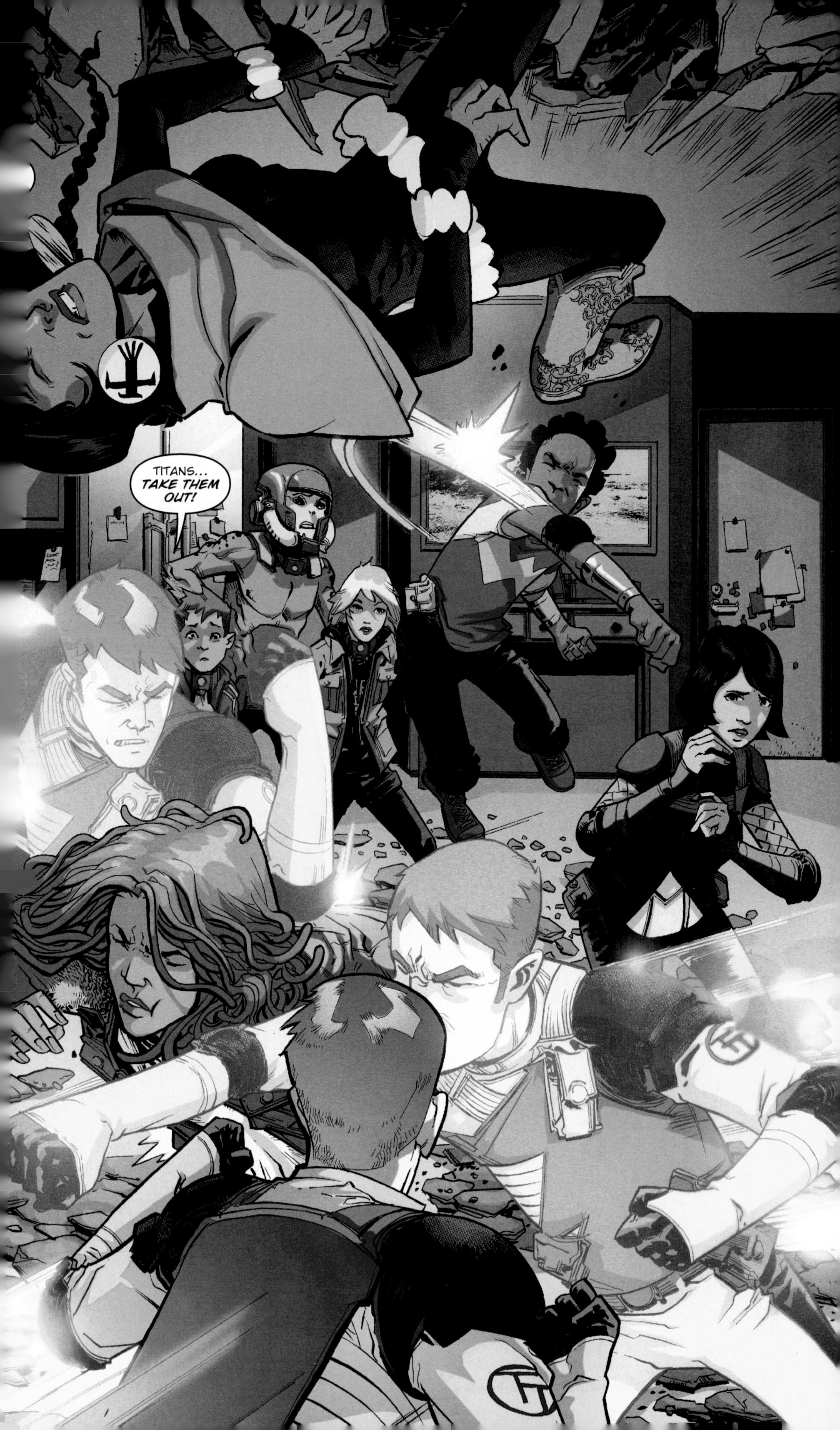
TITANS... TAKE THEM OUT!

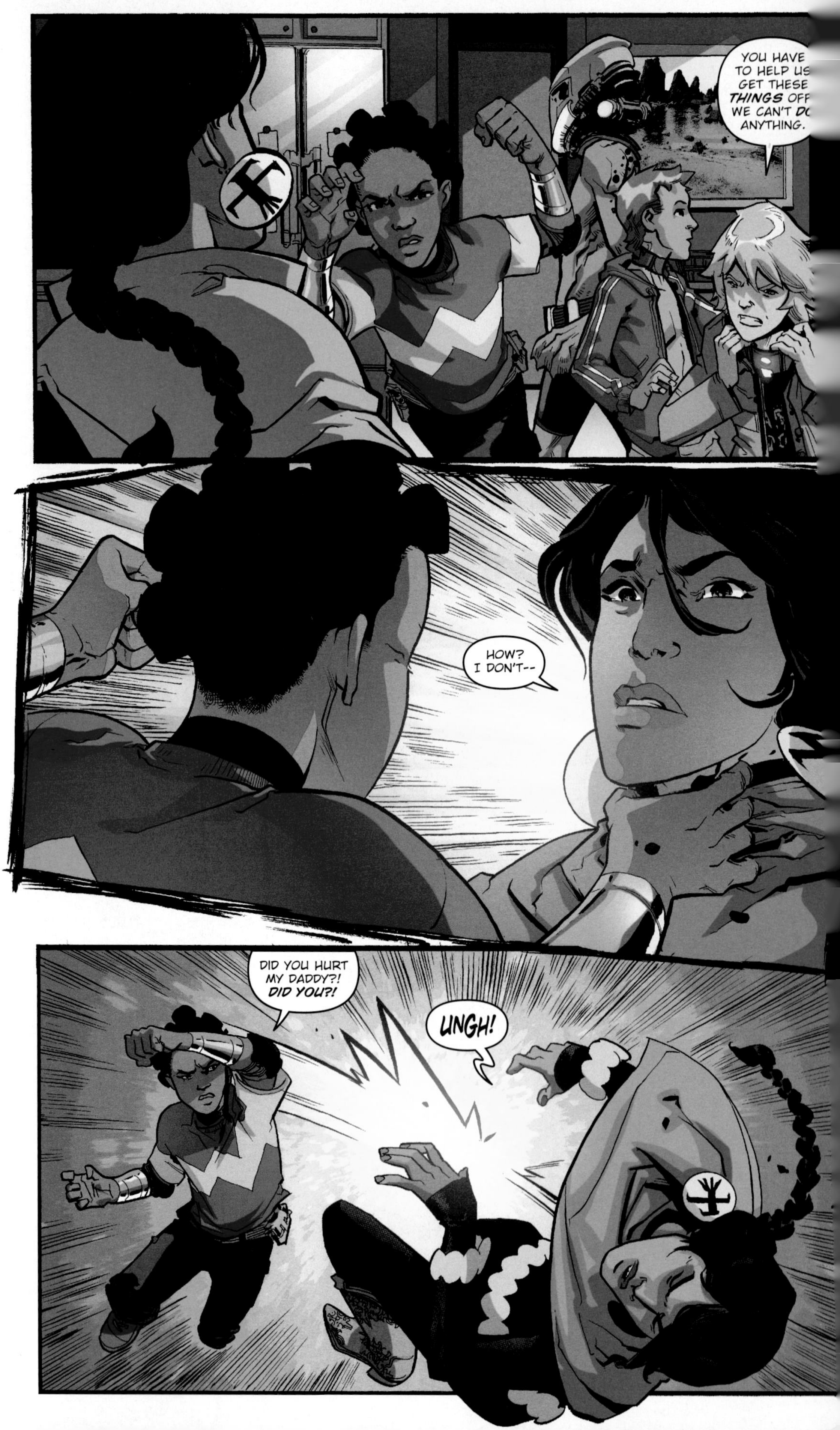
YOU HAVE TO HELP US GET THESE *THINGS* OFF WE CAN'T *DO* ANYTHING.
HOW? I DON'T--
DID YOU HURT MY DADDY?! *DID YOU?!*
UNGH!

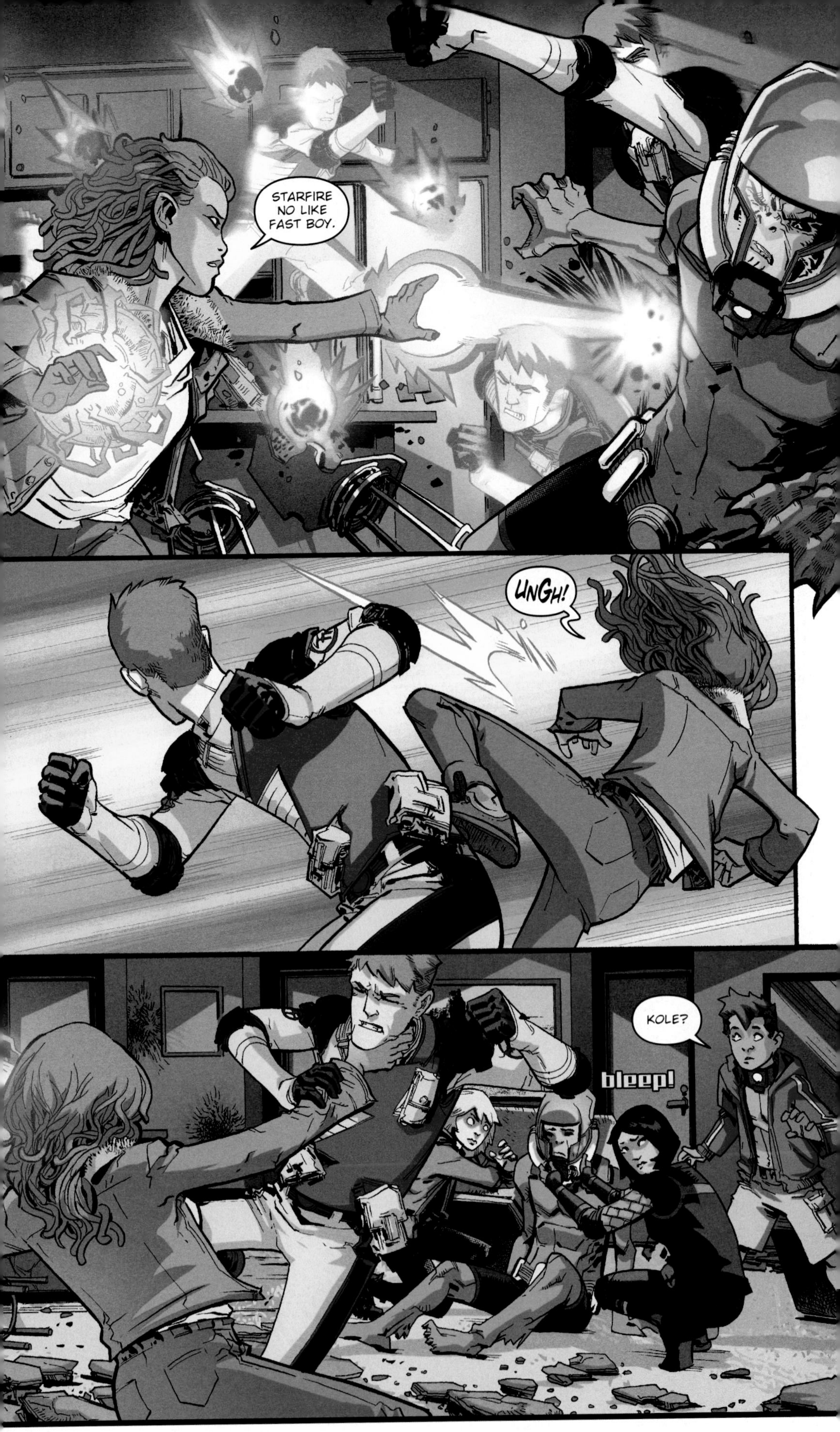
STARFIRE NO LIKE FAST BOY.
UNGH!
KOLE?
bleep!

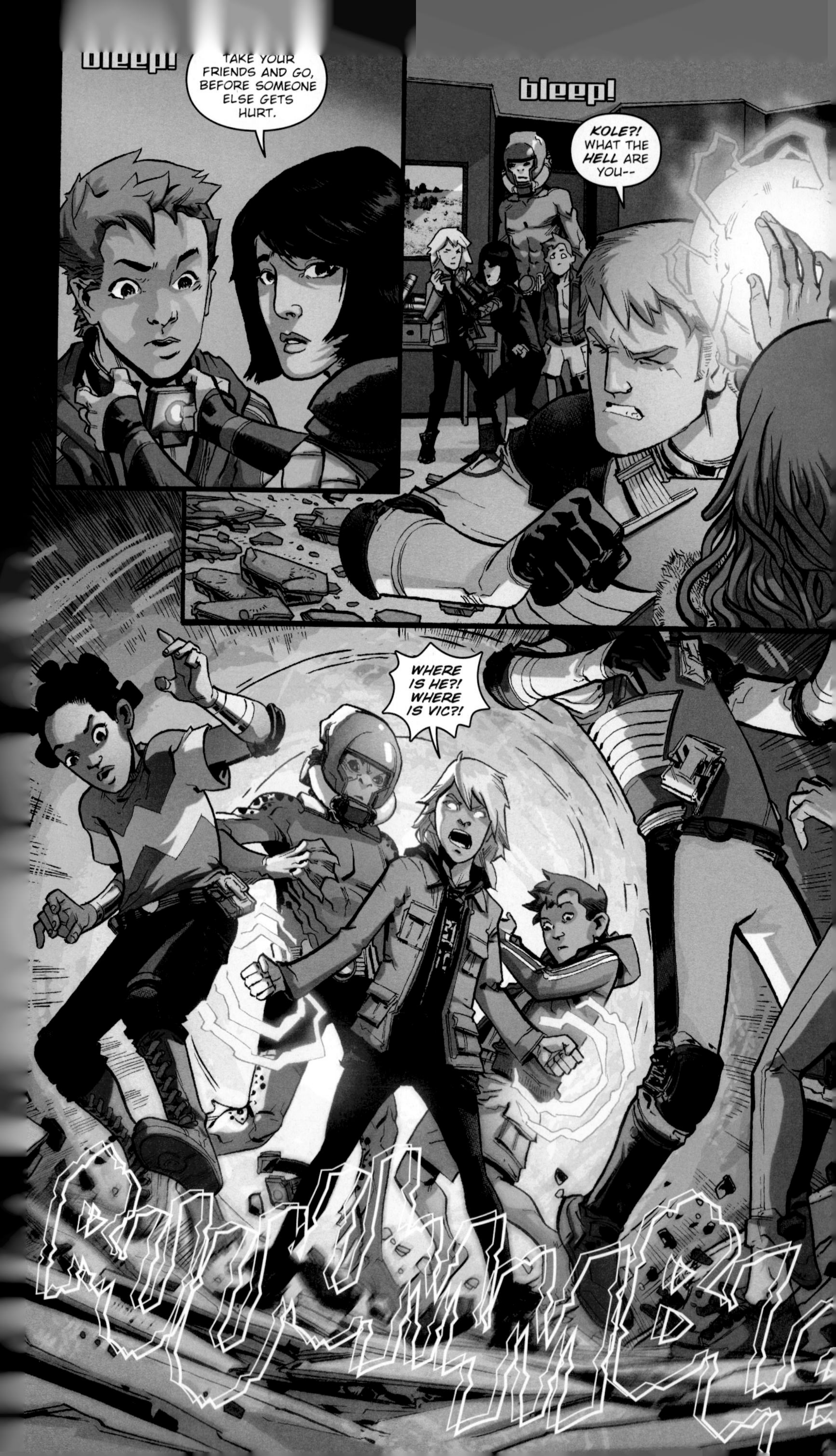
bleep!
TAKE YOUR FRIENDS AND GO, BEFORE SOMEONE ELSE GETS HURT.
bleep!
KOLE?! WHAT THE HELL ARE YOU--
WHERE IS HE?! WHERE IS VIC?!

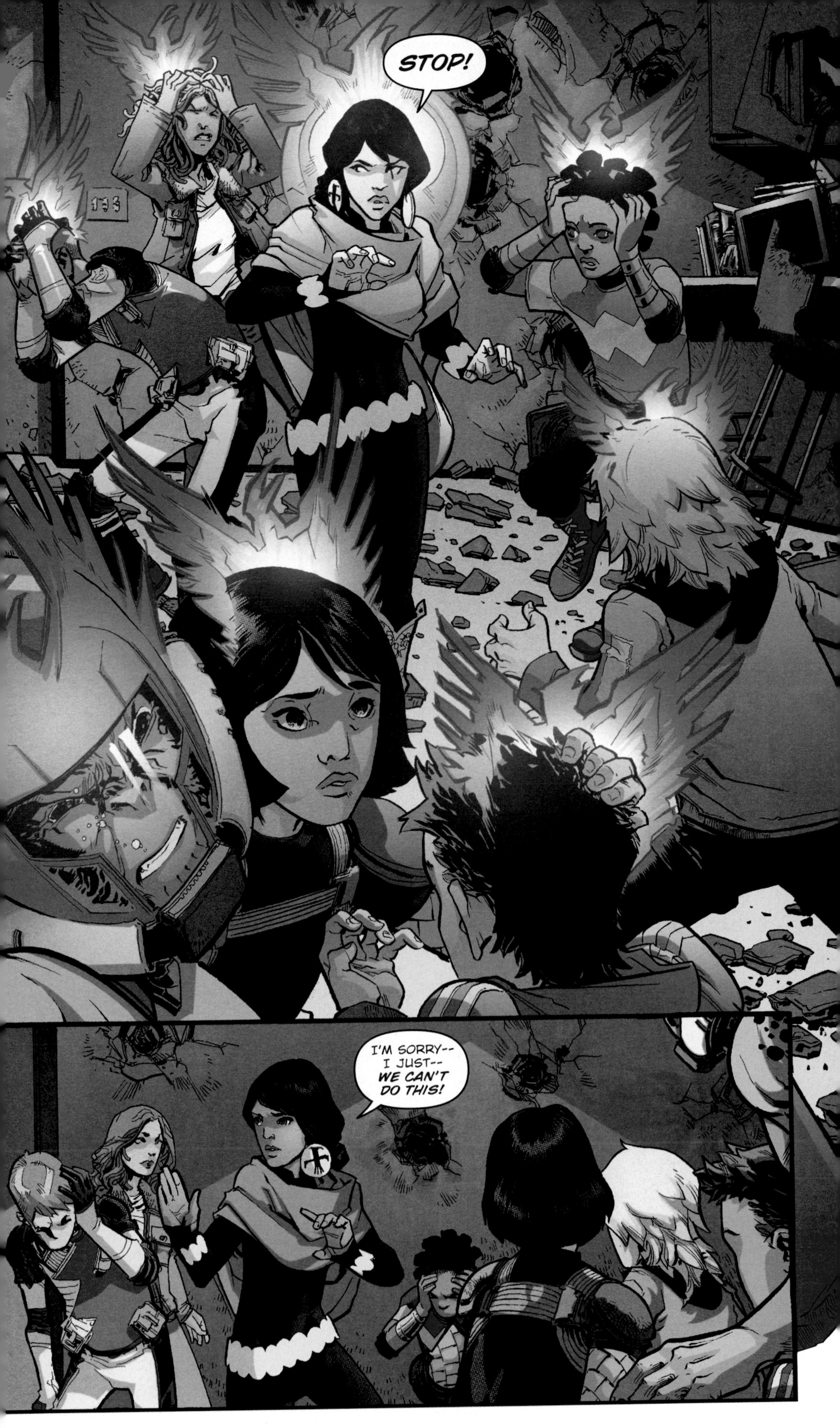
STOP!
I'M SORRY-- I JUST-- WE CAN'T DO THIS!

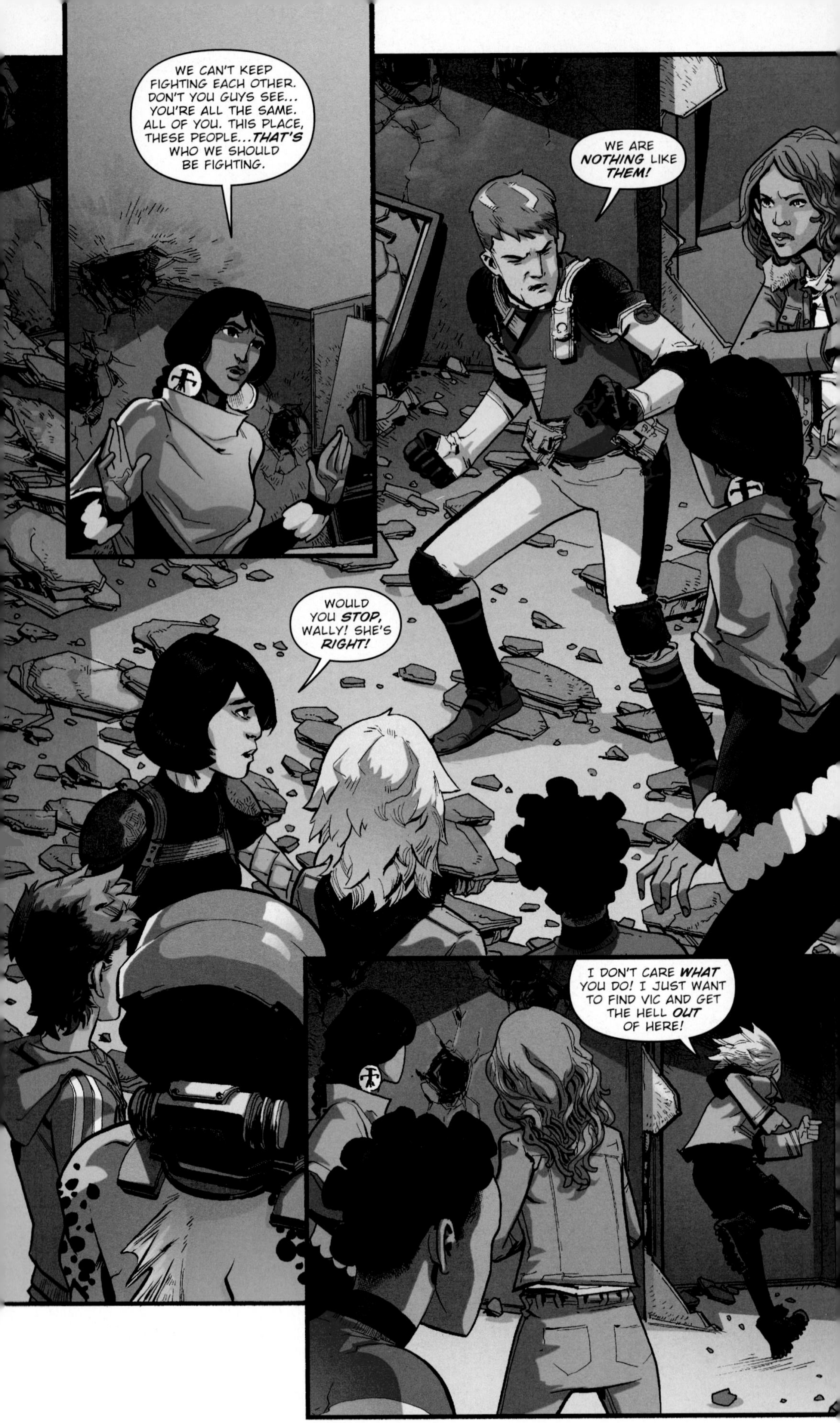
WE CAN'T KEEP FIGHTING EACH OTHER. DON'T YOU GUYS SEE... YOU'RE ALL THE SAME. ALL OF YOU. THIS PLACE, THESE PEOPLE...*THAT'S* WHO WE SHOULD BE FIGHTING.
WE ARE *NOTHING* LIKE *THEM!*
WOULD YOU *STOP,* WALLY! SHE'S *RIGHT!*
I DON'T CARE *WHAT* YOU DO! I JUST WANT TO FIND VIC AND GET THE HELL *OUT* OF HERE!

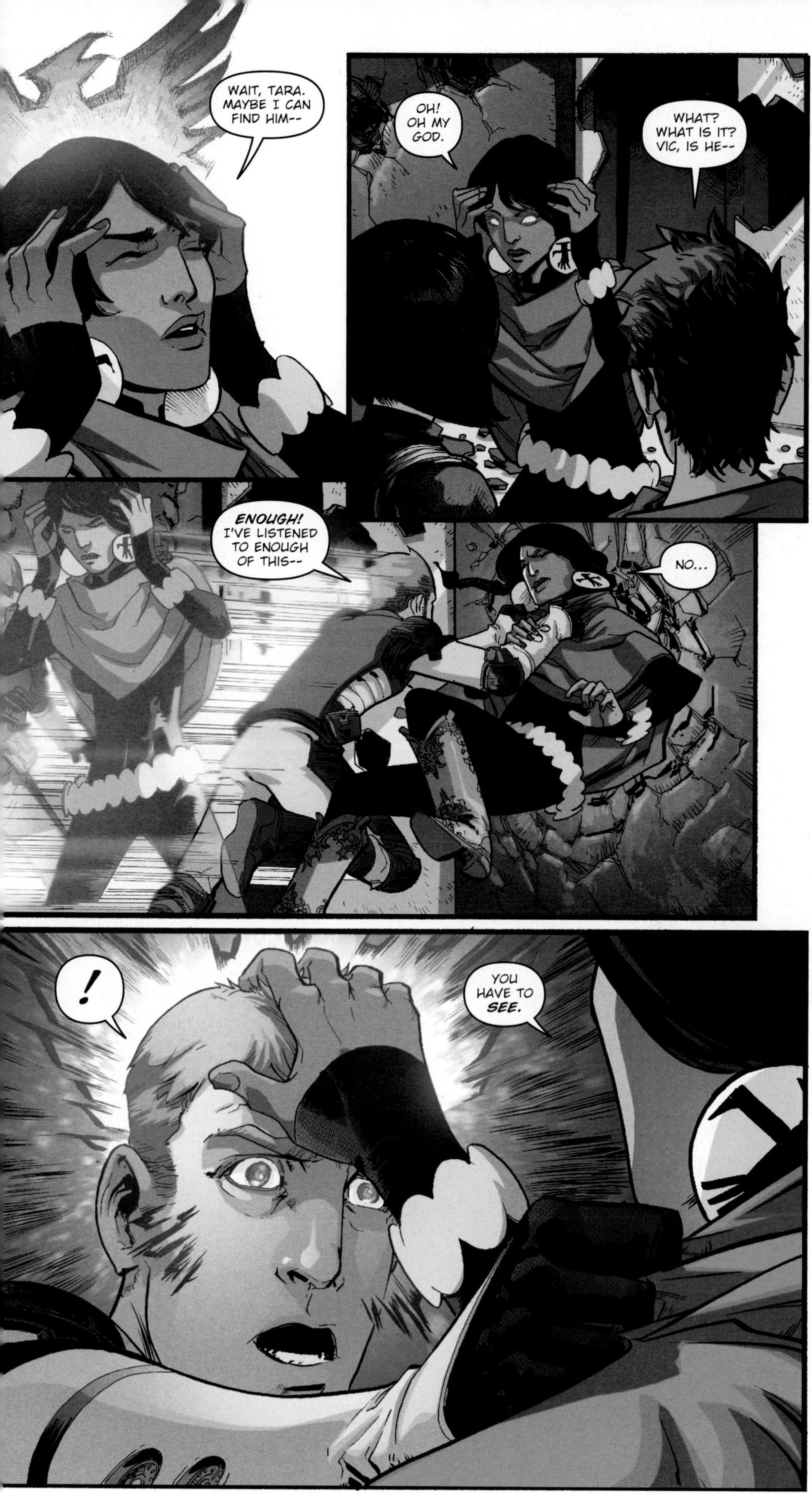
WAIT, TARA. MAYBE I CAN FIND HIM--
OH! OH MY GOD.
WHAT? WHAT IS IT? VIC, IS HE--
ENOUGH! I'VE LISTENED TO ENOUGH OF THIS--
NO...
!
YOU HAVE TO SEE.

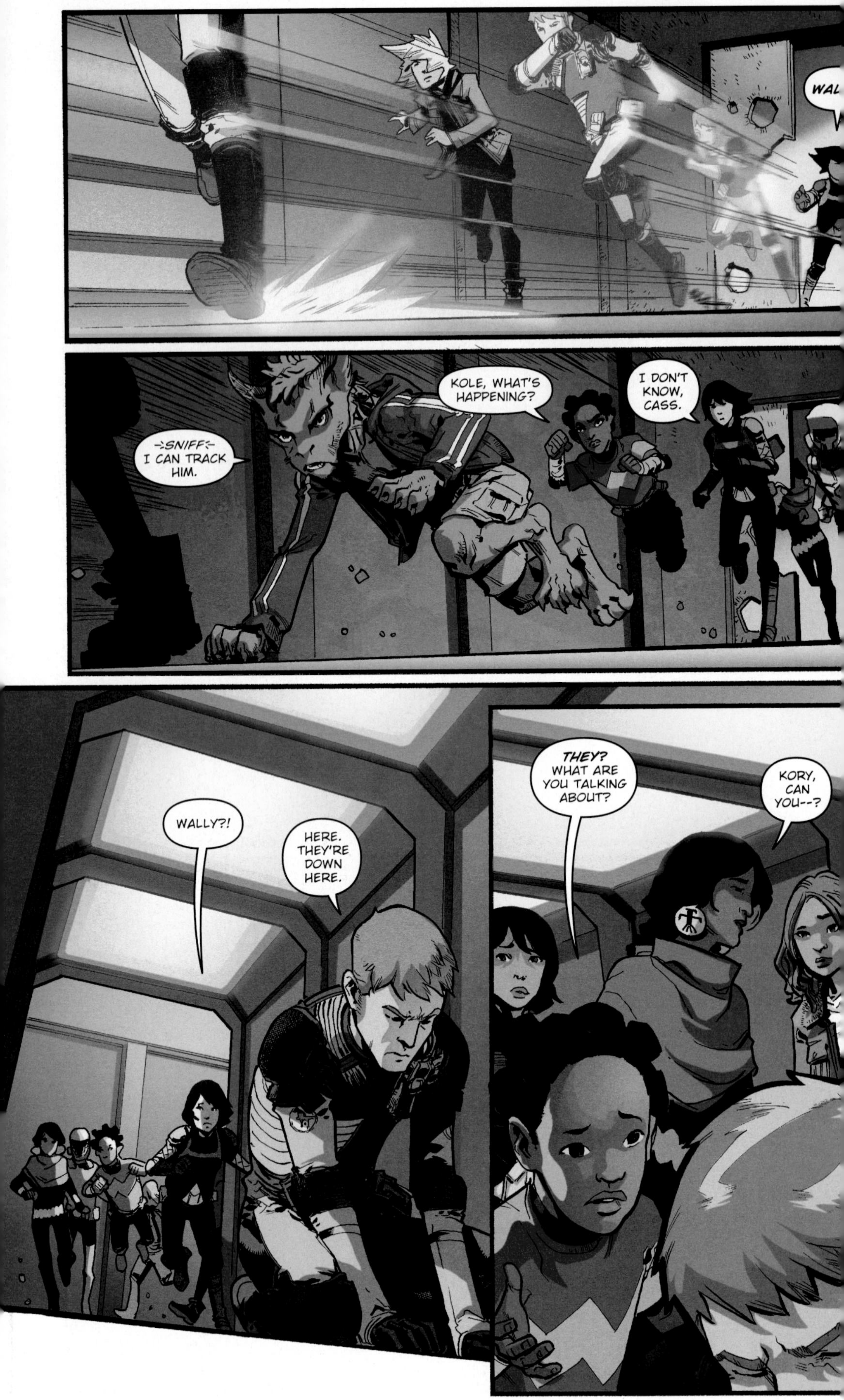
WAL
-SNIFF-
I CAN TRACK HIM.
KOLE, WHAT'S HAPPENING?
I DON'T KNOW, CASS.
WALLY?!
HERE. THEY'RE DOWN HERE.
THEY? WHAT ARE YOU TALKING ABOUT?
KORY, CAN YOU--?

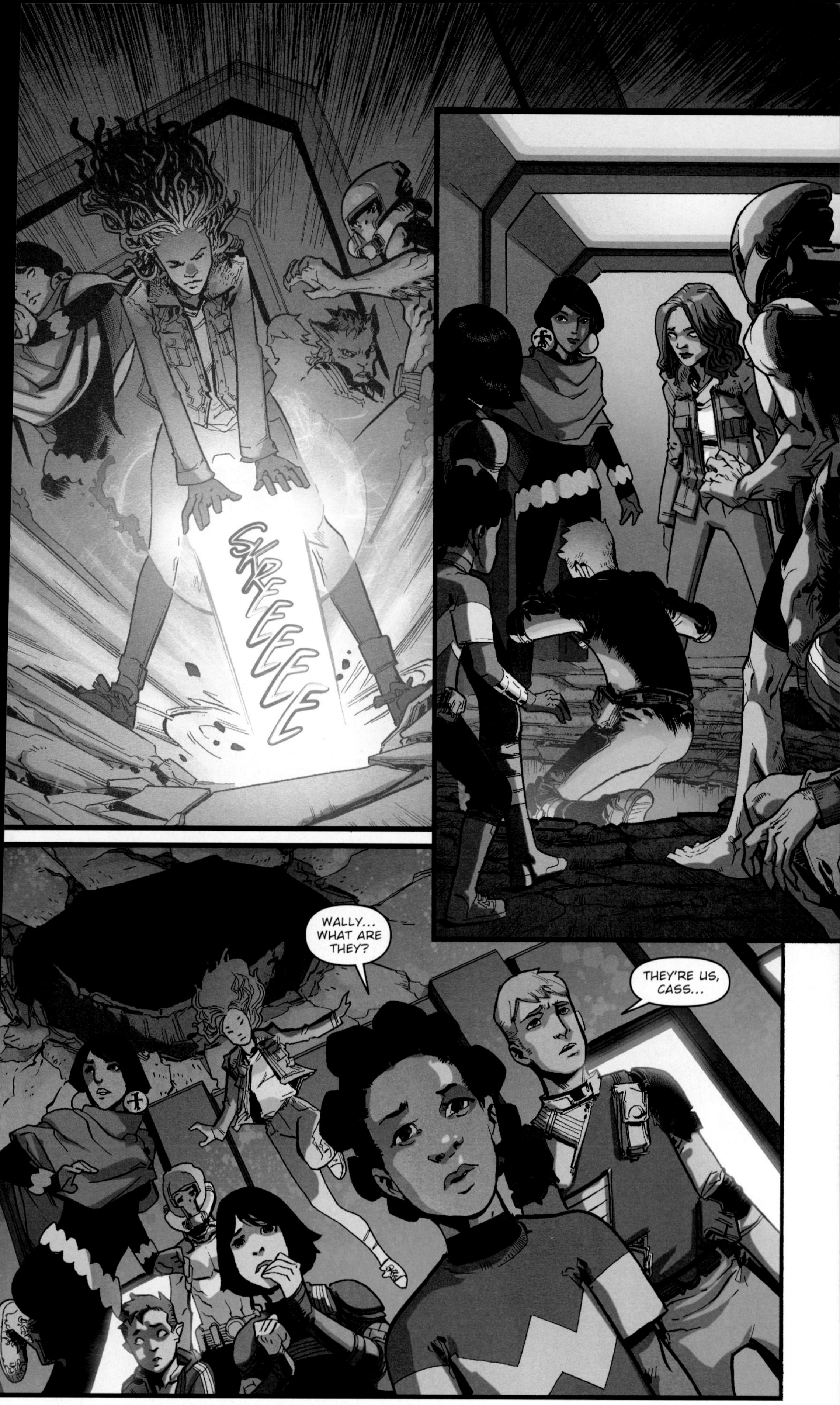
SKREEEEEE
WALLY... WHAT ARE THEY?
THEY'RE US, CASS...

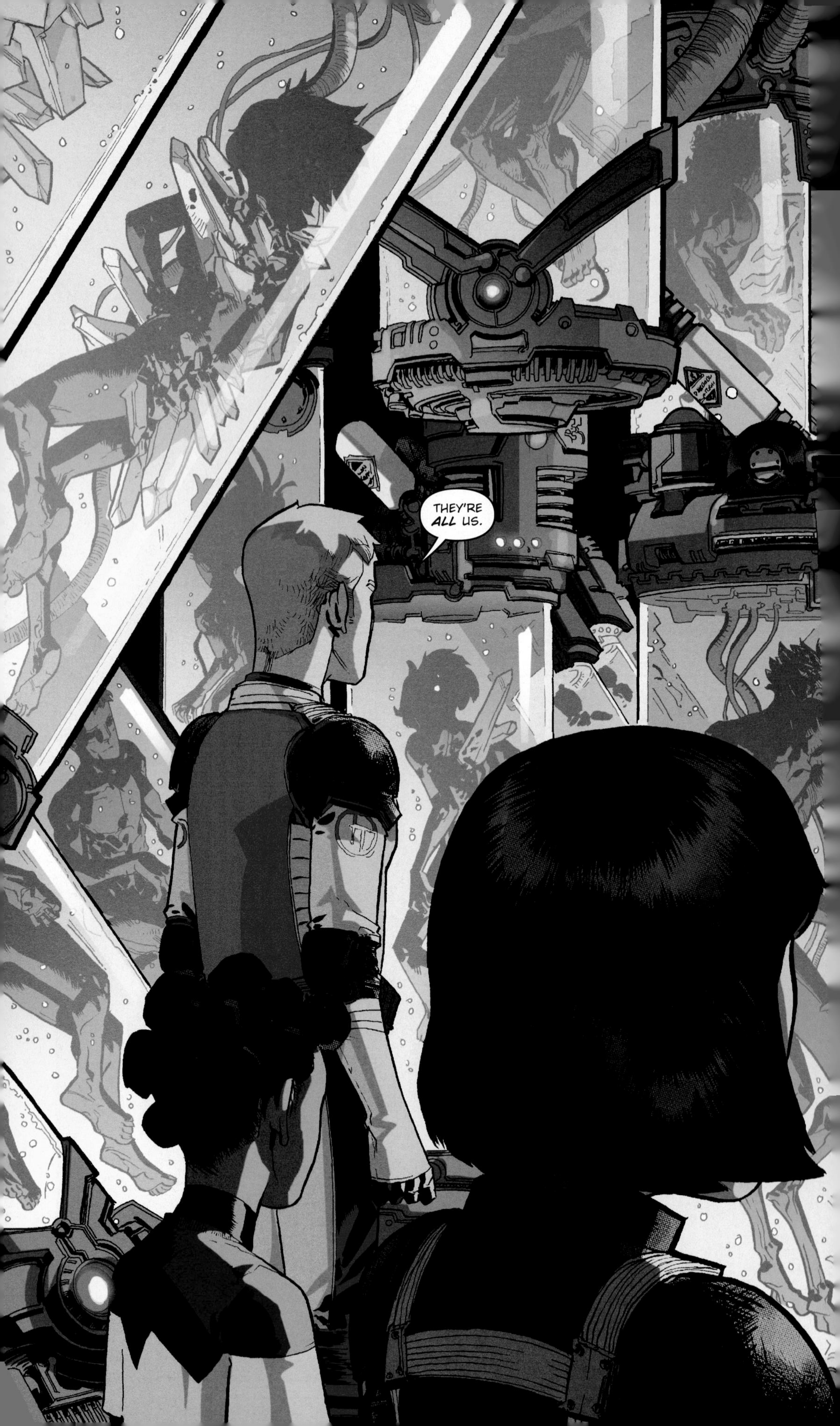
THEY'RE ALL US.

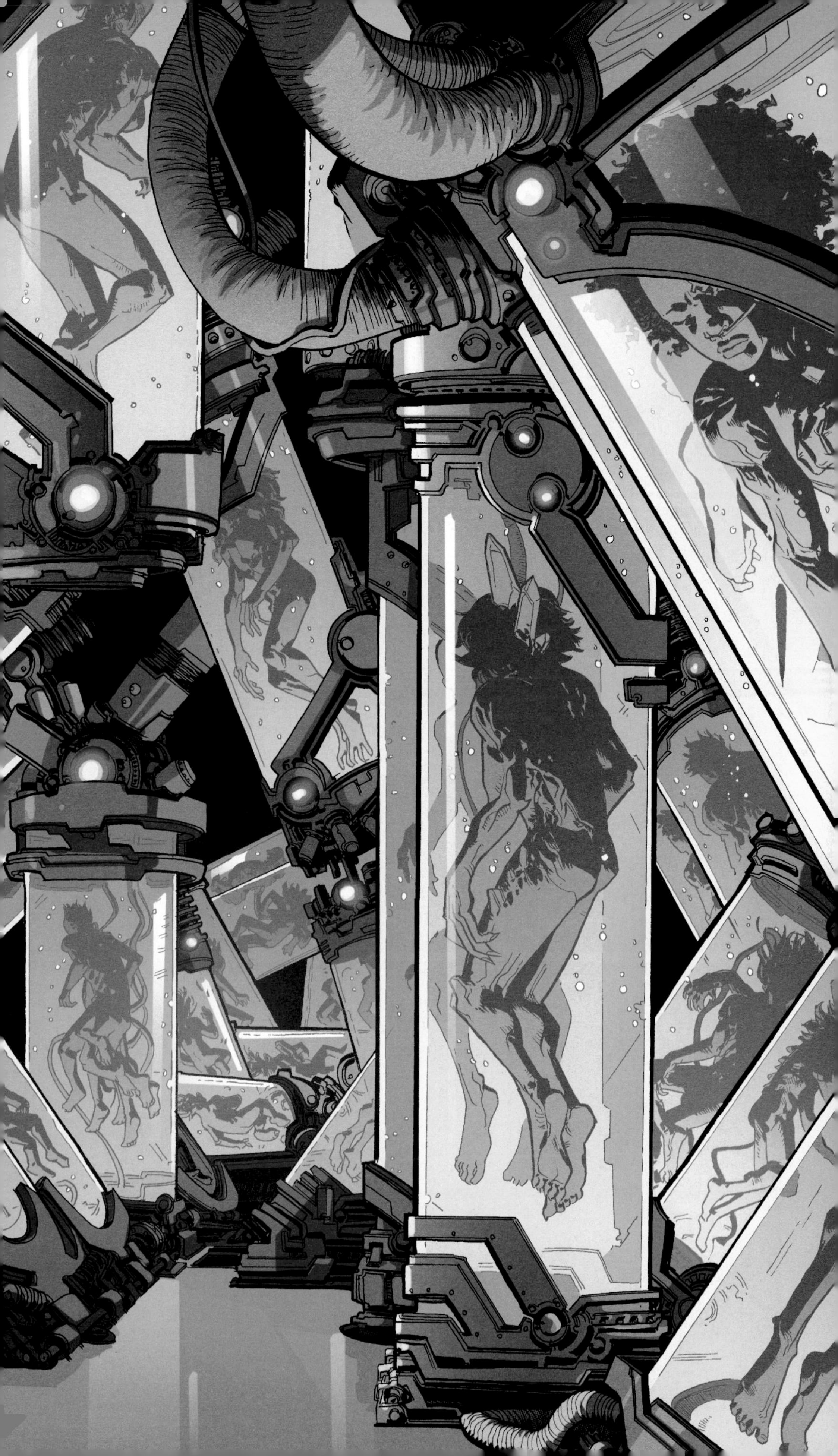

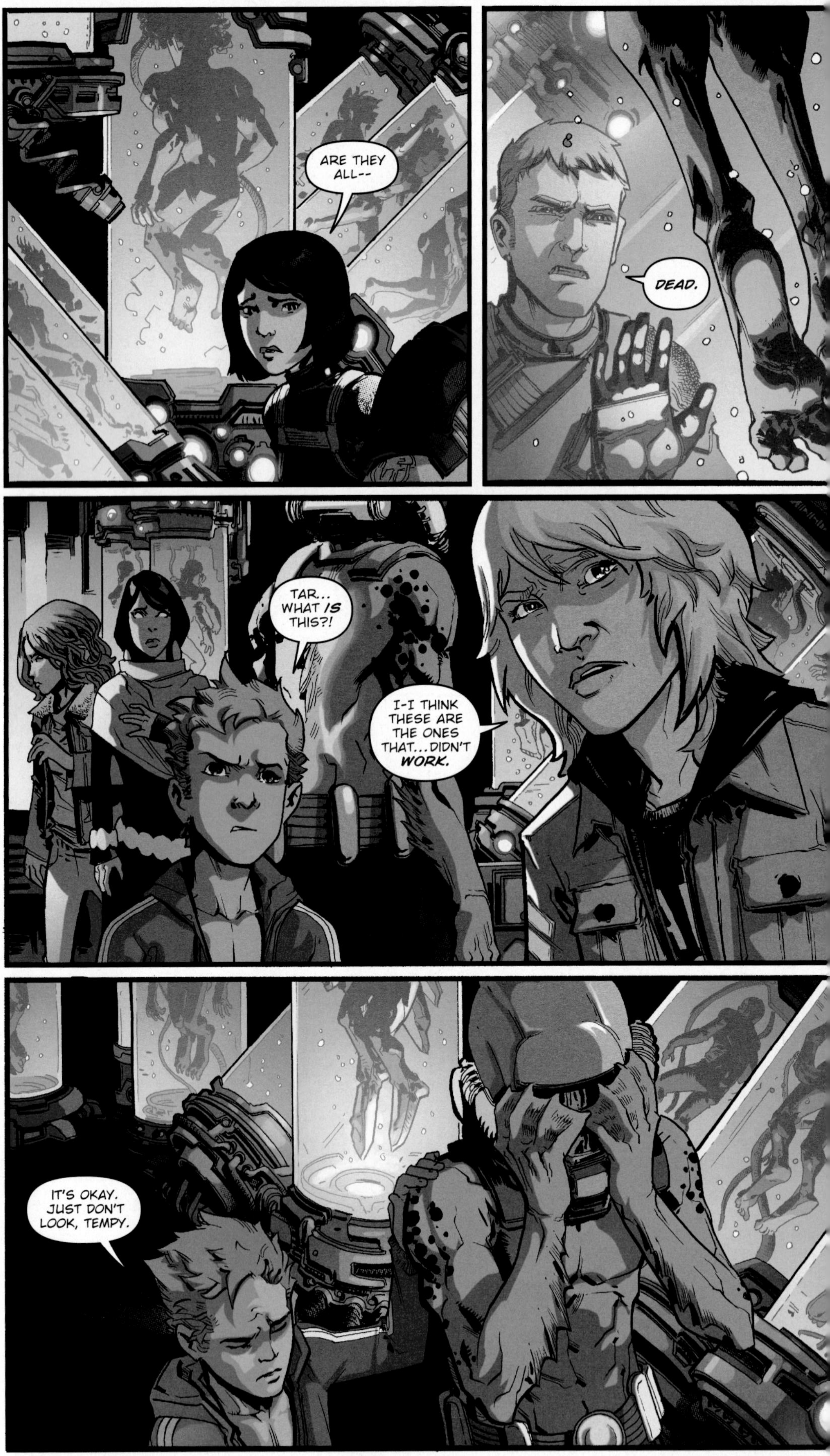
ARE THEY ALL--
DEAD.
TAR... WHAT IS THIS?!
I-I THINK THESE ARE THE ONES THAT...DIDN'T WORK.
IT'S OKAY. JUST DON'T LOOK, TEMPY.

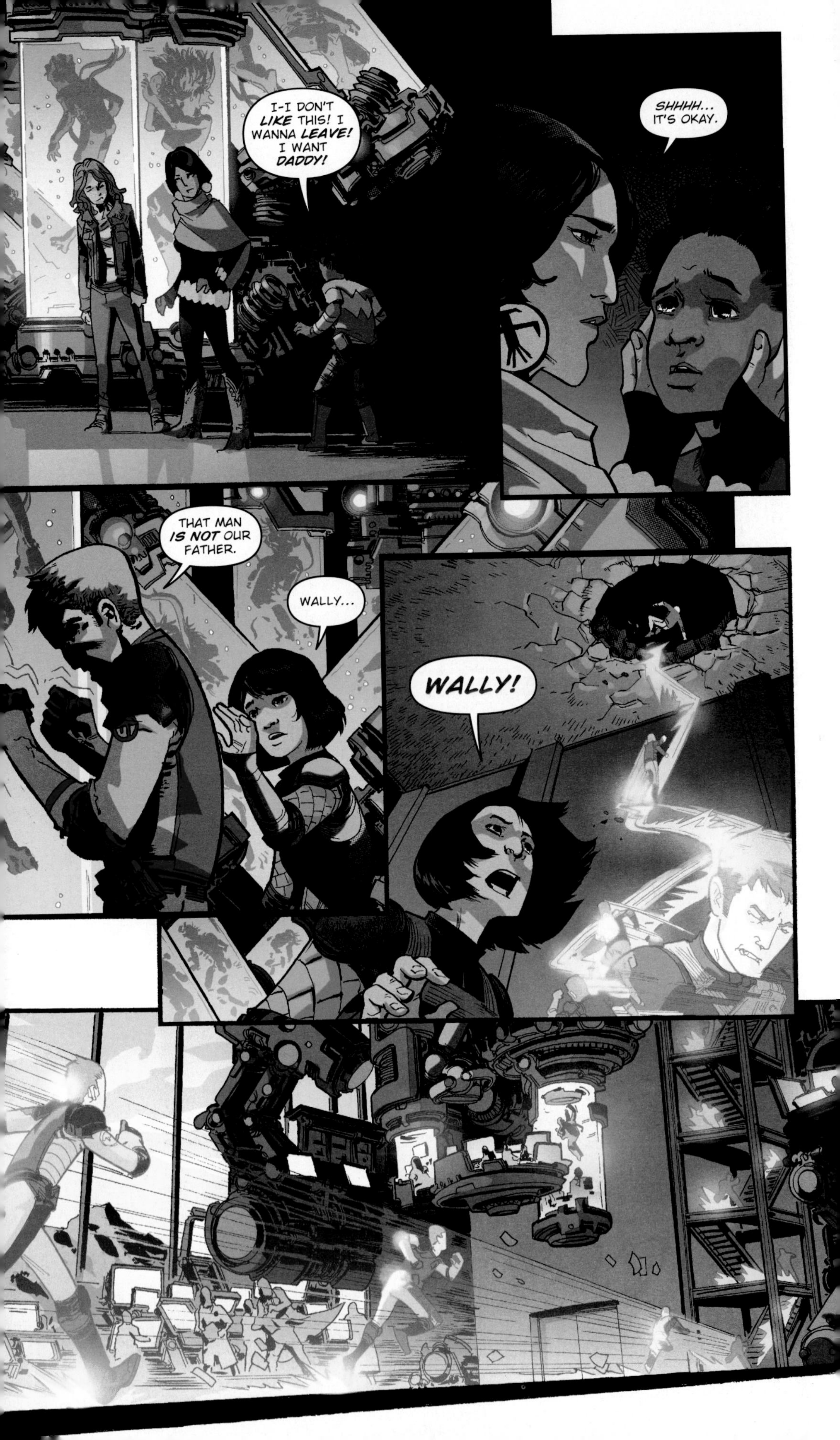

I-I DON'T LIKE THIS! I WANNA LEAVE! I WANT DADDY!
SHHHH... IT'S OKAY.
THAT MAN IS NOT OUR FATHER.
WALLY...
WALLY!

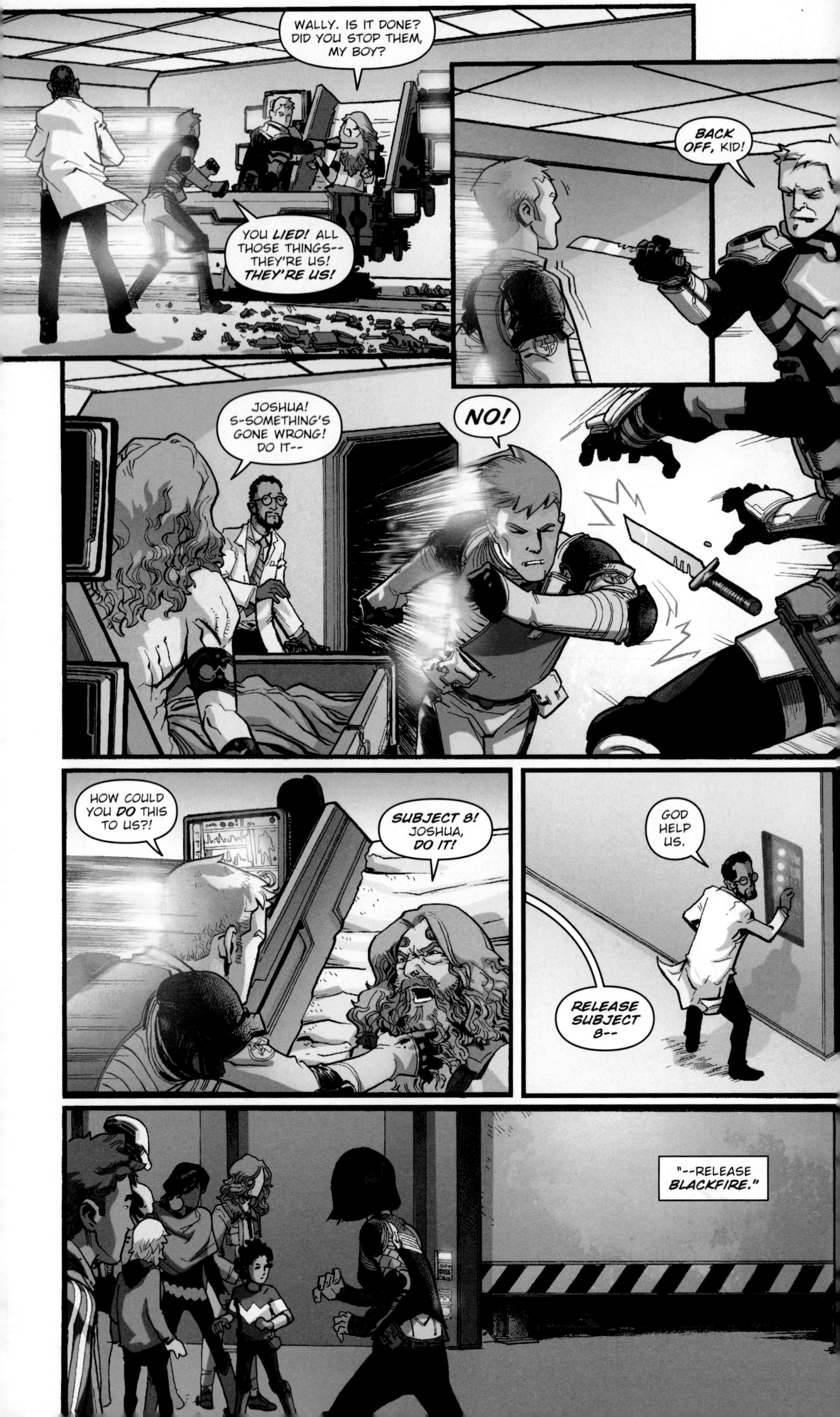

WALLY. IS IT DONE? DID YOU STOP THEM, MY BOY?
YOU LIED! ALL THOSE THINGS-- THEY'RE US! THEY'RE US!
BACK OFF, KID!
JOSHUA! S-SOMETHING'S GONE WRONG! DO IT--
NO!
HOW COULD YOU DO THIS TO US?!
SUBJECT 8! JOSHUA, DO IT!
GOD HELP US.
RELEASE SUBJECT 8--
"--RELEASE BLACKFIRE."

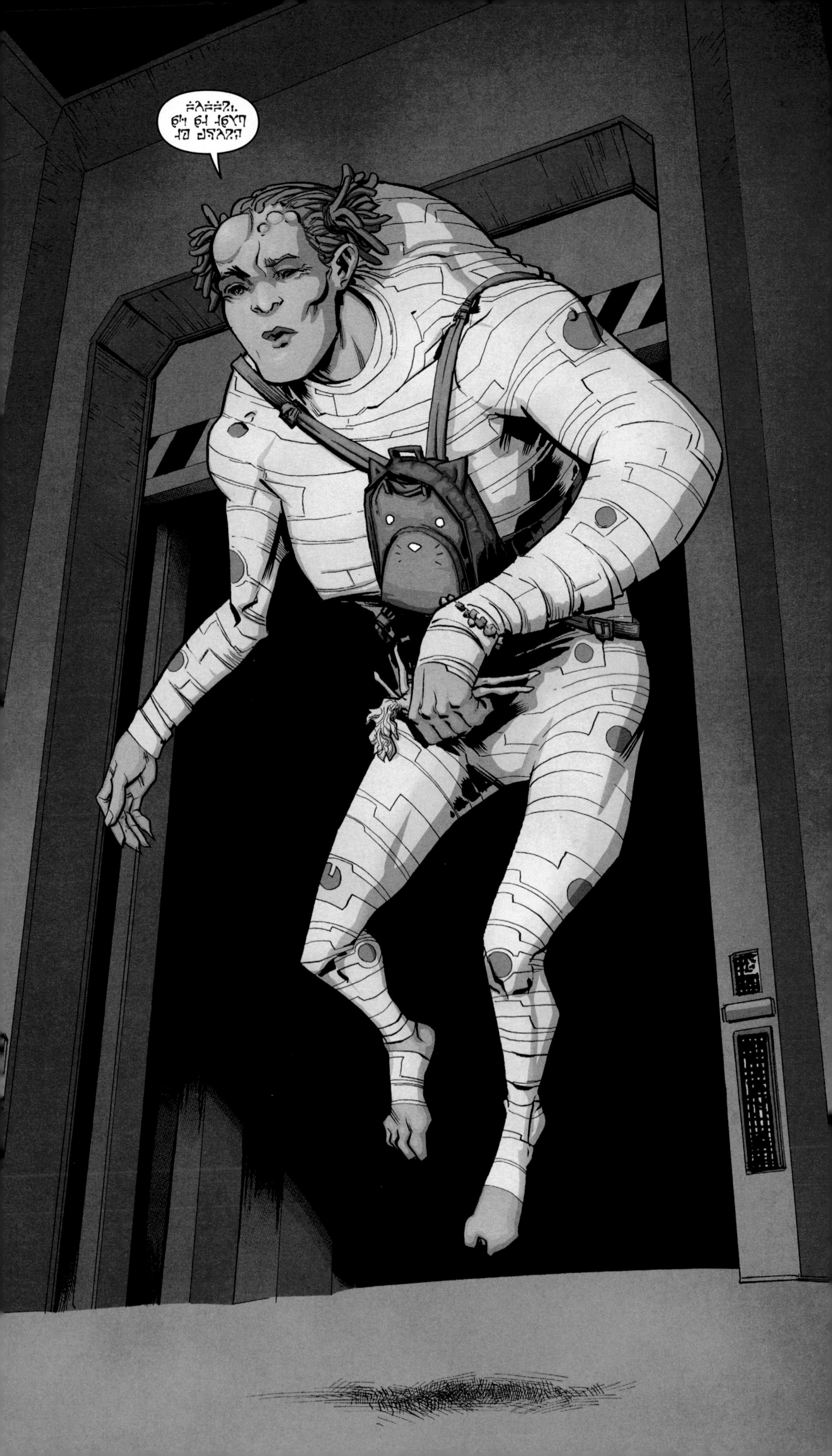

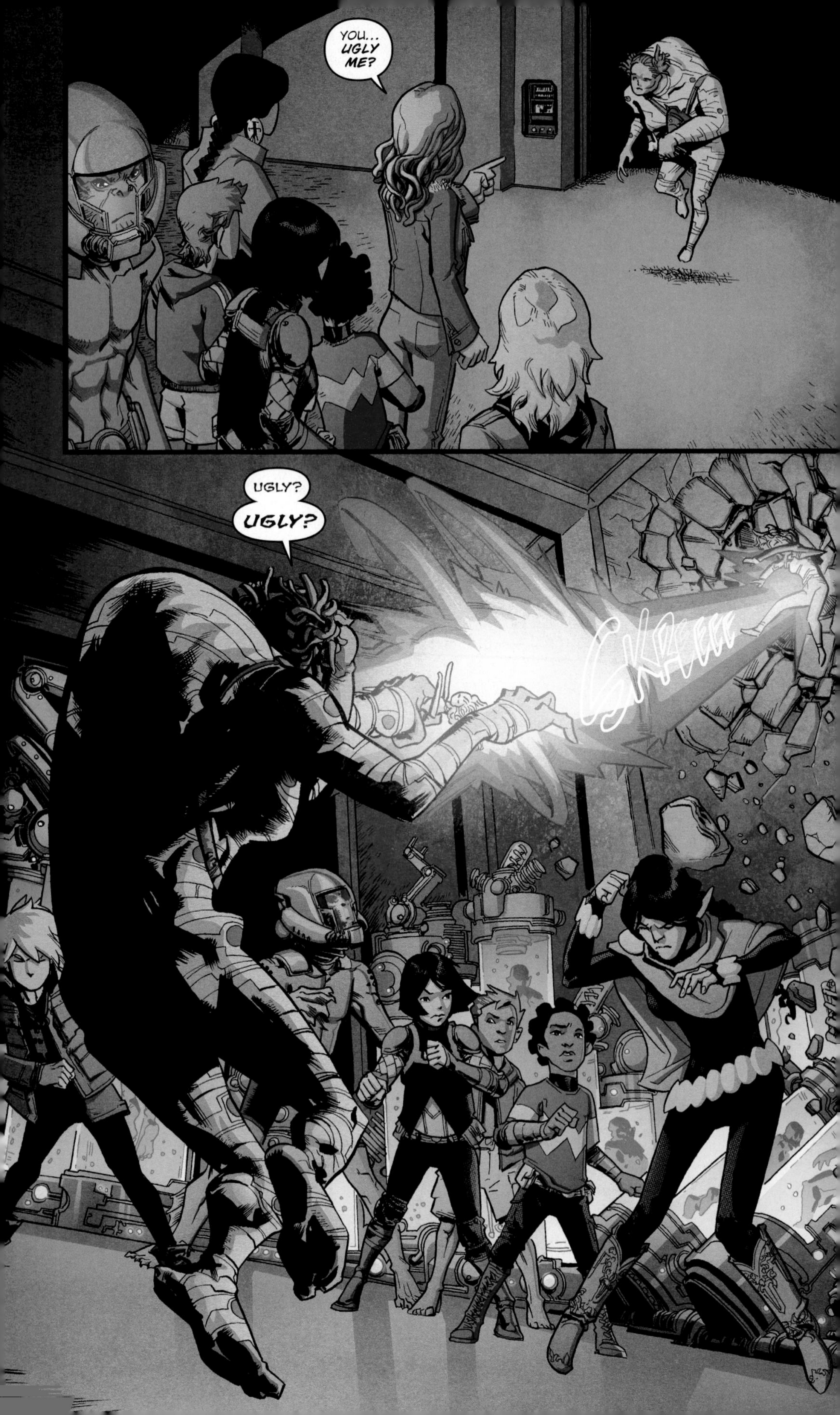
YOU...
UGLY
ME?
UGLY?
UGLY?

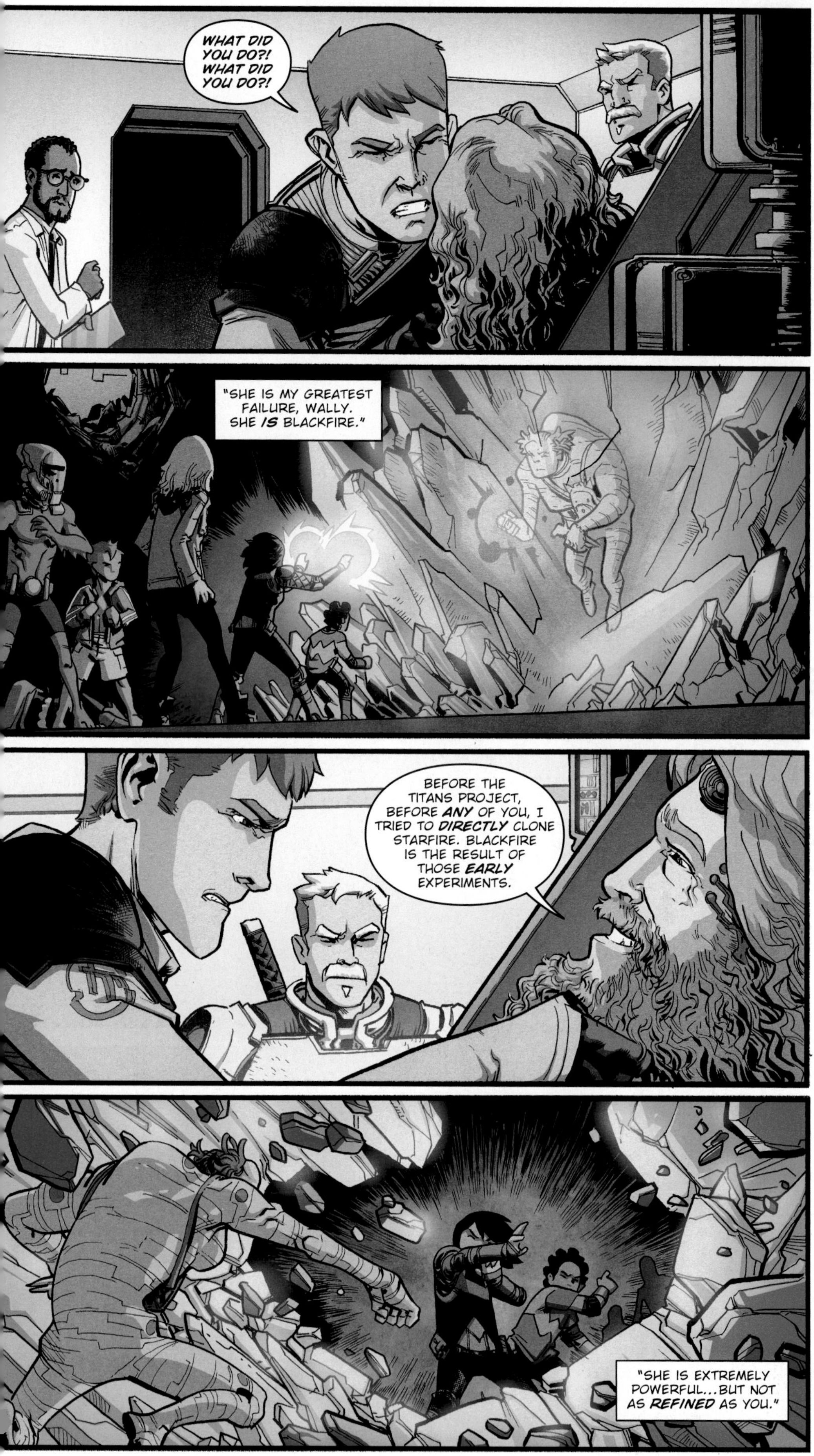
WHAT DID YOU DO?! WHAT DID YOU DO?!
"SHE IS MY GREATEST FAILURE, WALLY. SHE *IS* BLACKFIRE."
BEFORE THE TITANS PROJECT, BEFORE *ANY* OF YOU, I TRIED TO *DIRECTLY* CLONE STARFIRE. BLACKFIRE IS THE RESULT OF THOSE *EARLY* EXPERIMENTS.
"SHE IS EXTREMELY POWERFUL...BUT NOT AS *REFINED* AS YOU."

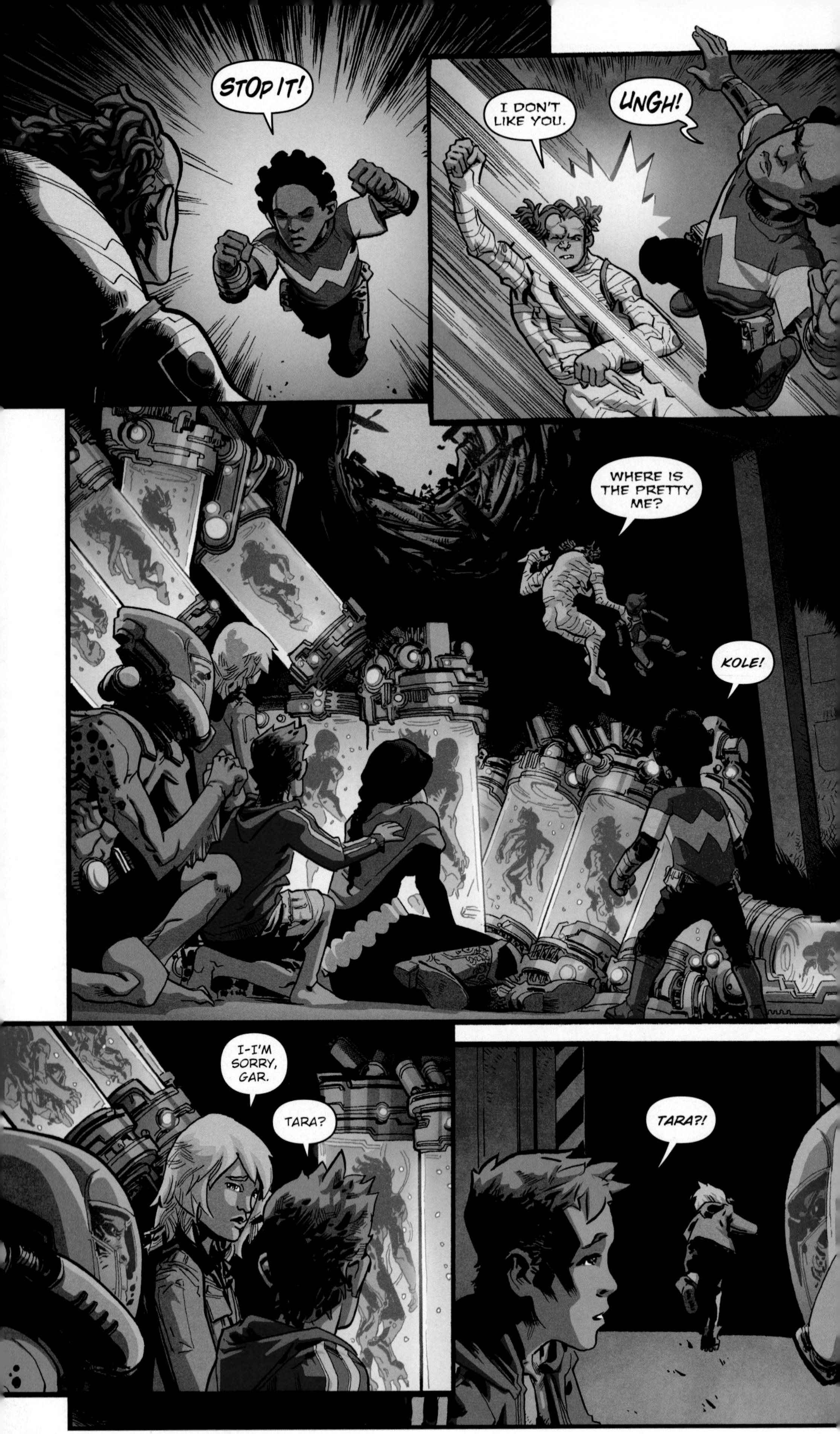
STOP IT!
I DON'T LIKE YOU.
UNGH!
WHERE IS THE PRETTY ME?
KOLE!
I-I'M SORRY, GAR.
TARA?
TARA?!

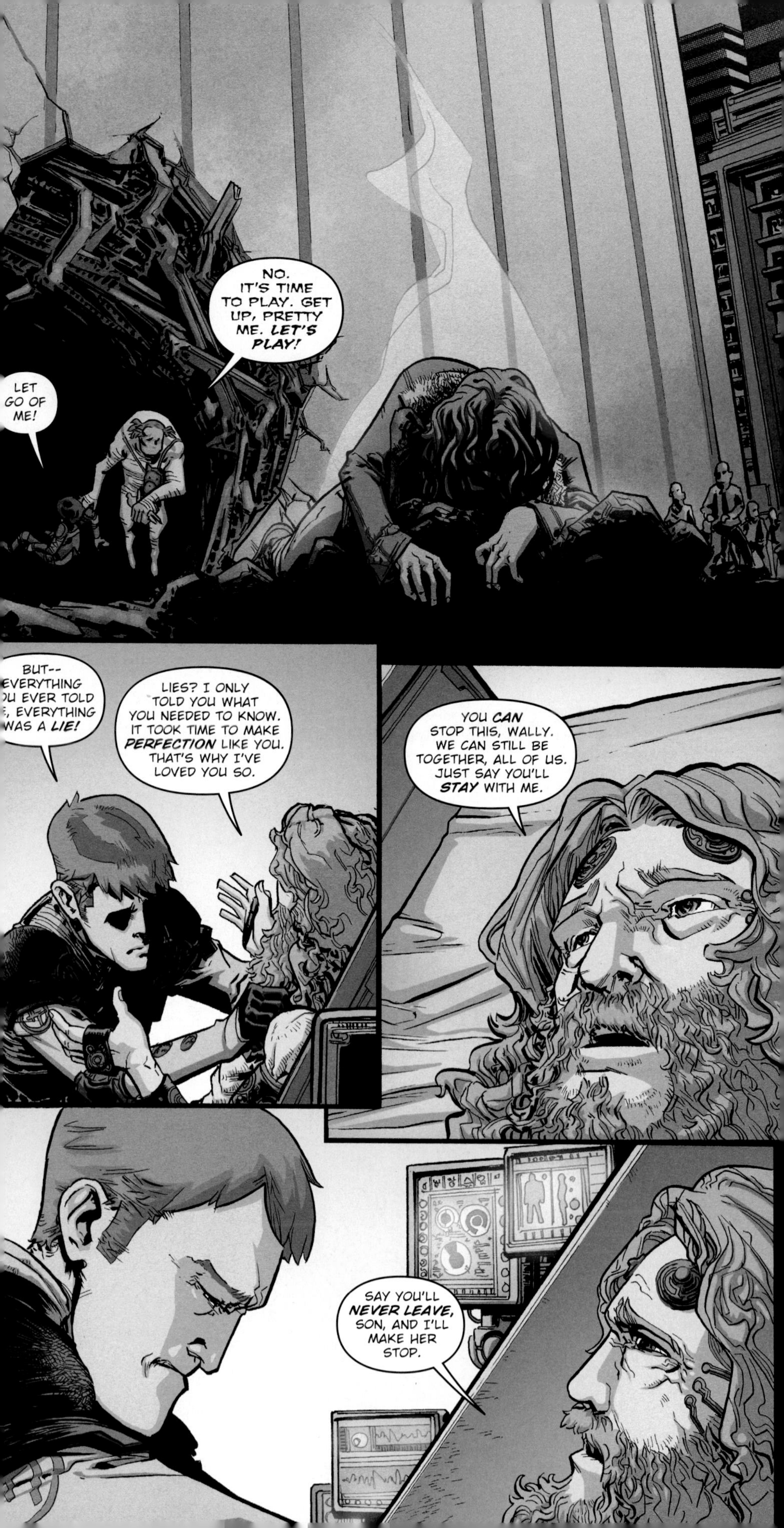

NO. IT'S TIME TO PLAY. GET UP, PRETTY ME. LET'S PLAY!
LET GO OF ME!
BUT-- EVERYTHING OU EVER TOLD E, EVERYTHING WAS A LIE!
LIES? I ONLY TOLD YOU WHAT YOU NEEDED TO KNOW. IT TOOK TIME TO MAKE PERFECTION LIKE YOU. THAT'S WHY I'VE LOVED YOU SO.
YOU CAN STOP THIS, WALLY. WE CAN STILL BE TOGETHER, ALL OF US. JUST SAY YOU'LL STAY WITH ME.
SAY YOU'LL NEVER LEAVE, SON, AND I'LL MAKE HER STOP.

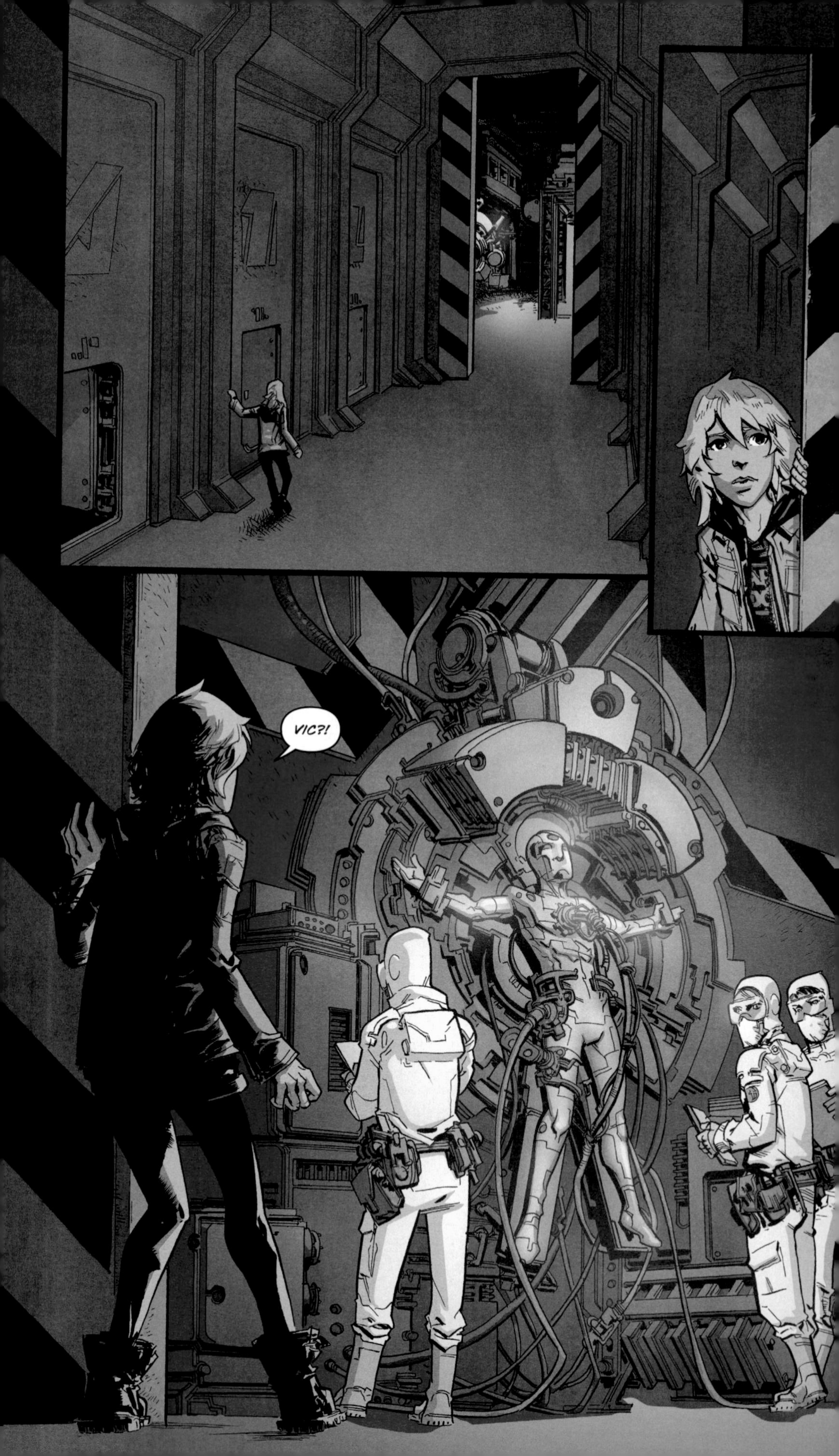
VIC?!

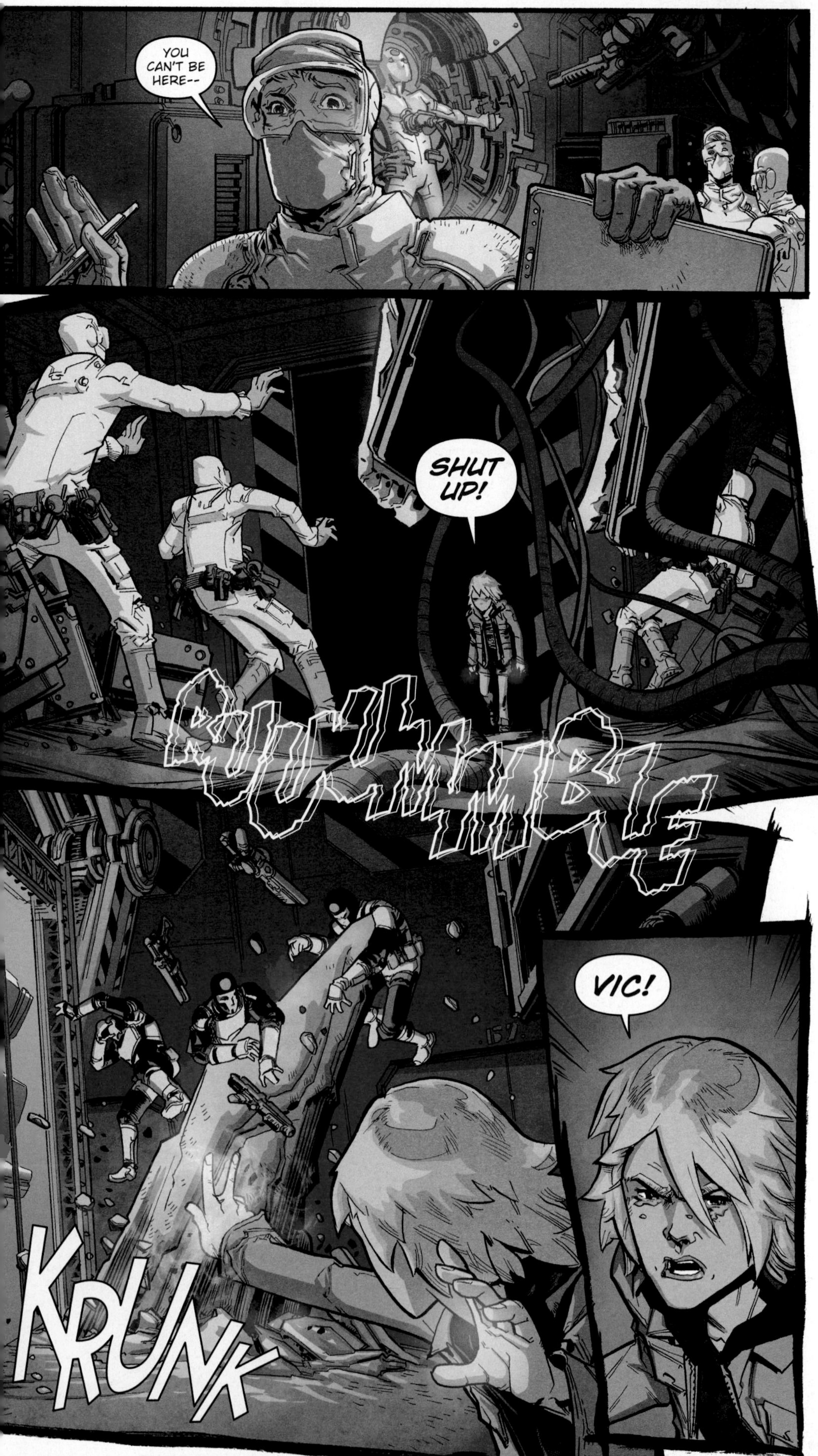
YOU CAN'T BE HERE--
SHUT UP!
KRUNK
VIC!

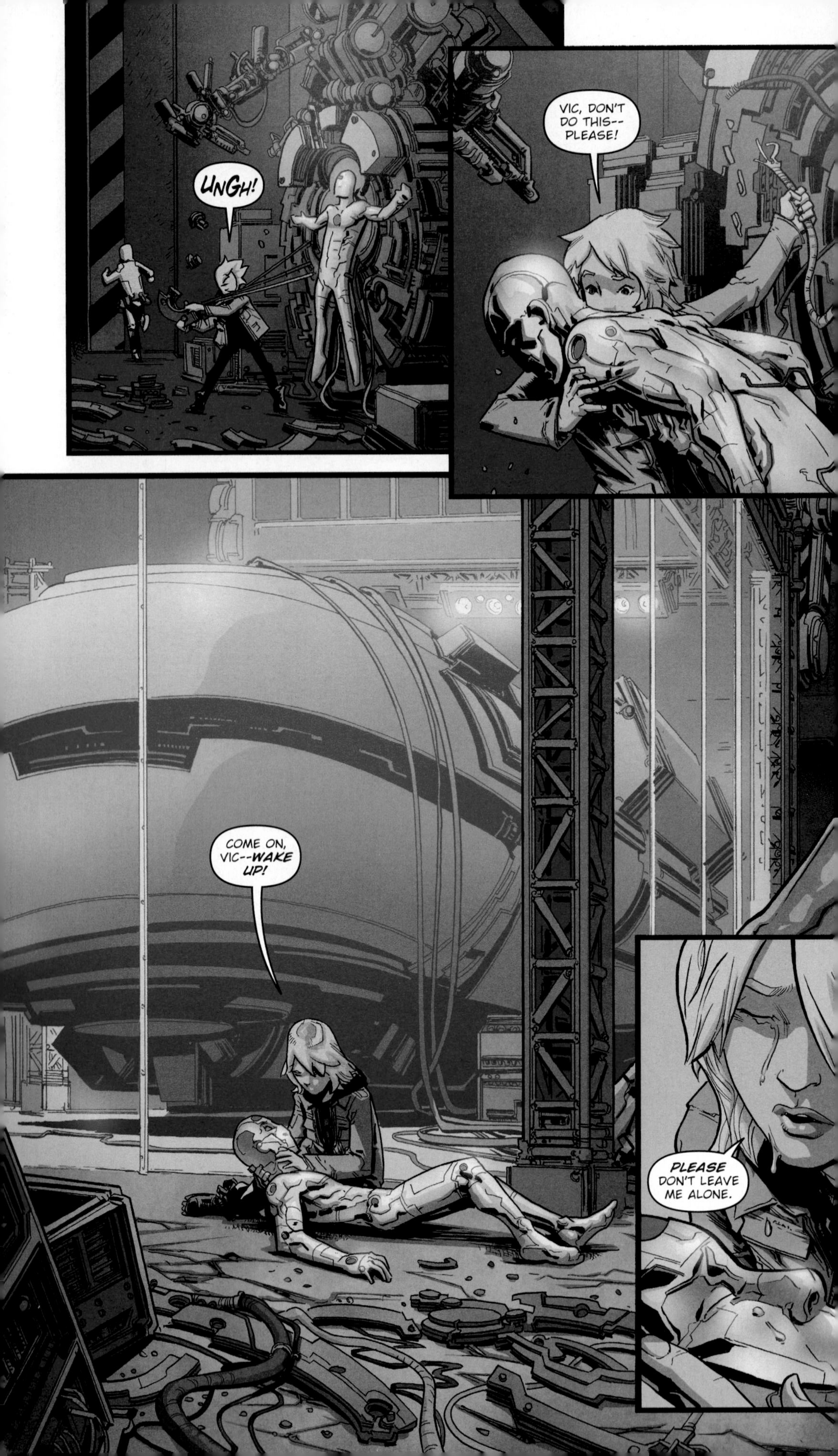
UNGH!
VIC, DON'T DO THIS-- PLEASE!
COME ON, VIC--WAKE UP!
PLEASE DON'T LEAVE ME ALONE.

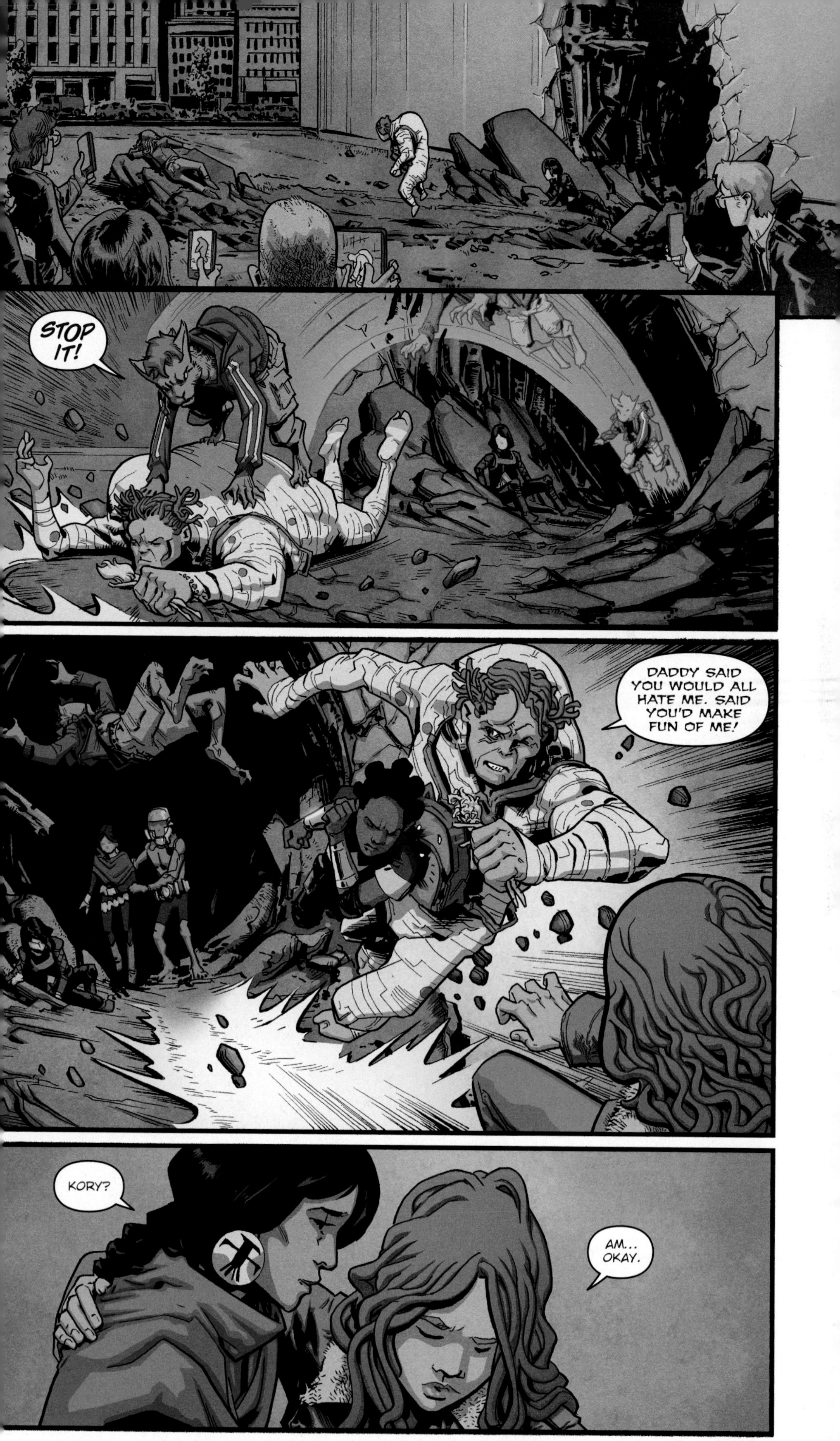
STOP IT!
DADDY SAID YOU WOULD ALL HATE ME. SAID YOU'D MAKE FUN OF ME!
KORY?
AM... OKAY.

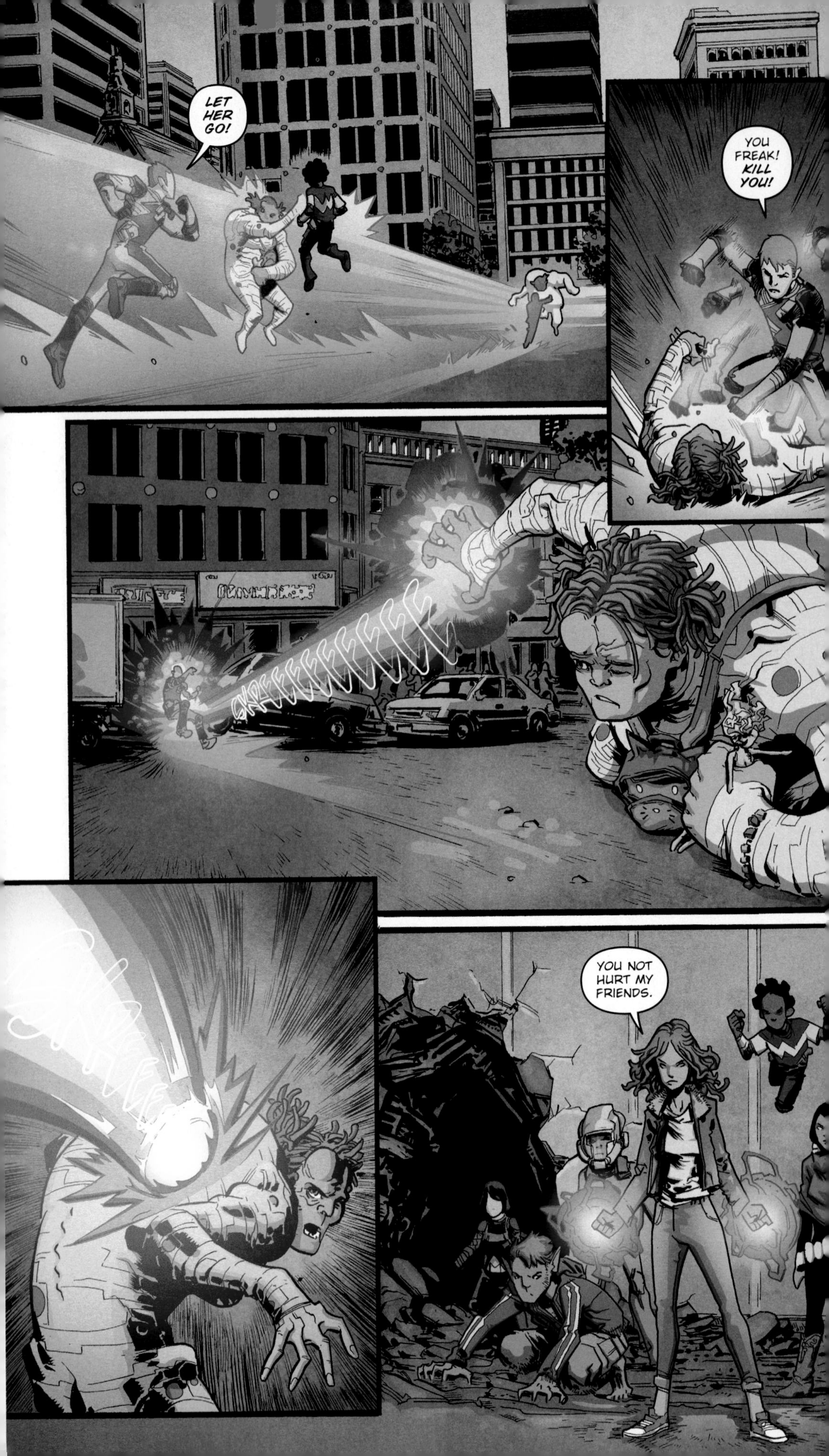

LET HER GO!
YOU FREAK! KILL YOU!
YOU NOT HURT MY FRIENDS.

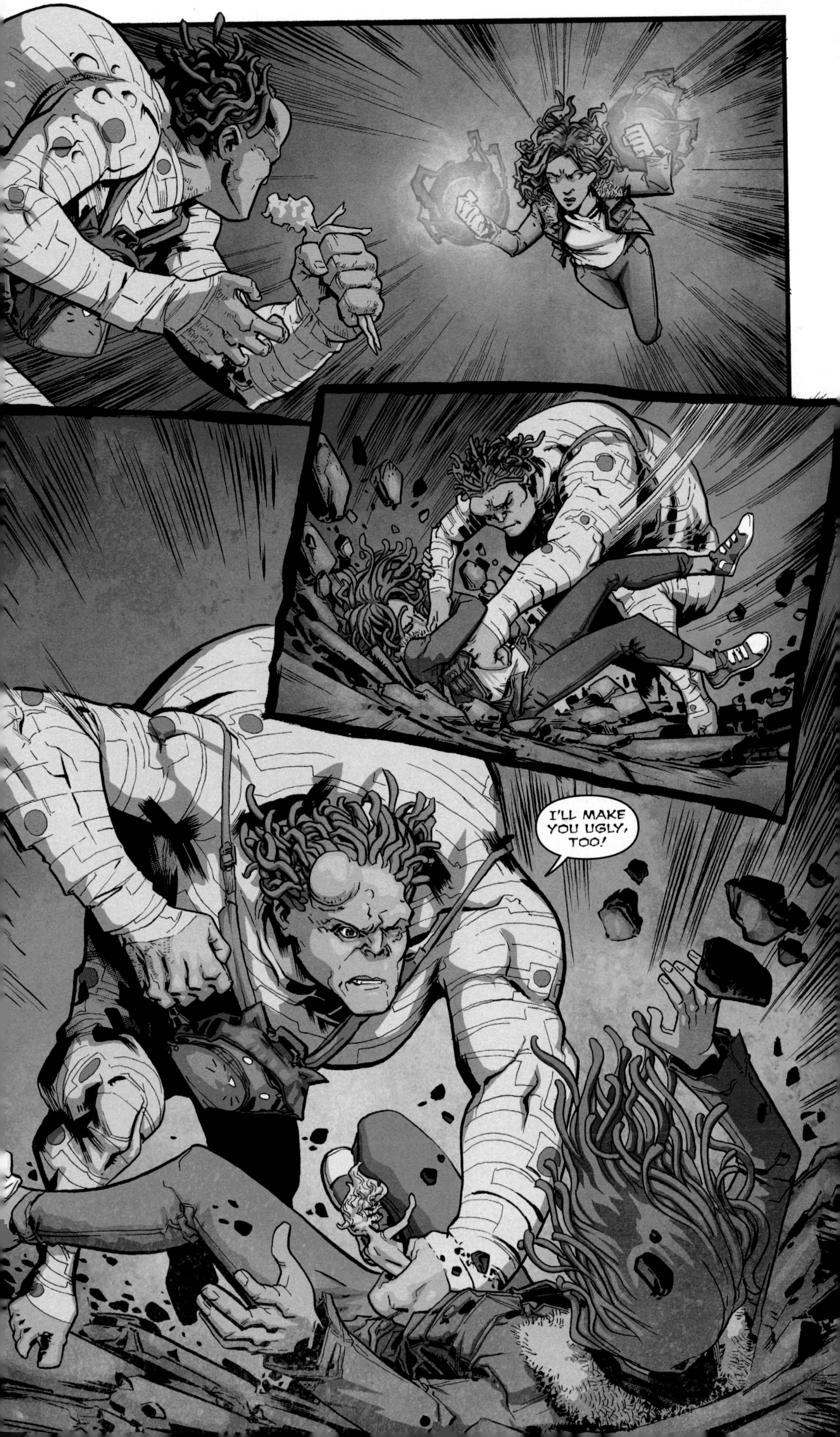
I'LL MAKE YOU UGLY, TOO!

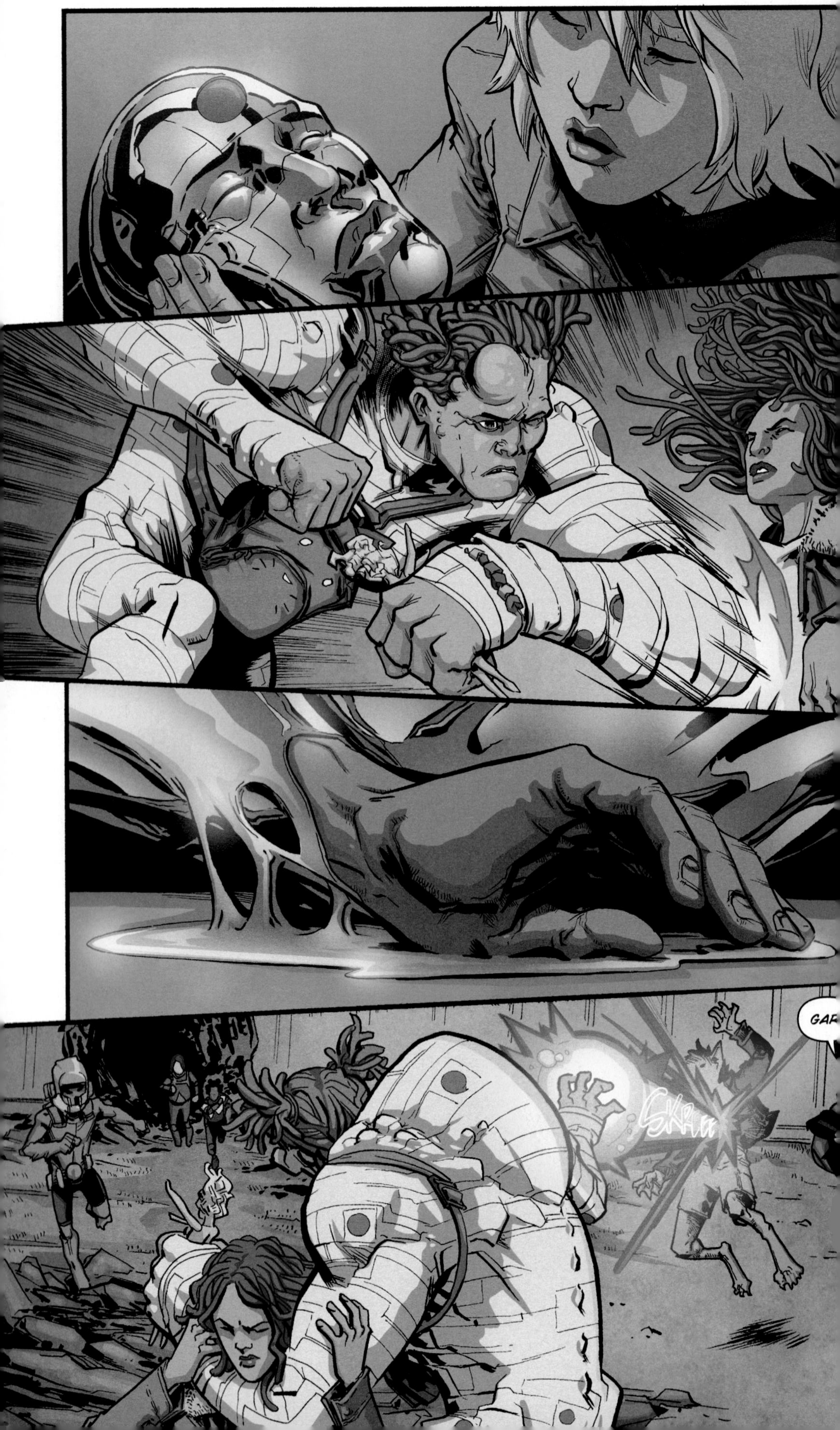
SKREE
GAR

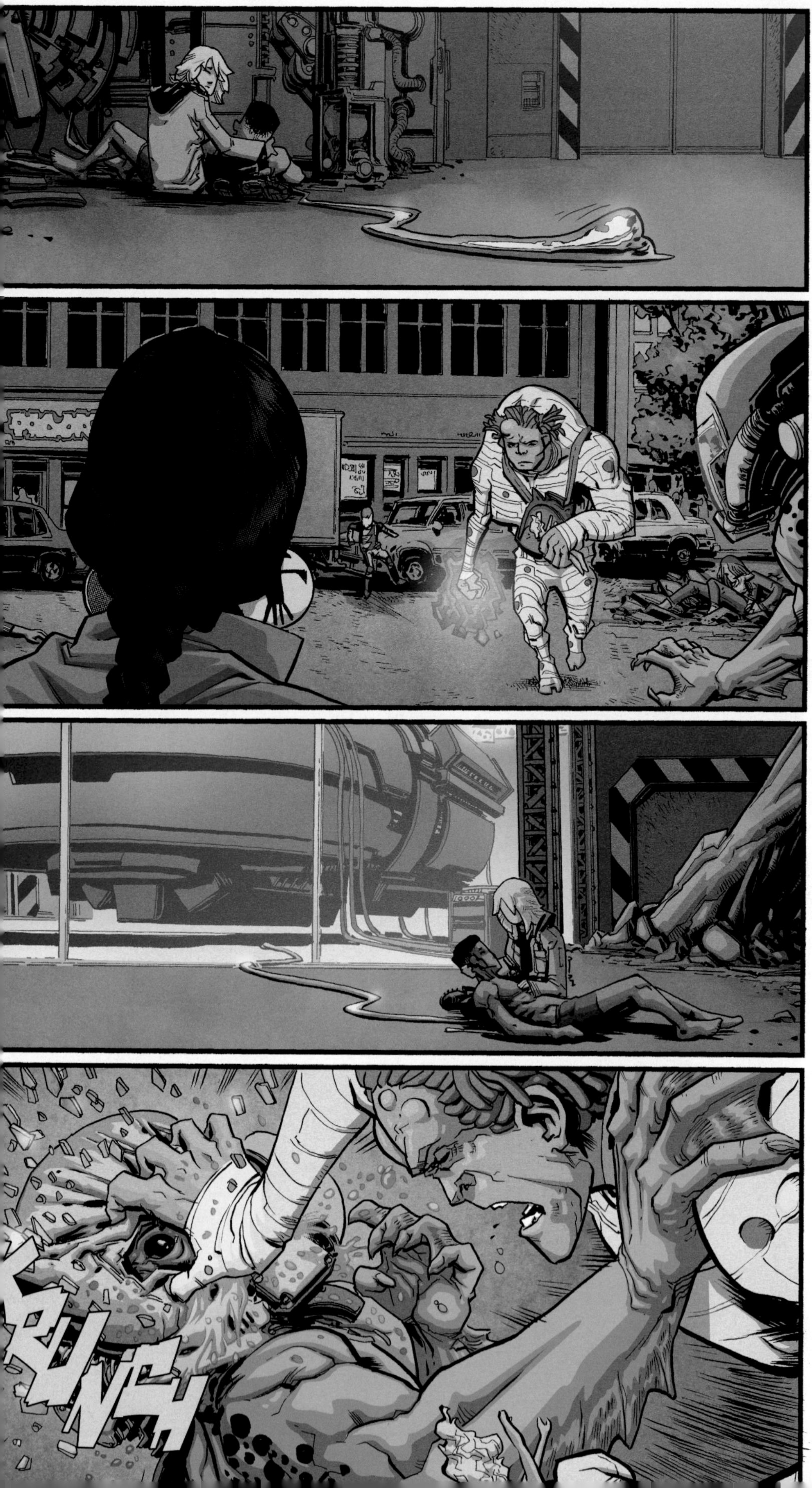
RUNCH

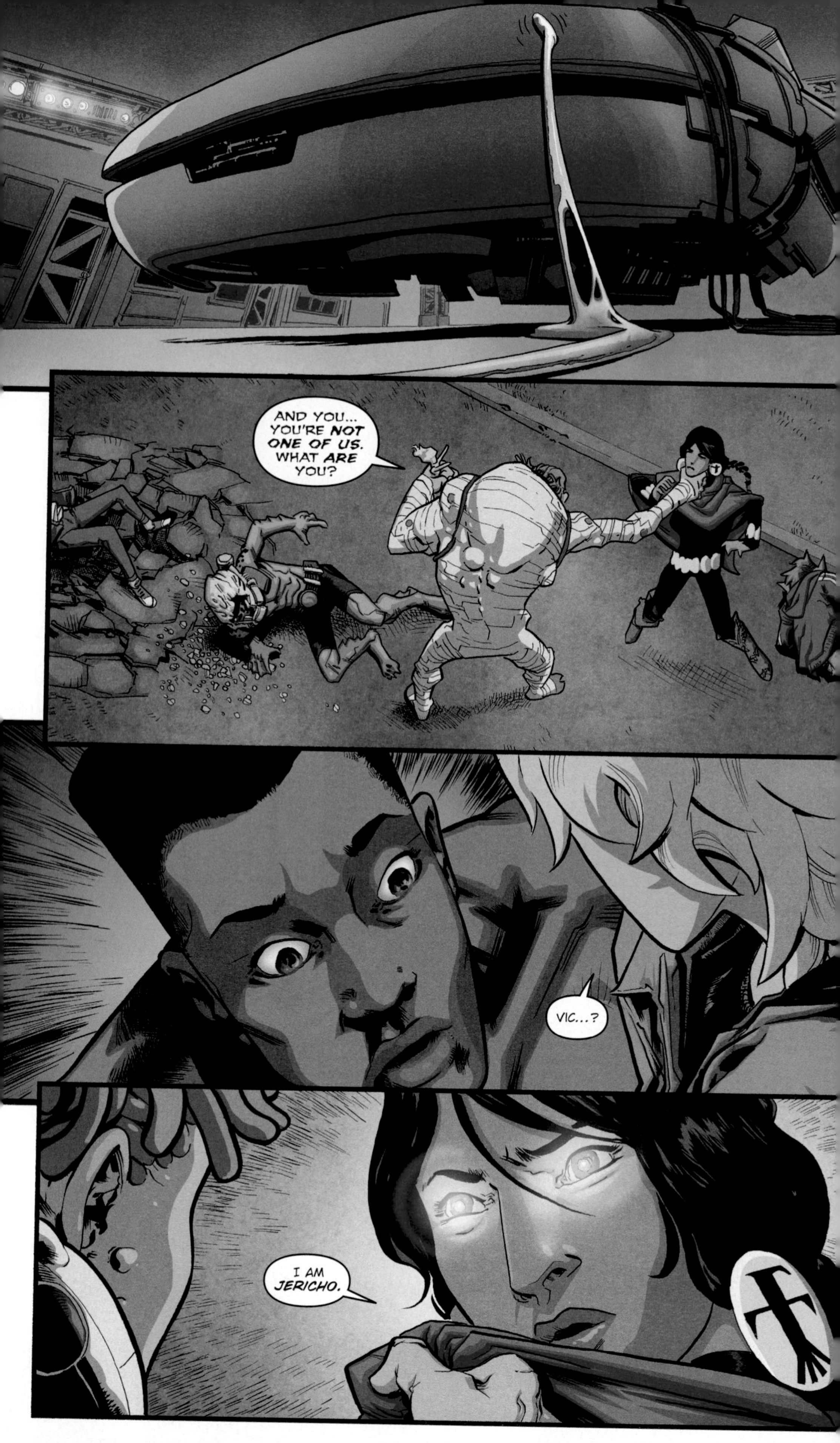
AND YOU... YOU'RE NOT ONE OF US. WHAT ARE YOU?
VIC...?
I AM JERICHO.

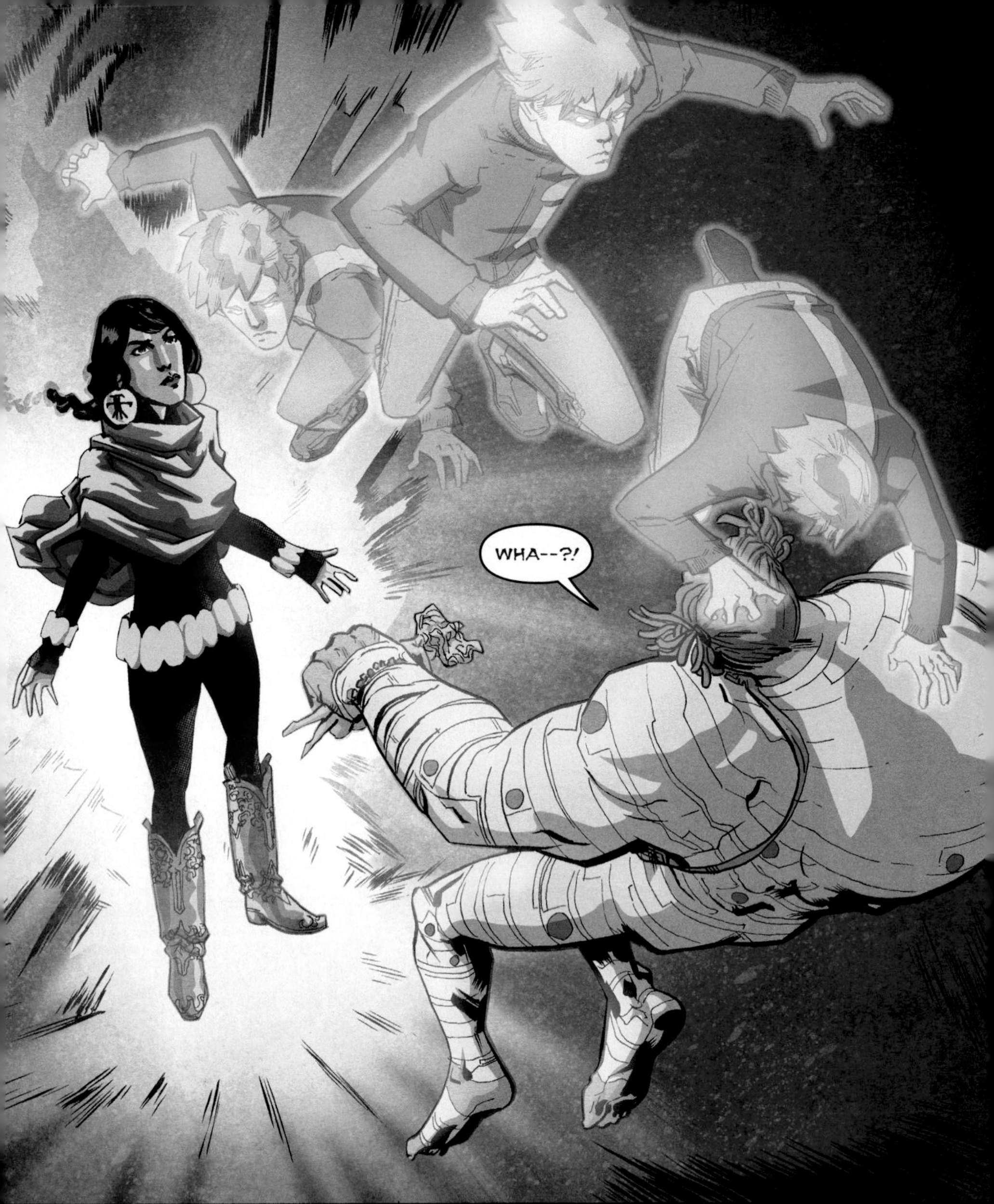
WHA--?!

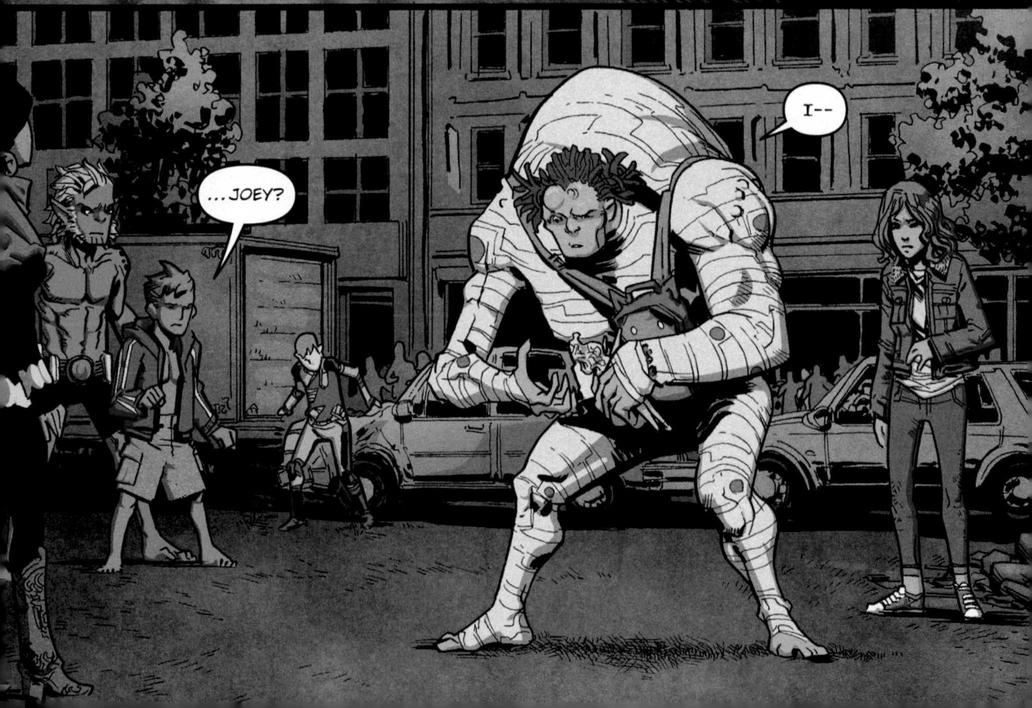
...JOEY?
I--

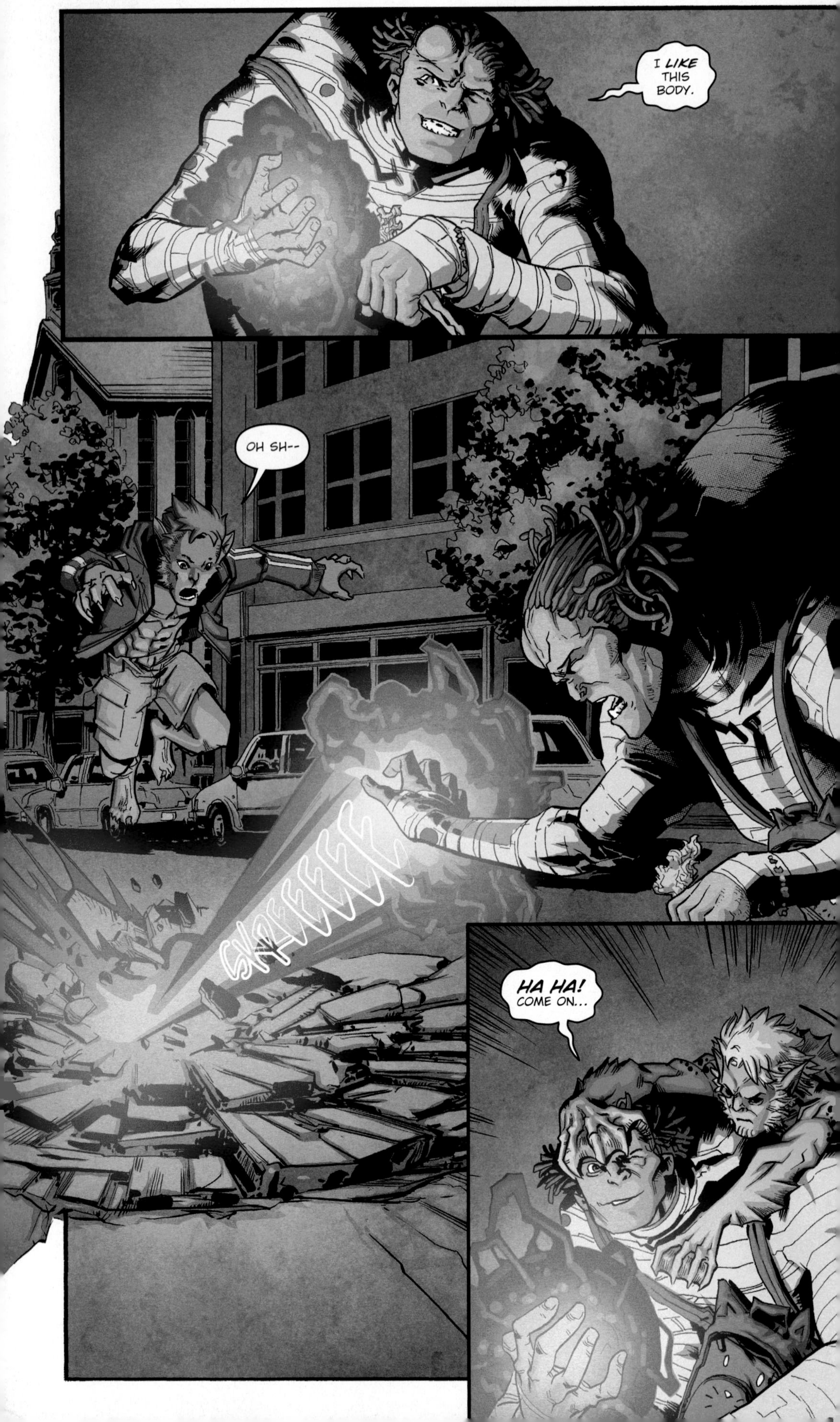
I LIKE THIS BODY.
OH SH--
SKREEEE
HA HA! COME ON...

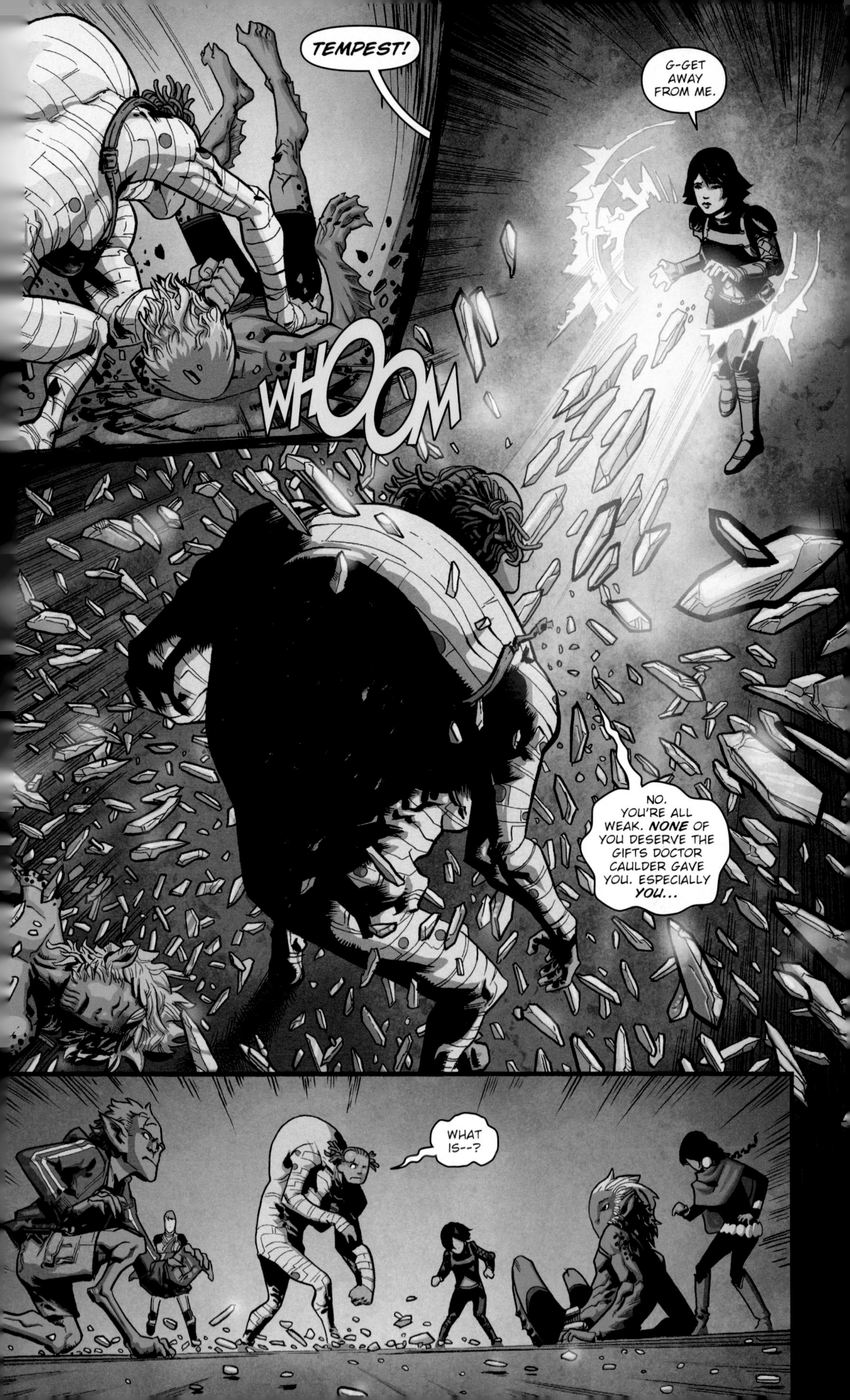
TEMPEST!
G-GET AWAY FROM ME.
WHOOM
NO. YOU'RE ALL WEAK. NONE OF YOU DESERVE THE GIFTS DOCTOR CAULDER GAVE YOU. ESPECIALLY YOU...
WHAT IS--?

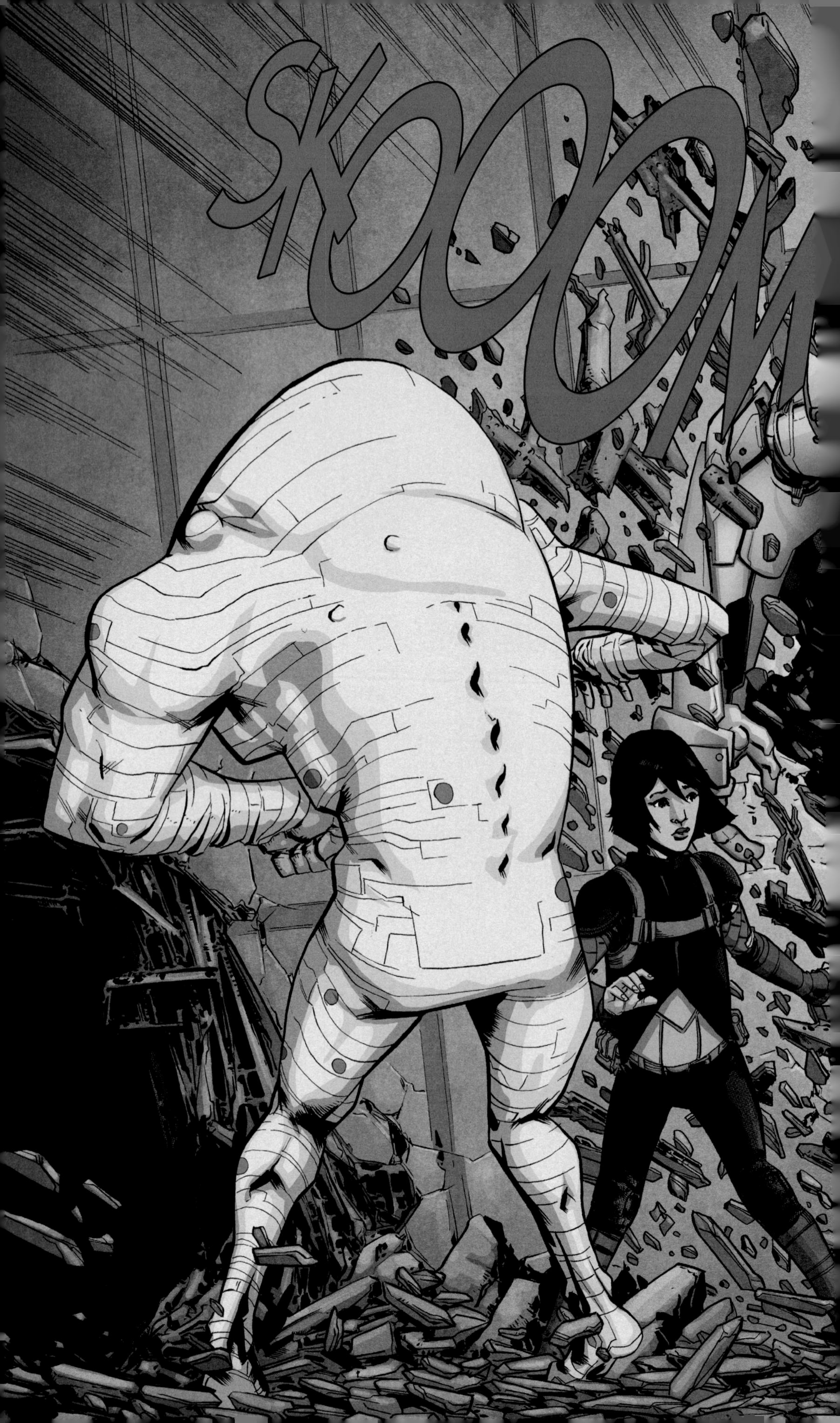
SKOOM

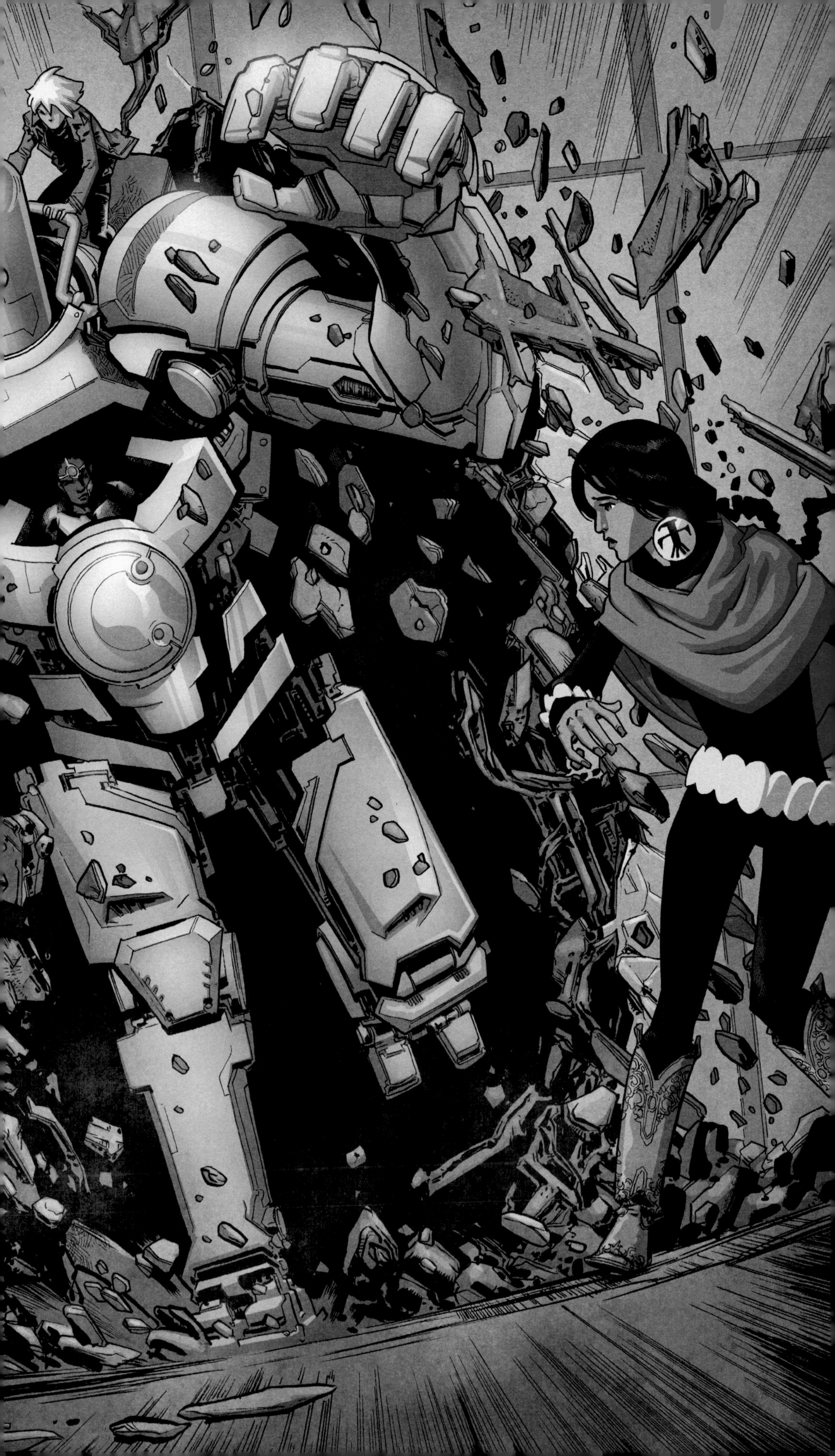

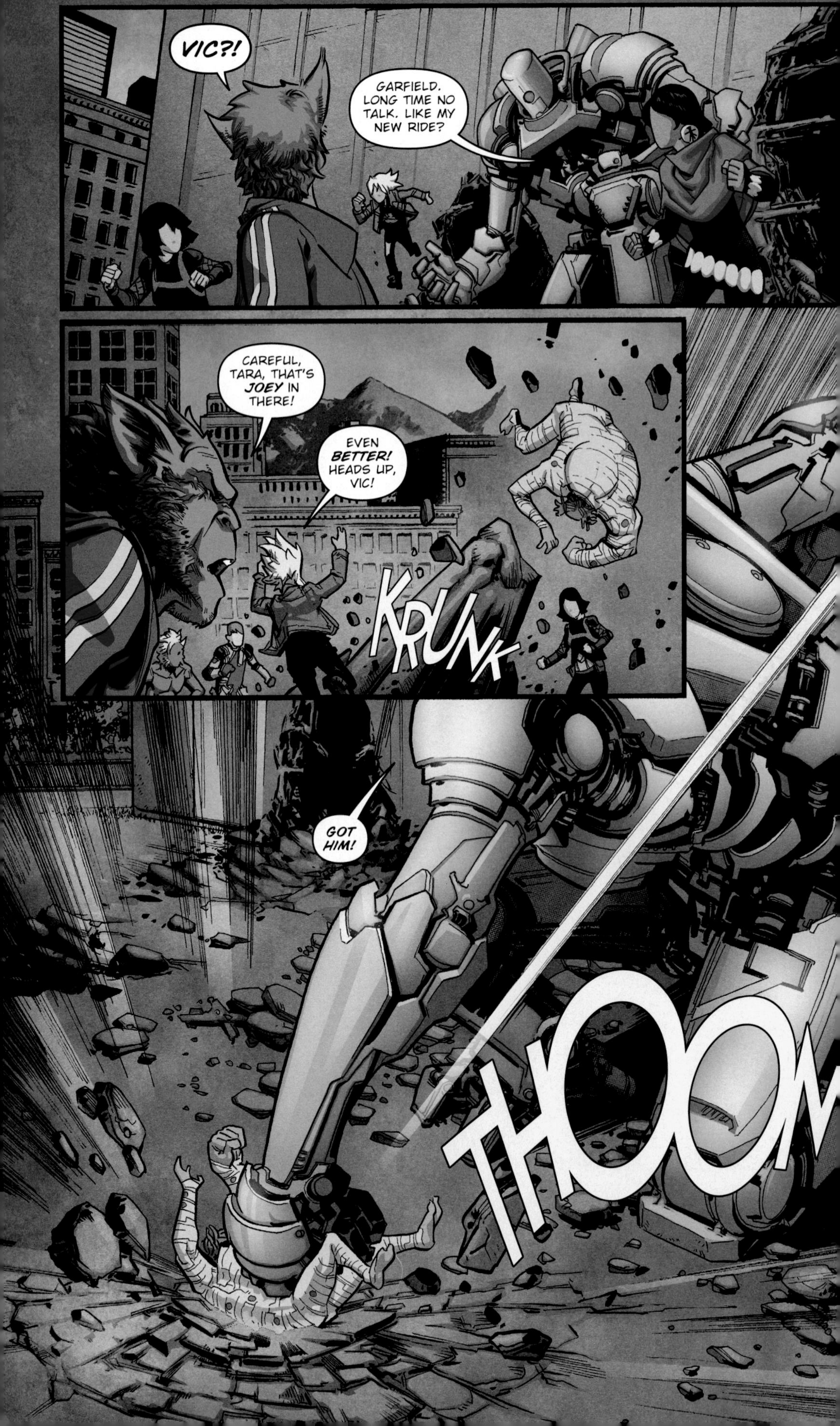
VIC?!
GARFIELD. LONG TIME NO TALK. LIKE MY NEW RIDE?
CAREFUL, TARA, THAT'S JOEY IN THERE!
EVEN BETTER! HEADS UP, VIC!
KRUNK
GOT HIM!
THOOM

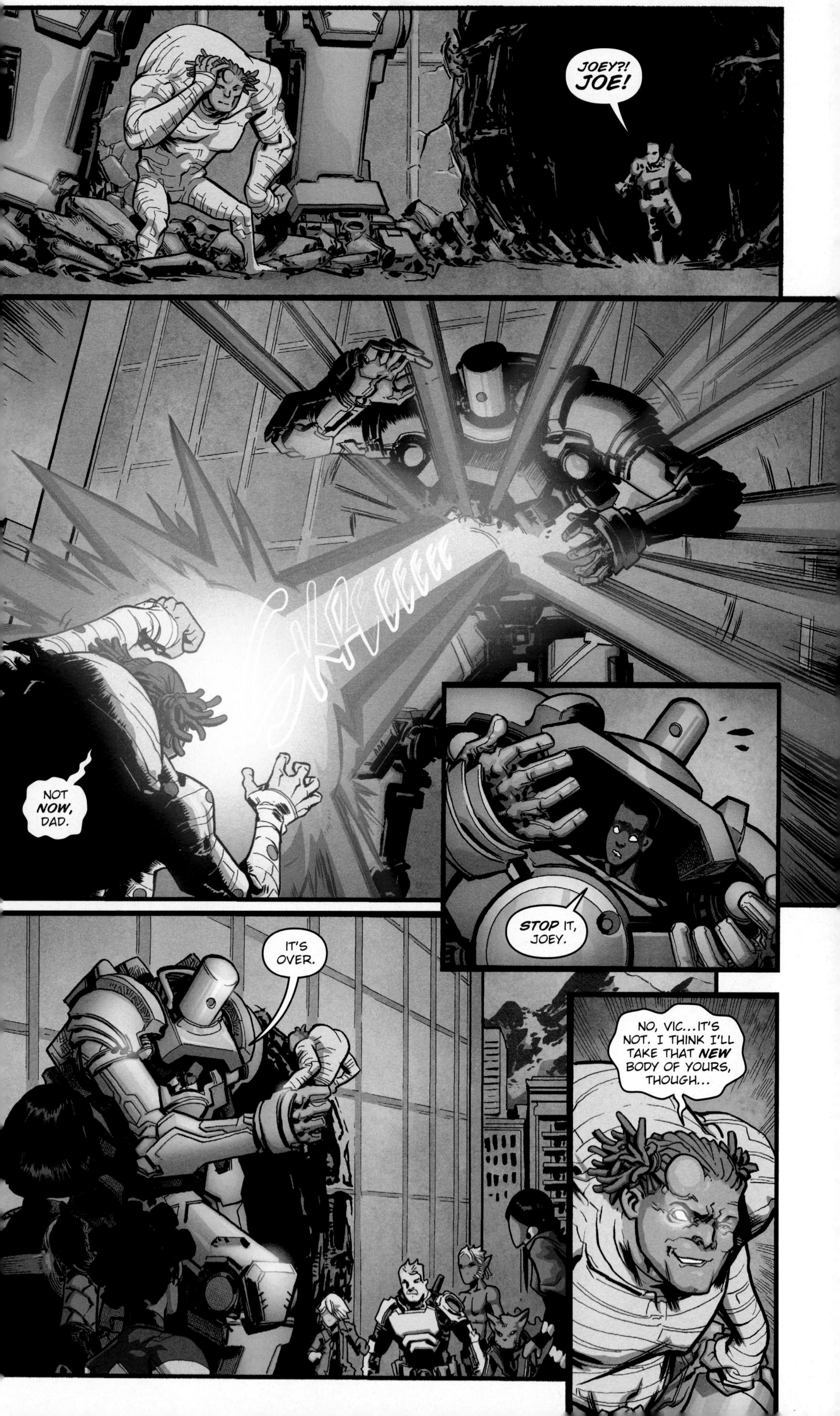

JOEY?! JOE!
NOT NOW, DAD.
STOP IT, JOEY.
IT'S OVER.
NO, VIC...IT'S NOT. I THINK I'LL TAKE THAT NEW BODY OF YOURS, THOUGH...

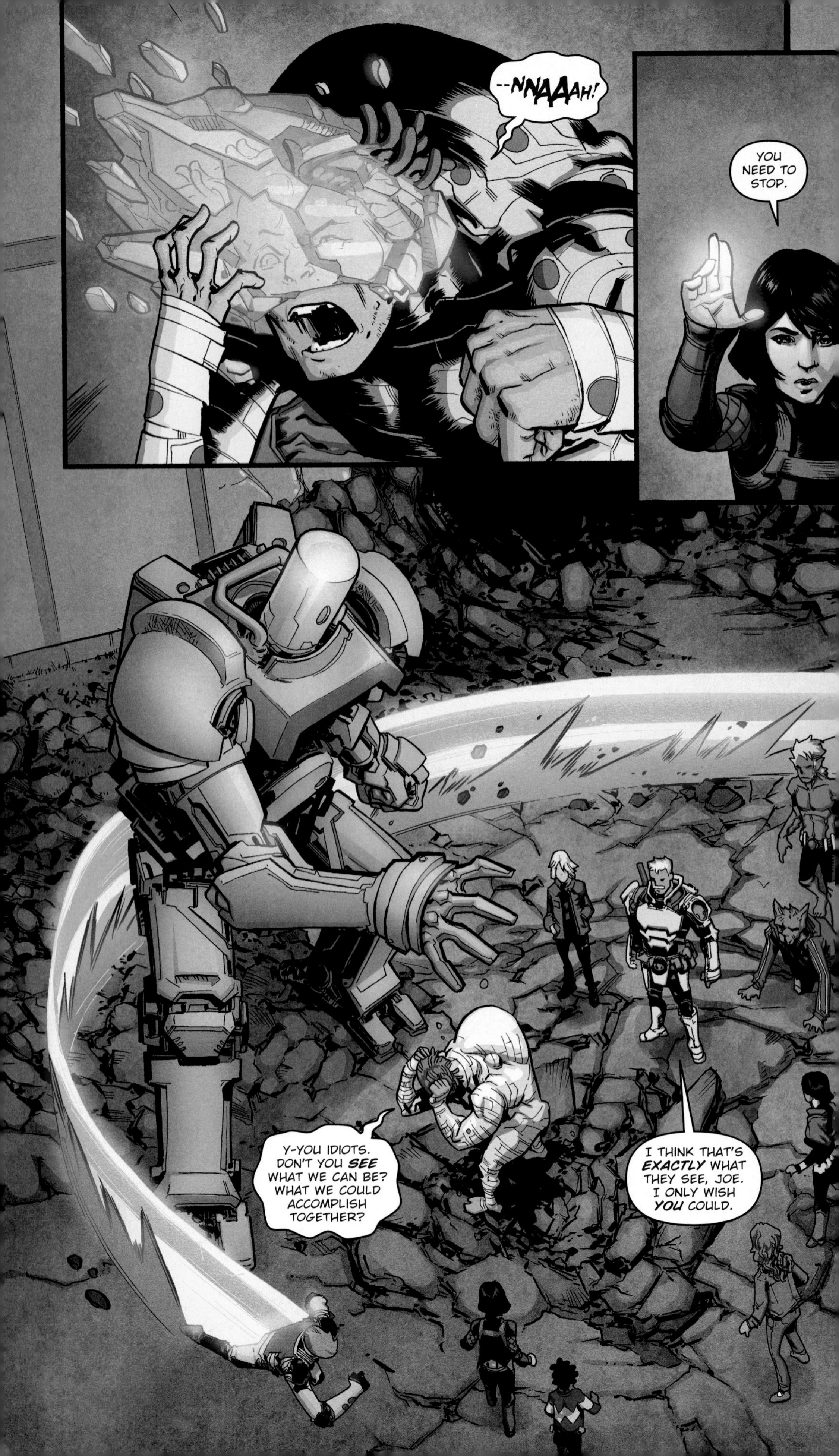
--NNAAAH!
YOU NEED TO STOP.
Y-YOU IDIOTS. DON'T YOU SEE WHAT WE CAN BE? WHAT WE COULD ACCOMPLISH TOGETHER?
I THINK THAT'S EXACTLY WHAT THEY SEE, JOE. I ONLY WISH YOU COULD.

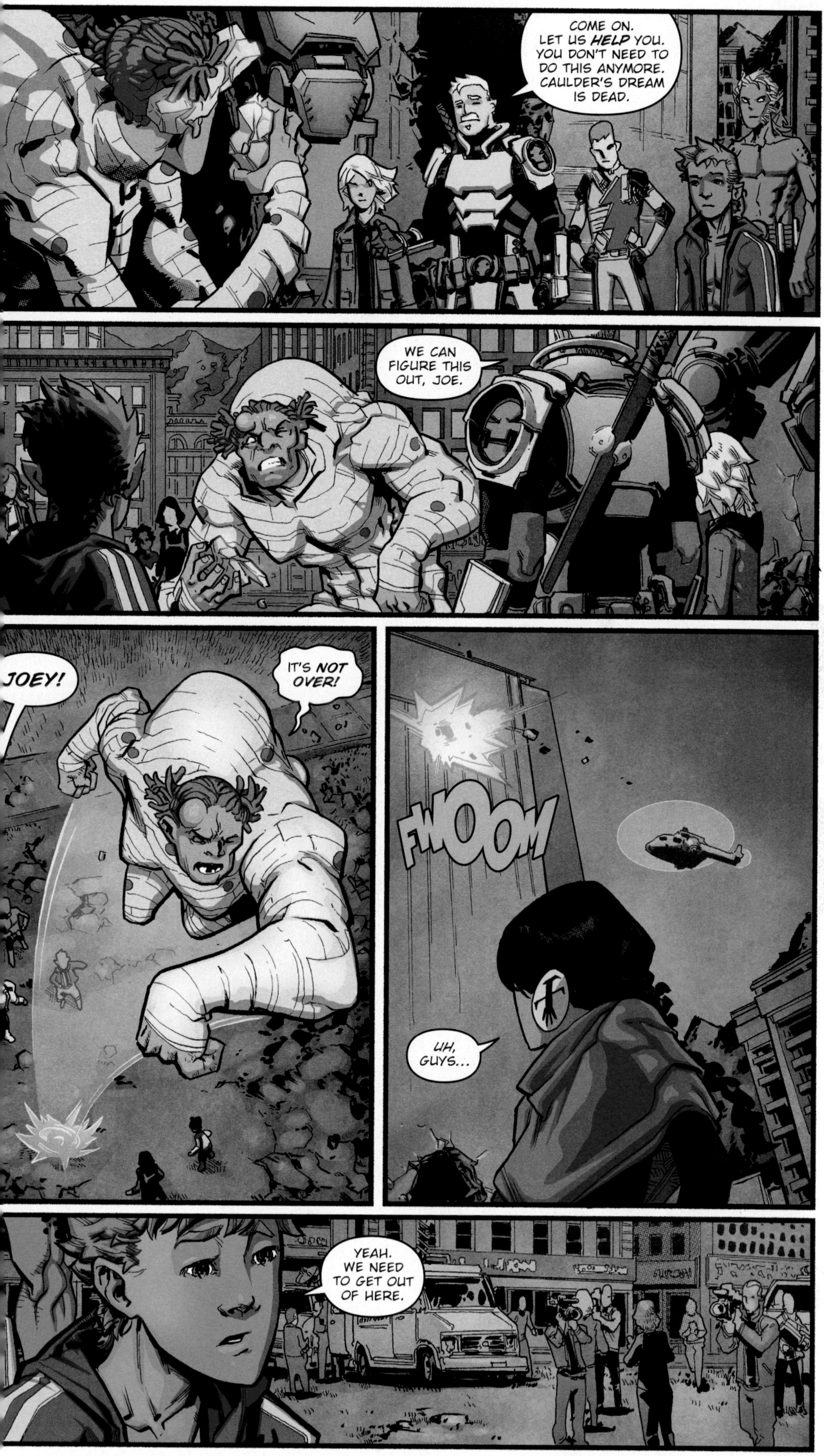
COME ON. LET US *HELP* YOU. YOU DON'T NEED TO DO THIS ANYMORE. CAULDER'S DREAM IS DEAD.
WE CAN FIGURE THIS OUT, JOE.
JOEY!
IT'S *NOT OVER!*
FWOOM
UH, GUYS...
YEAH. WE NEED TO GET OUT OF HERE.

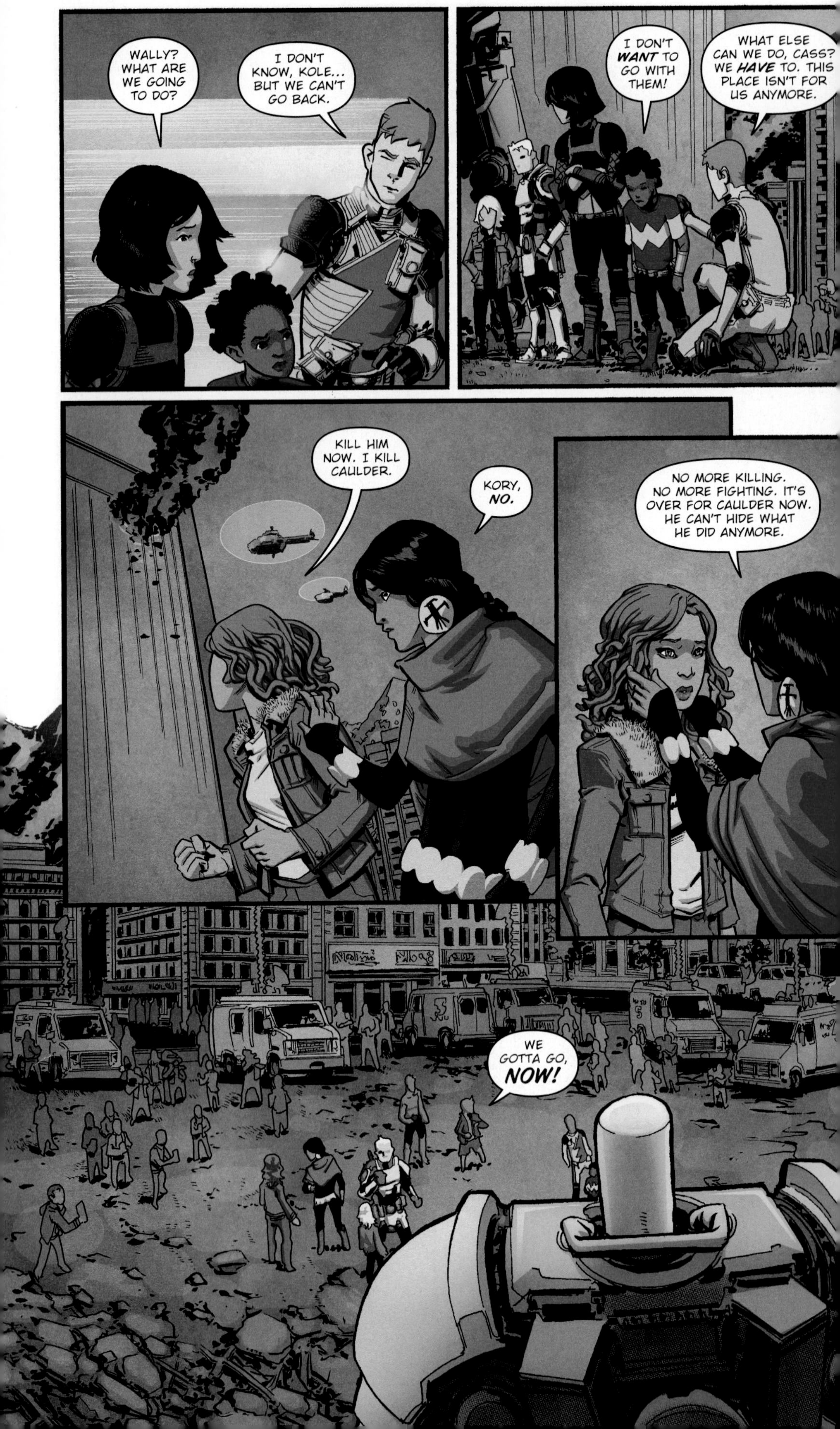
WALLY? WHAT ARE WE GOING TO DO?
I DON'T KNOW, KOLE... BUT WE CAN'T GO BACK.
I DON'T *WANT* TO GO WITH THEM!
WHAT ELSE CAN WE DO, CASS? WE *HAVE* TO. THIS PLACE ISN'T FOR US ANYMORE.
KILL HIM NOW. I KILL CAULDER.
KORY, *NO.*
NO MORE KILLING. NO MORE FIGHTING. IT'S OVER FOR CAULDER NOW. HE CAN'T HIDE WHAT HE DID ANYMORE.
WE GOTTA GO, *NOW!*

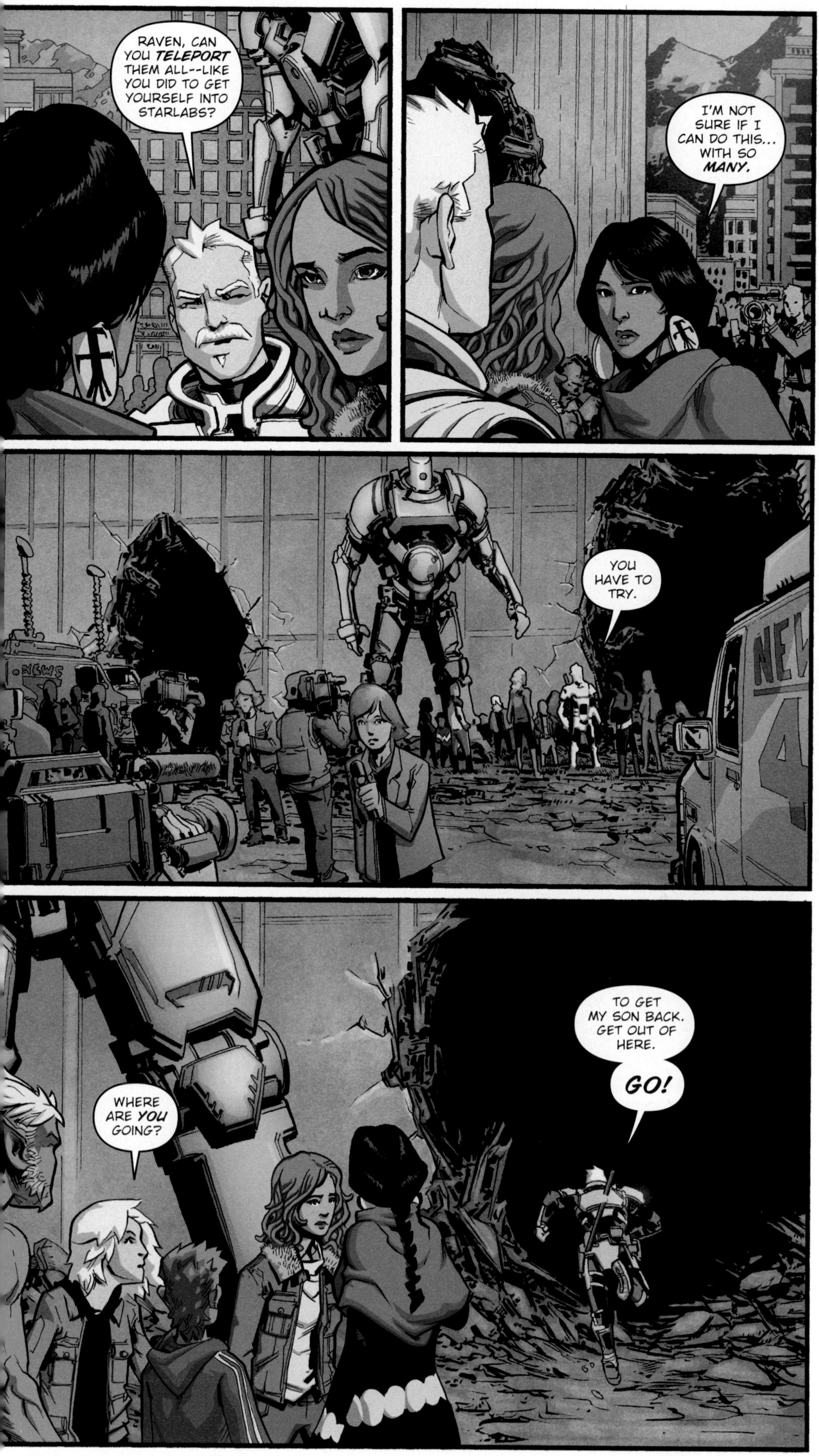
RAVEN, CAN YOU TELEPORT THEM ALL--LIKE YOU DID TO GET YOURSELF INTO STARLABS?
I'M NOT SURE IF I CAN DO THIS... WITH SO MANY.
NEWS
YOU HAVE TO TRY.
NEWS 4
WHERE ARE YOU GOING?
TO GET MY SON BACK. GET OUT OF HERE.
GO!

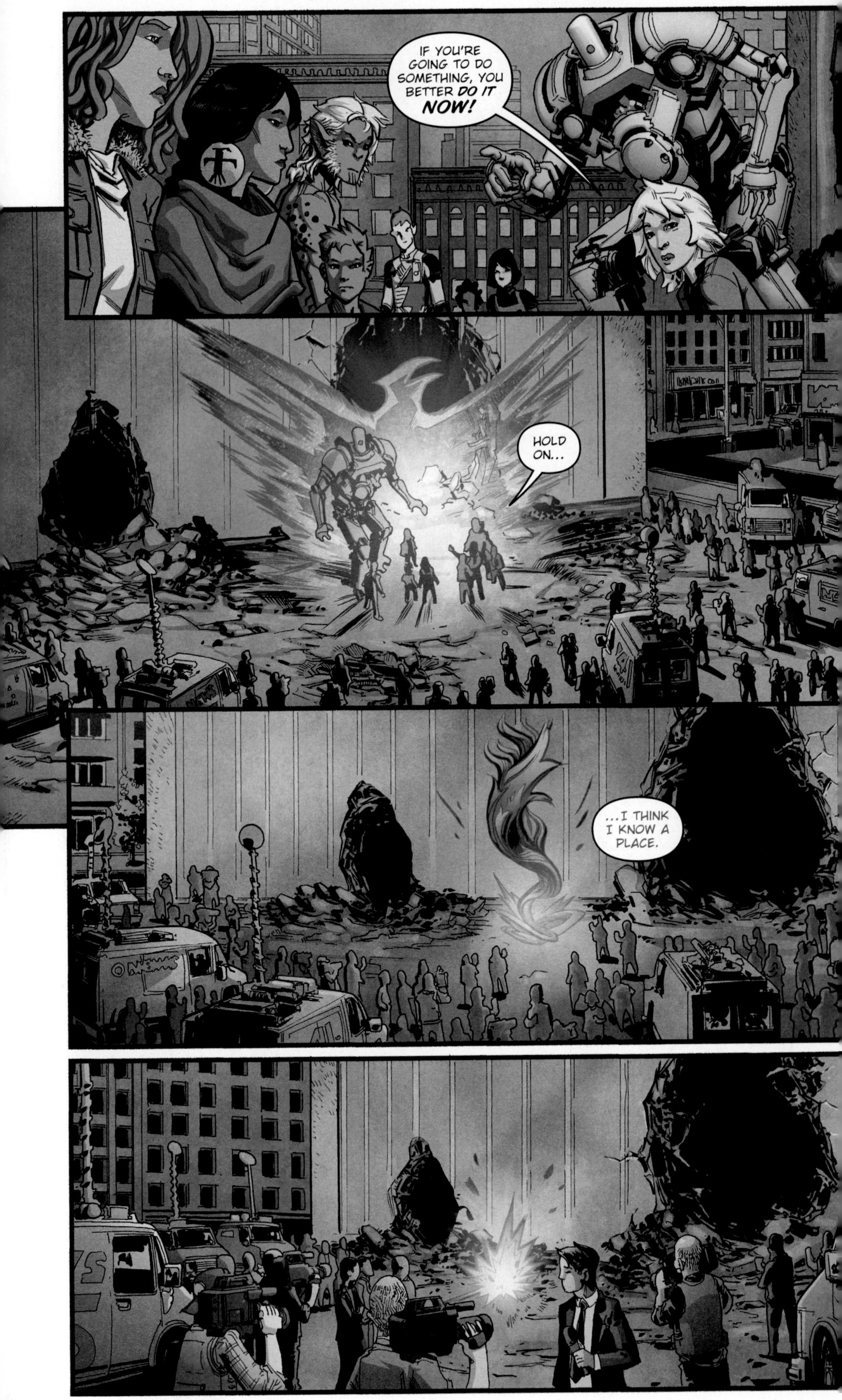
IF YOU'RE GOING TO DO SOMETHING, YOU BETTER *DO IT* *NOW!*
HOLD ON...
...I THINK I KNOW A PLACE.

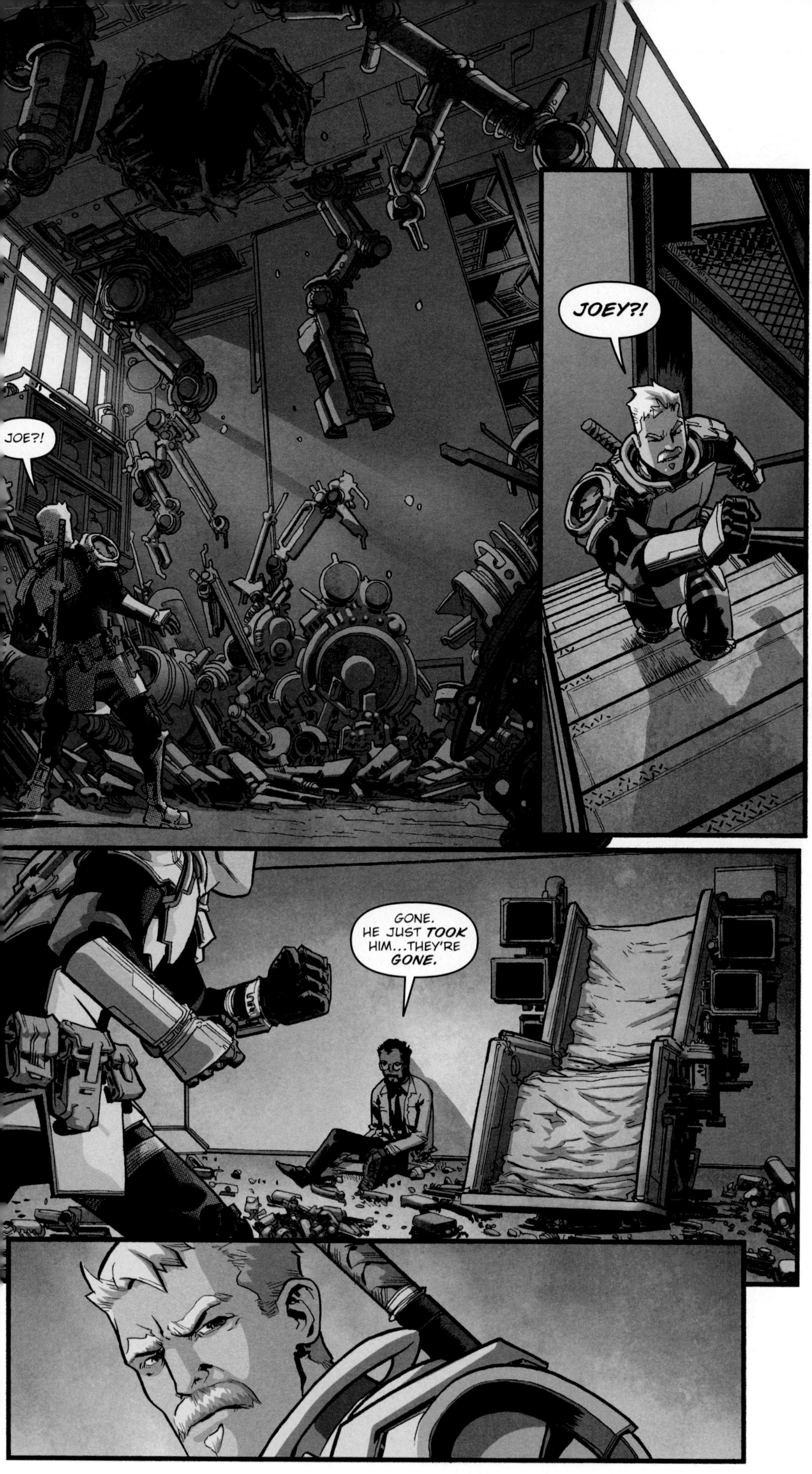

JOE?!
JOEY?!
GONE. HE JUST TOOK HIM...THEY'RE GONE.

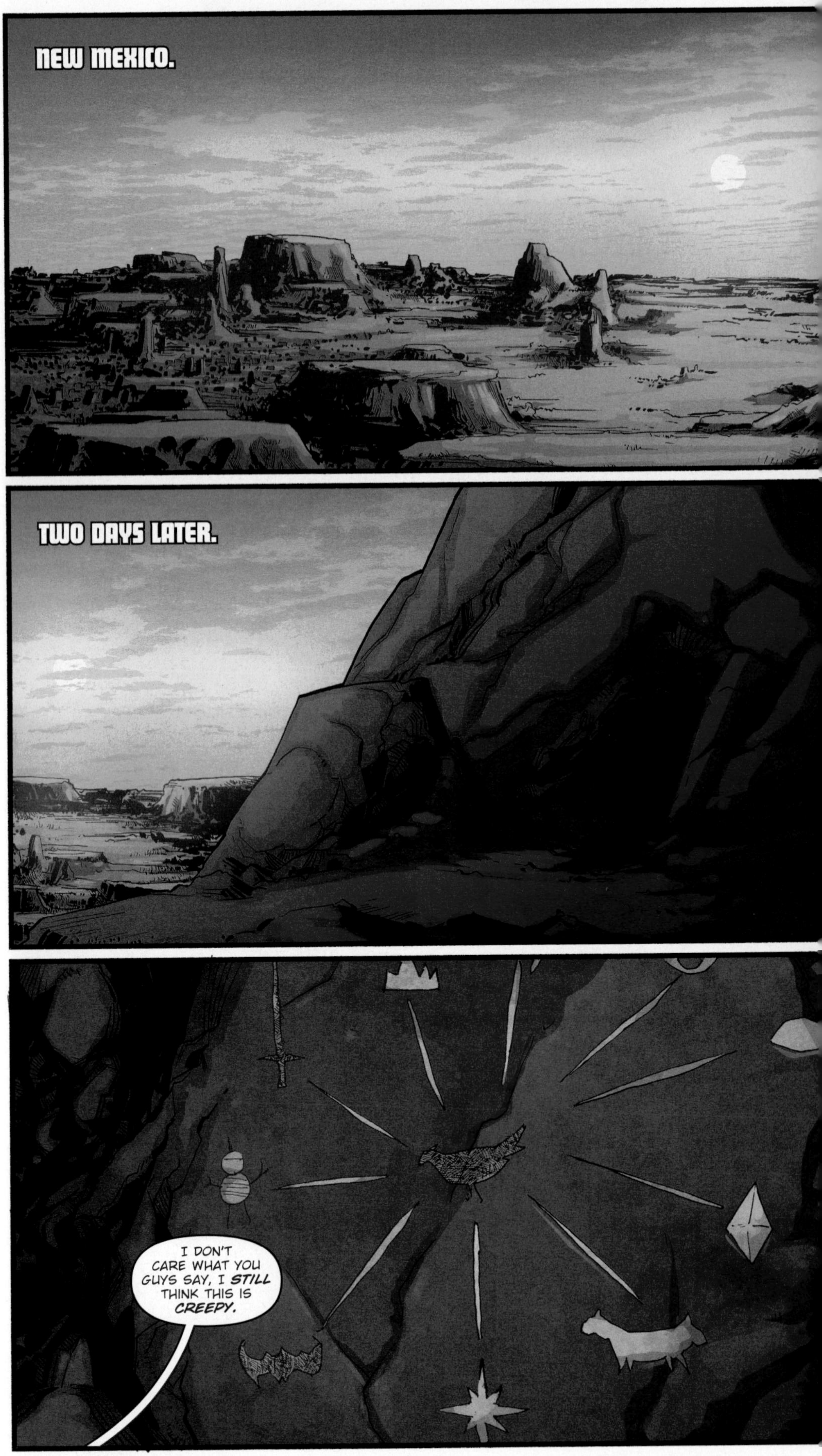
NEW MEXICO.
TWO DAYS LATER.
I DON'T CARE WHAT YOU GUYS SAY, I STILL THINK THIS IS CREEPY.

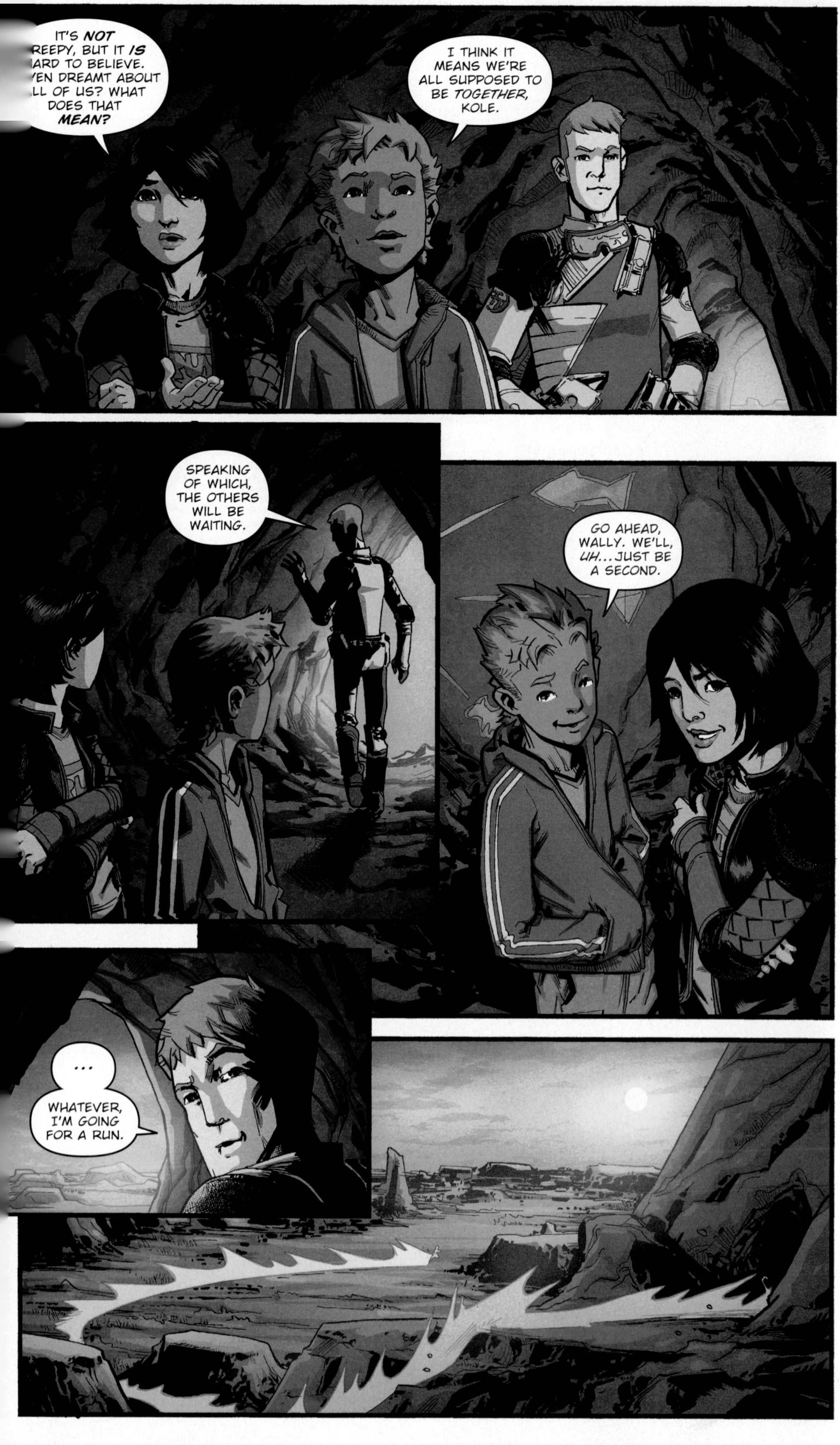

IT'S NOT REEPY, BUT IT IS ARD TO BELIEVE. YEN DREAMT ABOUT LL OF US? WHAT DOES THAT MEAN?
I THINK IT MEANS WE'RE ALL SUPPOSED TO BE TOGETHER, KOLE.
SPEAKING OF WHICH, THE OTHERS WILL BE WAITING.
GO AHEAD, WALLY. WE'LL, UH... JUST BE A SECOND.
...
WHATEVER, I'M GOING FOR A RUN.

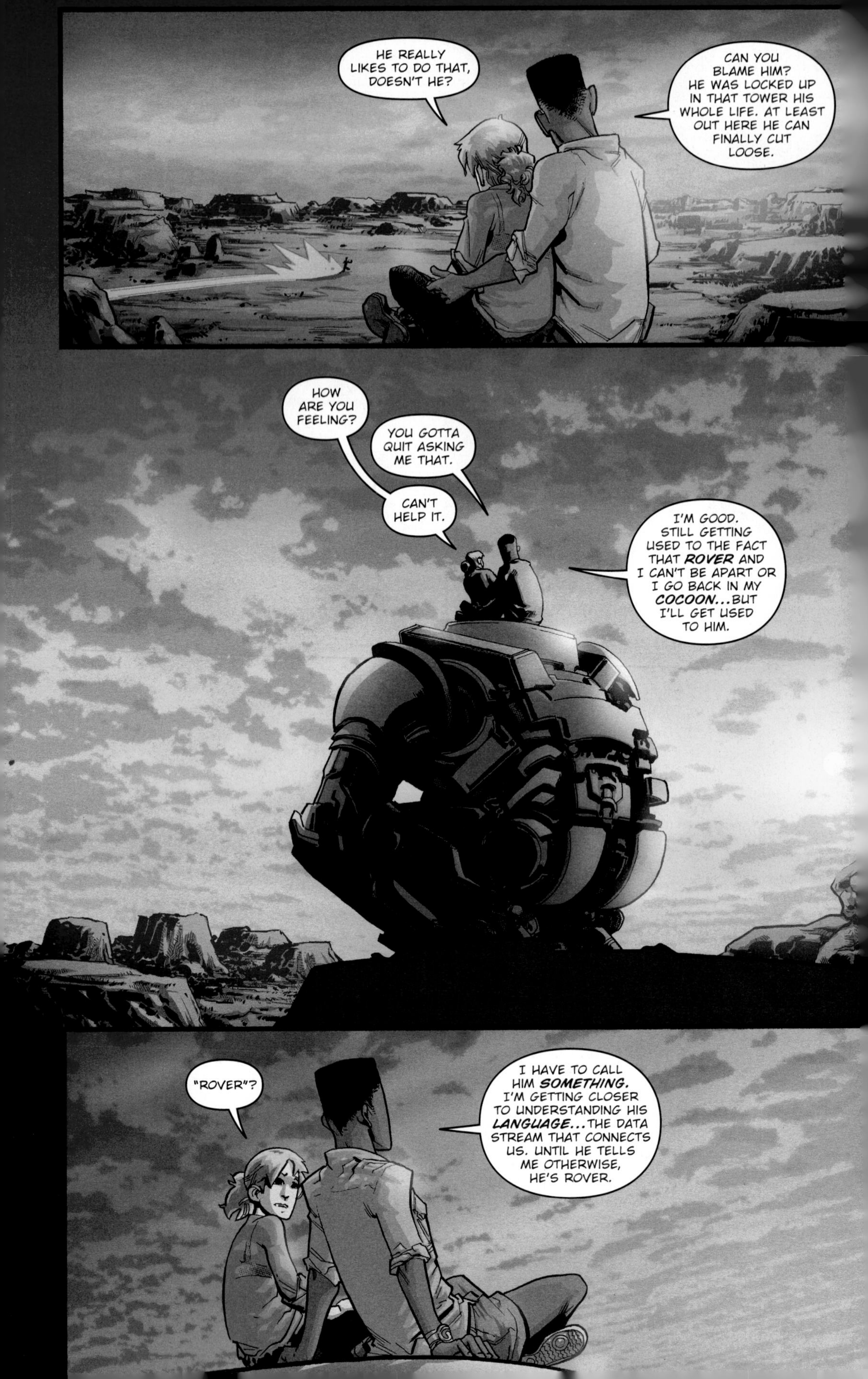
HE REALLY LIKES TO DO THAT, DOESN'T HE?
CAN YOU BLAME HIM? HE WAS LOCKED UP IN THAT TOWER HIS WHOLE LIFE. AT LEAST OUT HERE HE CAN FINALLY CUT LOOSE.
HOW ARE YOU FEELING?
YOU GOTTA QUIT ASKING ME THAT.
CAN'T HELP IT.
I'M GOOD. STILL GETTING USED TO THE FACT THAT ROVER AND I CAN'T BE APART OR I GO BACK IN MY COCOON...BUT I'LL GET USED TO HIM.
"ROVER"?
I HAVE TO CALL HIM SOMETHING. I'M GETTING CLOSER TO UNDERSTANDING HIS LANGUAGE...THE DATA STREAM THAT CONNECTS US. UNTIL HE TELLS ME OTHERWISE, HE'S ROVER.

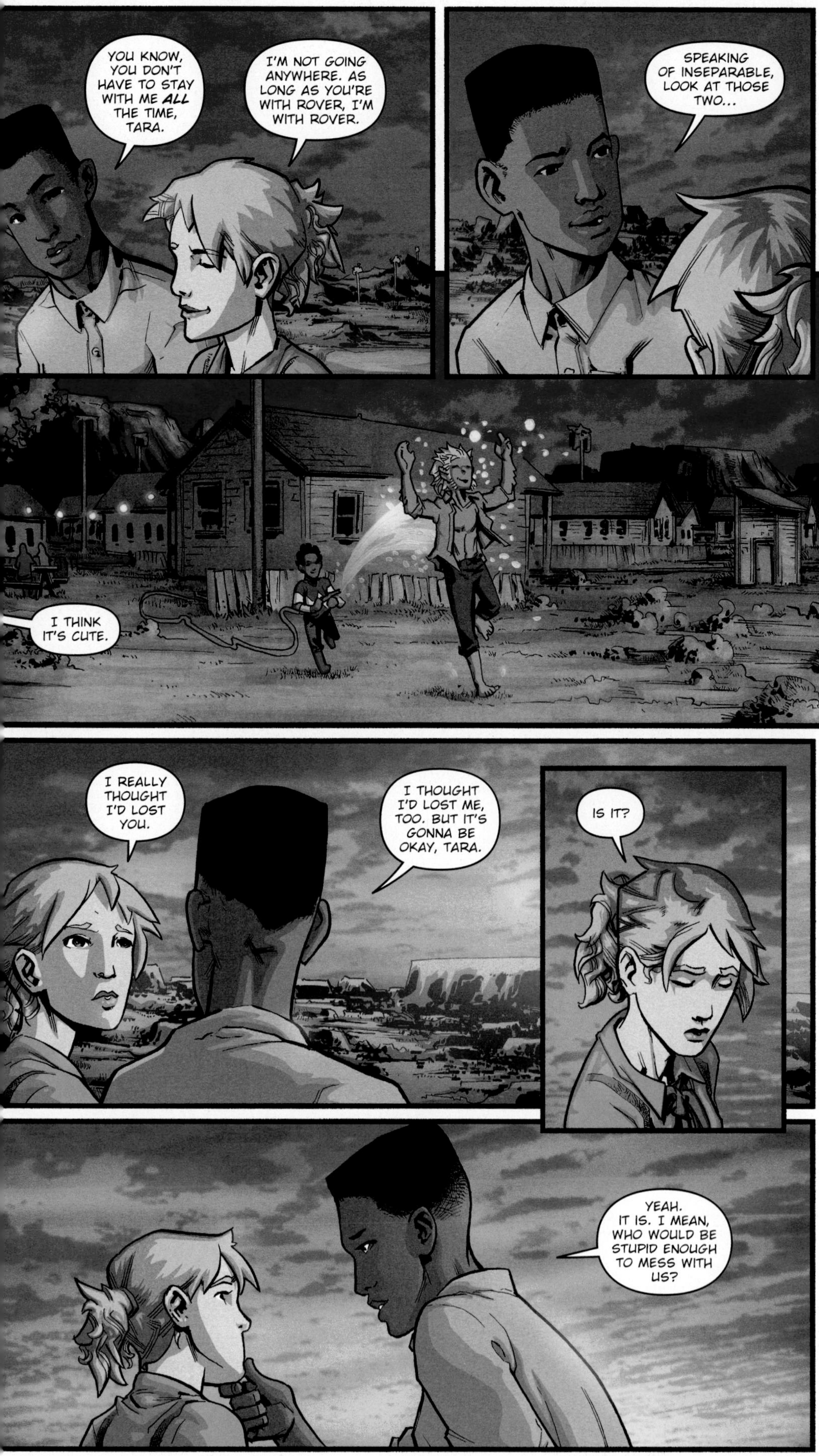
YOU KNOW, YOU DON'T HAVE TO STAY WITH ME ***ALL*** THE TIME, TARA.
I'M NOT GOING ANYWHERE. AS LONG AS YOU'RE WITH ROVER, I'M WITH ROVER.
SPEAKING OF INSEPARABLE, LOOK AT THOSE TWO...
I THINK IT'S CUTE.
I REALLY THOUGHT I'D LOST YOU.
I THOUGHT I'D LOST ME, TOO. BUT IT'S GONNA BE OKAY, TARA.
IS IT?
YEAH. IT IS. I MEAN, WHO WOULD BE STUPID ENOUGH TO MESS WITH US?

THE COPS STILL HAVEN'T FOUND CAULDER.

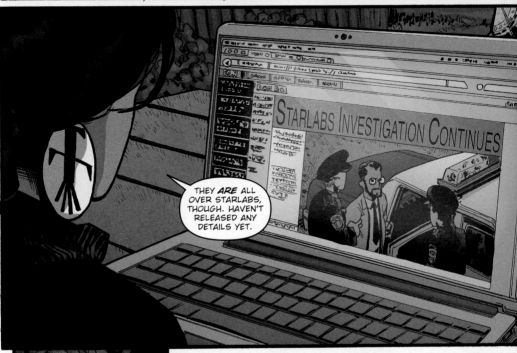

THEY **ARE** ALL OVER STARLABS, THOUGH. HAVEN'T RELEASED ANY DETAILS YET.

STARLABS INVESTIGATION CONTINUES

CLICK

MIRACLE TEENS STILL MISSING

IT'S ONLY A MATTER OF TIME UNTIL THEY FIND US, TOO, KORY. WE CAN'T HIDE OUT HERE FOREVER.

NOT TODAY. THEY NOT FIND US TODAY, RAVEN.

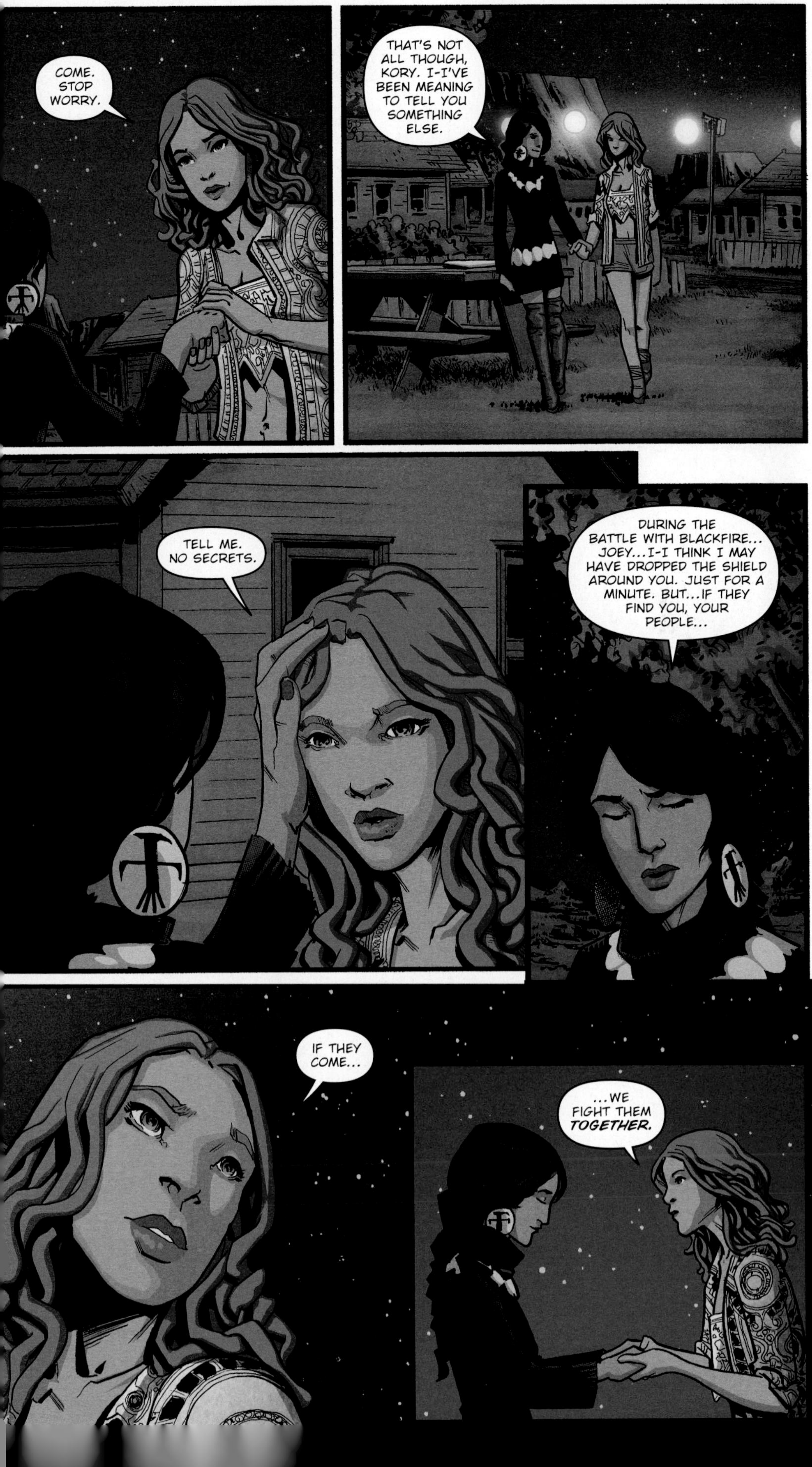

COME. STOP WORRY.
THAT'S NOT ALL THOUGH, KORY. I-I'VE BEEN MEANING TO TELL YOU SOMETHING ELSE.
TELL ME. NO SECRETS.
DURING THE BATTLE WITH BLACKFIRE... JOEY...I-I THINK I MAY HAVE DROPPED THE SHIELD AROUND YOU. JUST FOR A MINUTE. BUT...IF THEY FIND YOU, YOUR PEOPLE...
IF THEY COME...
...WE FIGHT THEM *TOGETHER.*

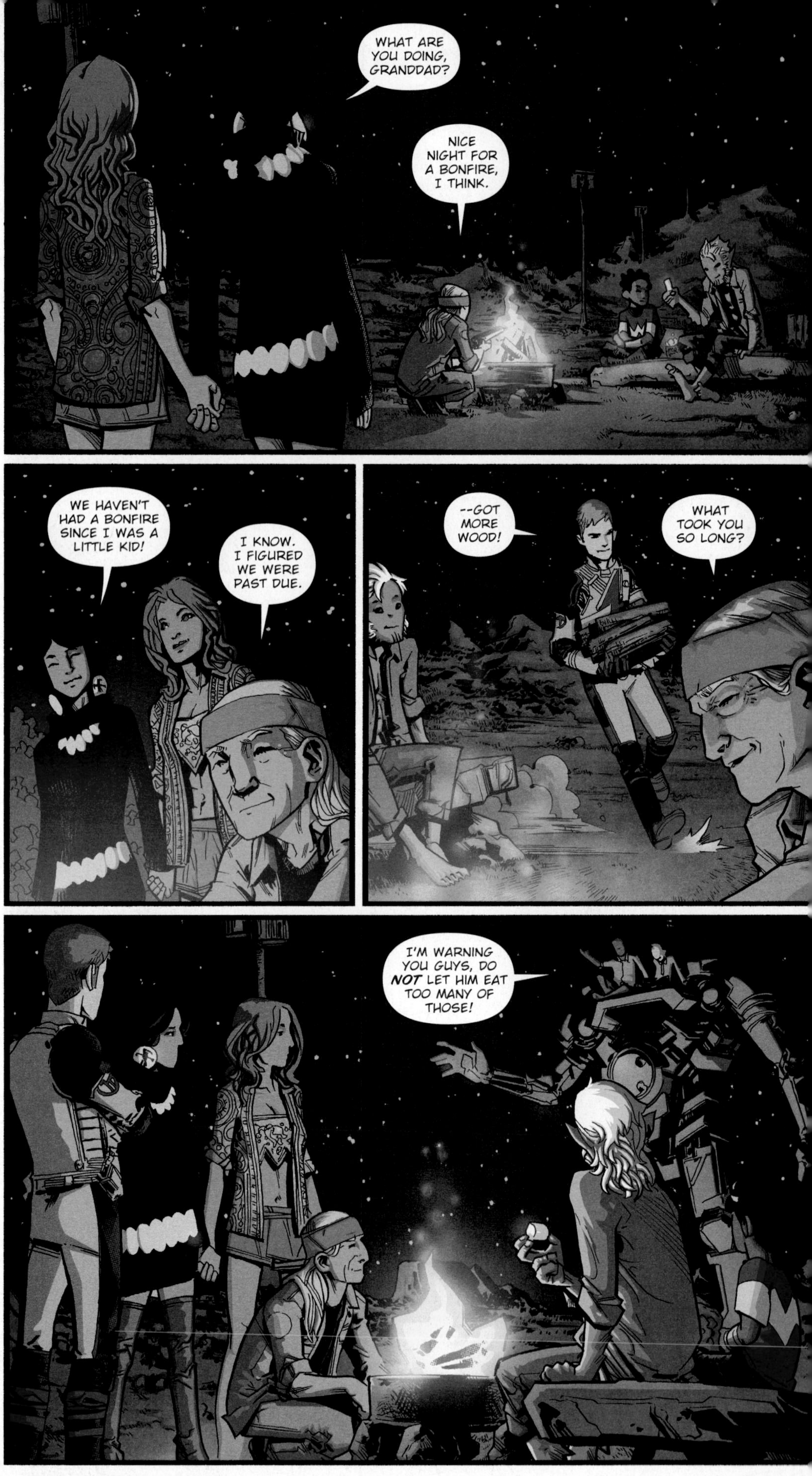
WHAT ARE YOU DOING, GRANDDAD?
NICE NIGHT FOR A BONFIRE, I THINK.
WE HAVEN'T HAD A BONFIRE SINCE I WAS A LITTLE KID!
I KNOW. I FIGURED WE WERE PAST DUE.
--GOT MORE WOOD!
WHAT TOOK YOU SO LONG?
I'M WARNING YOU GUYS, DO *NOT* LET HIM EAT TOO MANY OF THOSE!

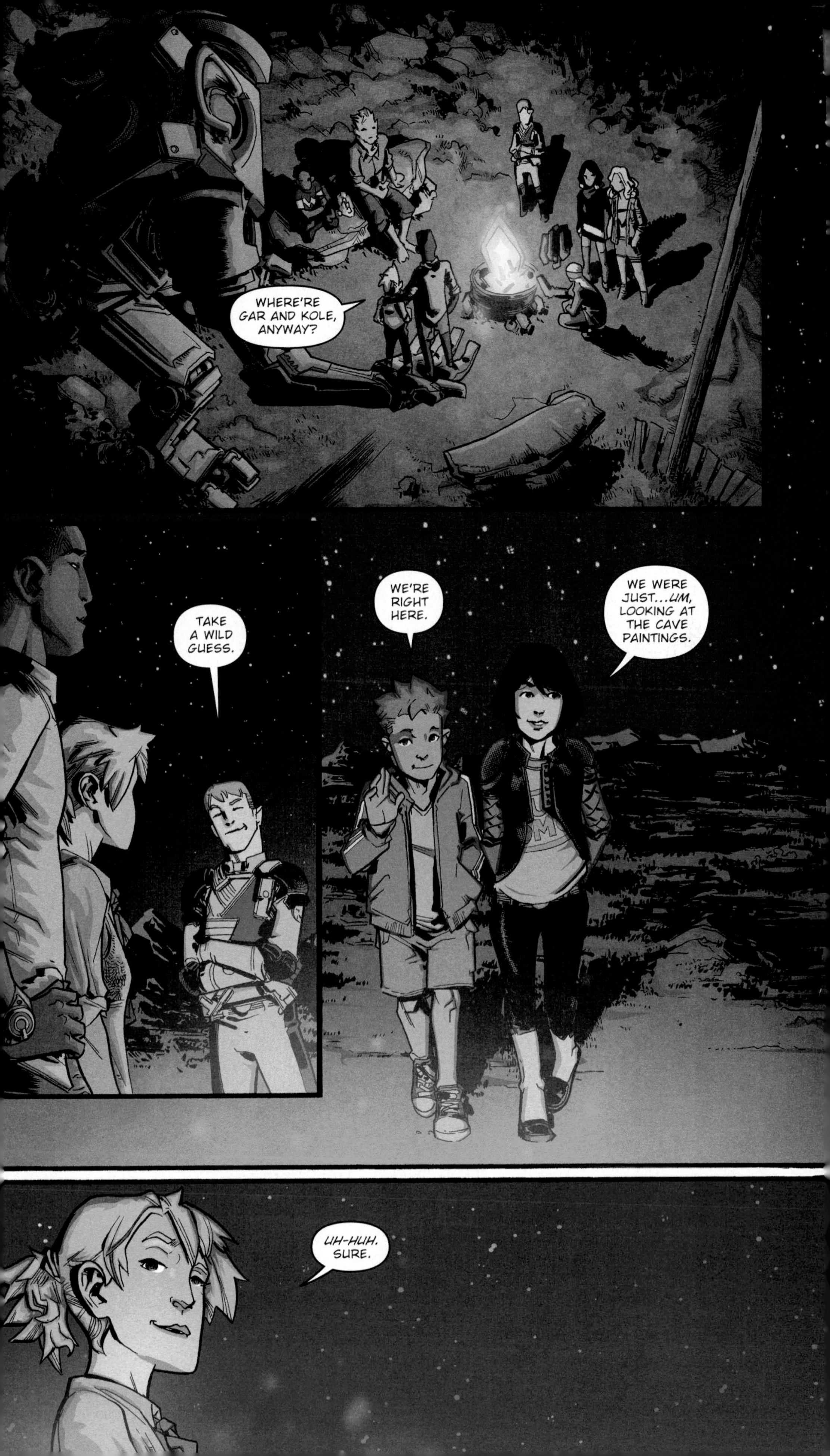
WHERE'RE GAR AND KOLE, ANYWAY?
TAKE A WILD GUESS.
WE'RE RIGHT HERE.
WE WERE JUST...UM, LOOKING AT THE CAVE PAINTINGS.
UH-HUH. SURE.

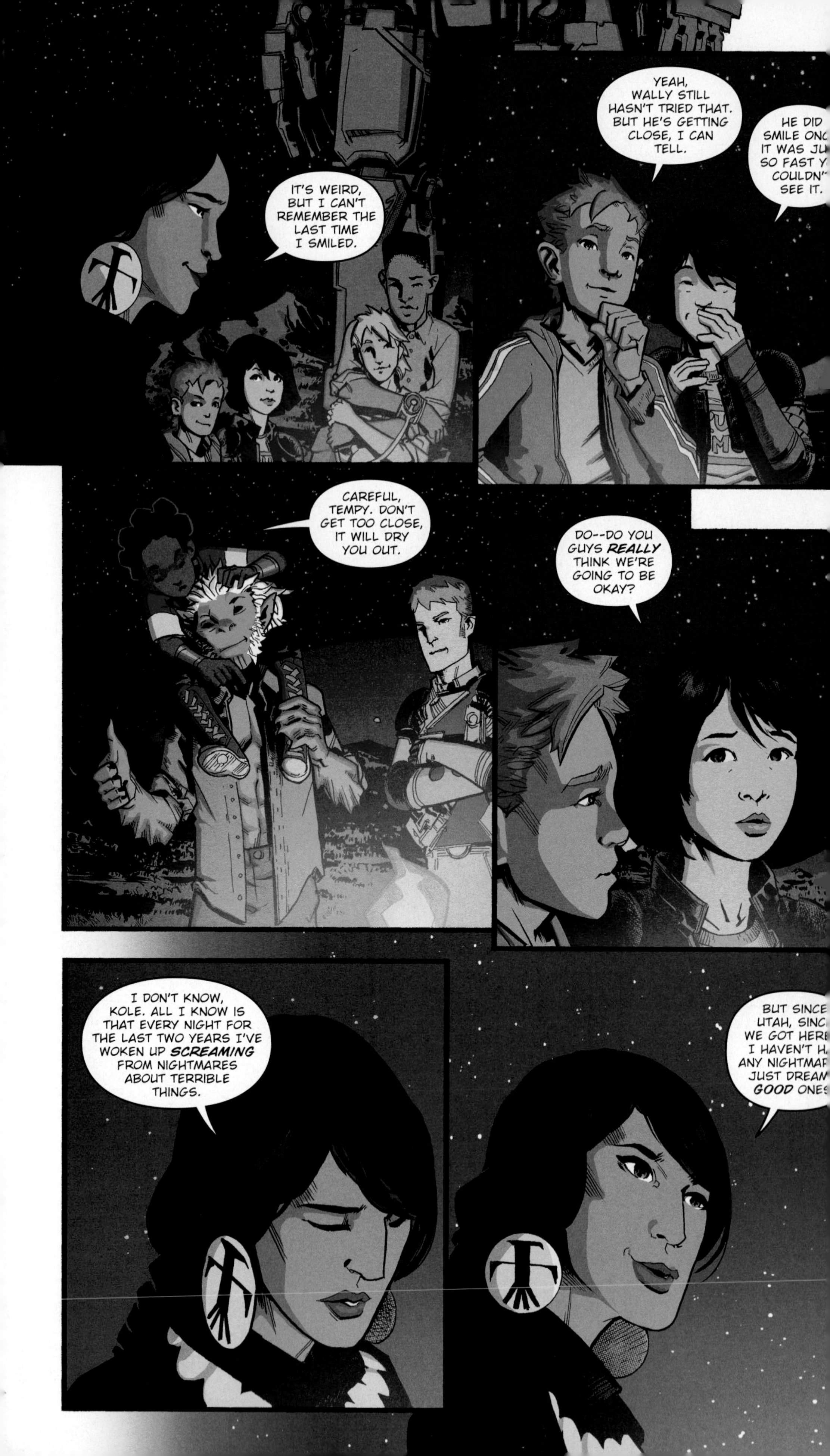
IT'S WEIRD, BUT I CAN'T REMEMBER THE LAST TIME I SMILED.
YEAH, WALLY STILL HASN'T TRIED THAT. BUT HE'S GETTING CLOSE, I CAN TELL.
HE DID SMILE ONC IT WAS JU SO FAST Y COULDN' SEE IT.
CAREFUL, TEMPY. DON'T GET TOO CLOSE, IT WILL DRY YOU OUT.
DO--DO YOU GUYS REALLY THINK WE'RE GOING TO BE OKAY?
I DON'T KNOW, KOLE. ALL I KNOW IS THAT EVERY NIGHT FOR THE LAST TWO YEARS I'VE WOKEN UP SCREAMING FROM NIGHTMARES ABOUT TERRIBLE THINGS.
BUT SINCE UTAH, SINC WE GOT HER I HAVEN'T H ANY NIGHTMA JUST DREAM GOOD ONES

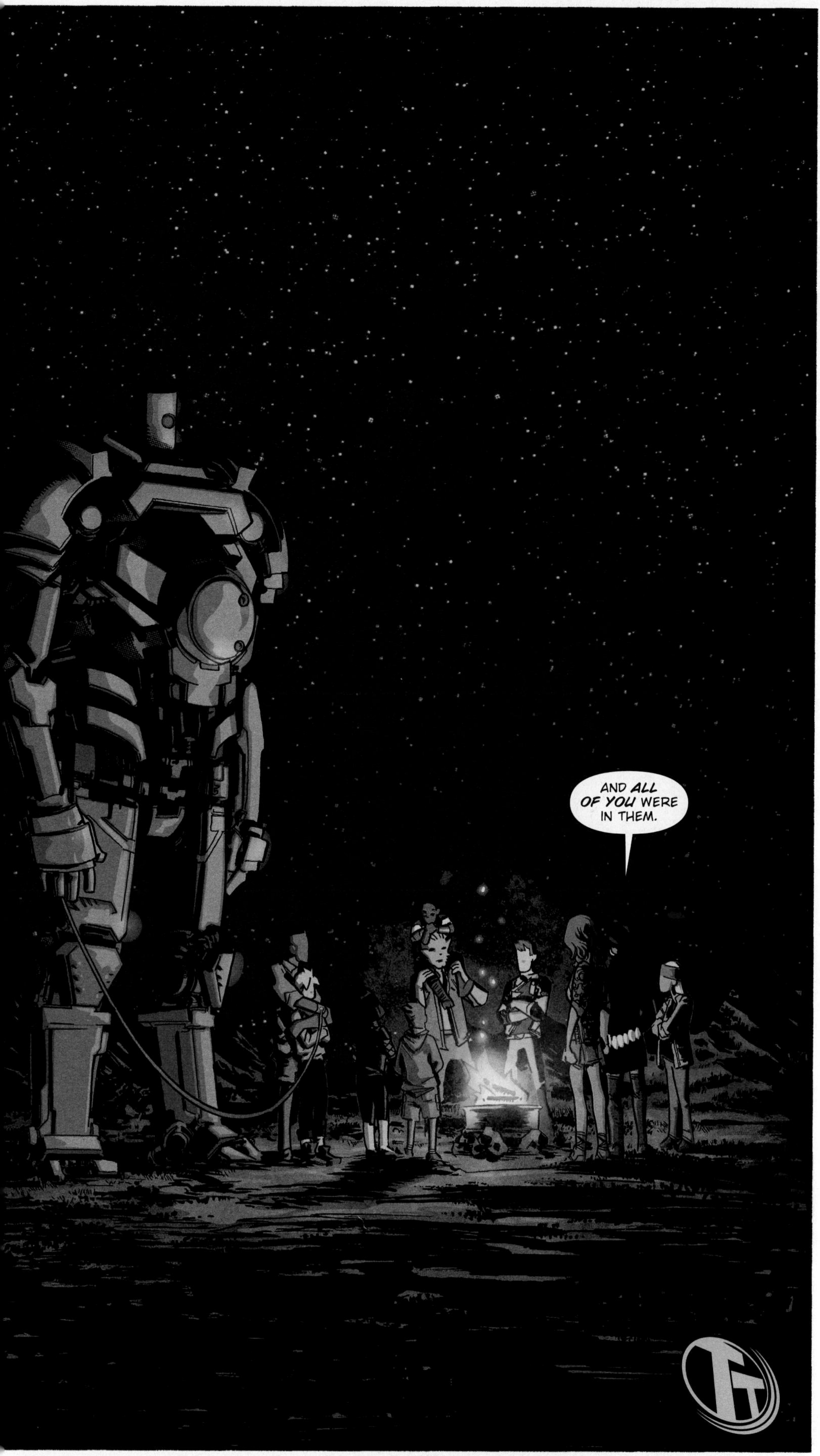
AND ALL OF YOU WERE IN THEM.

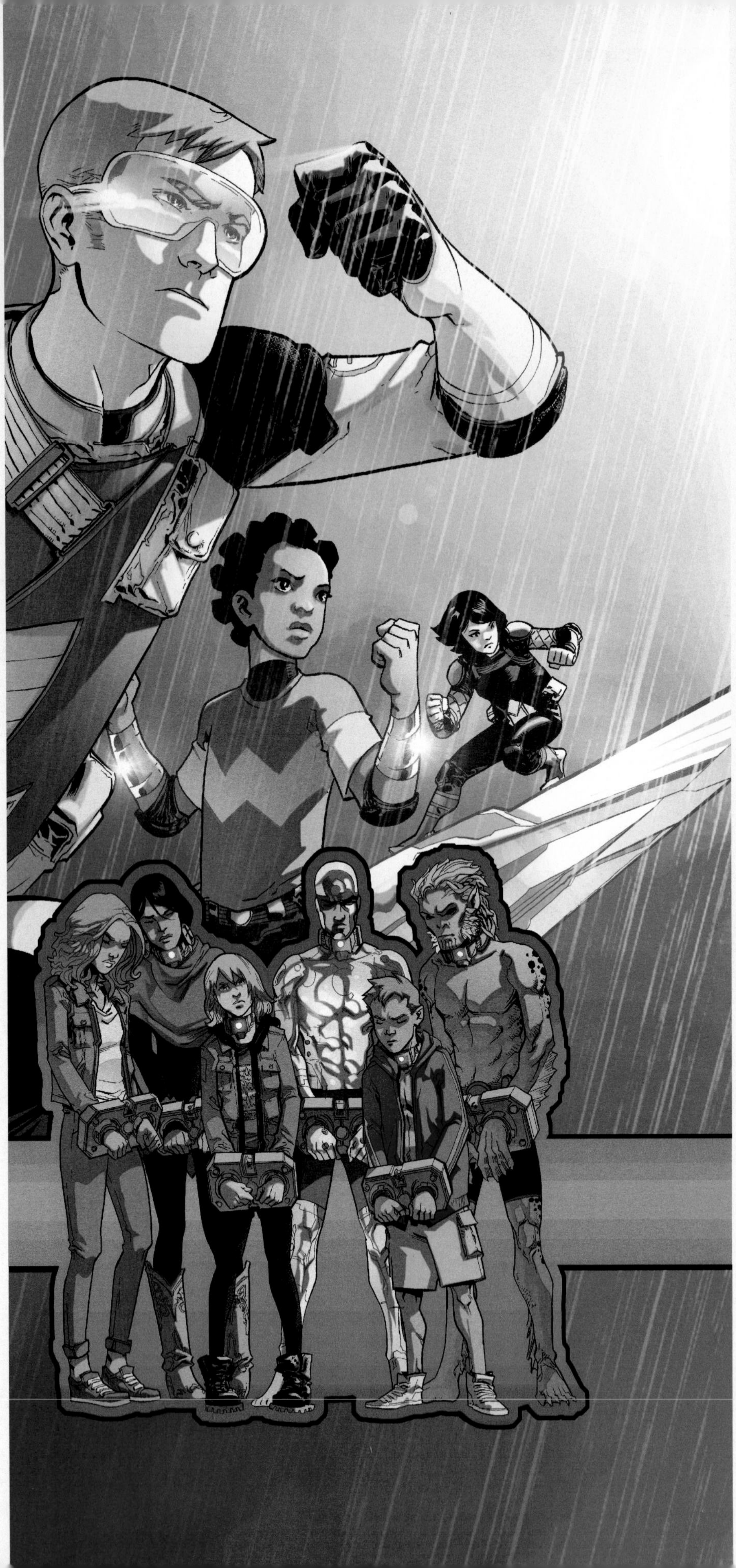

Unused cover art by Andy MacDonald and Brad Anderson.

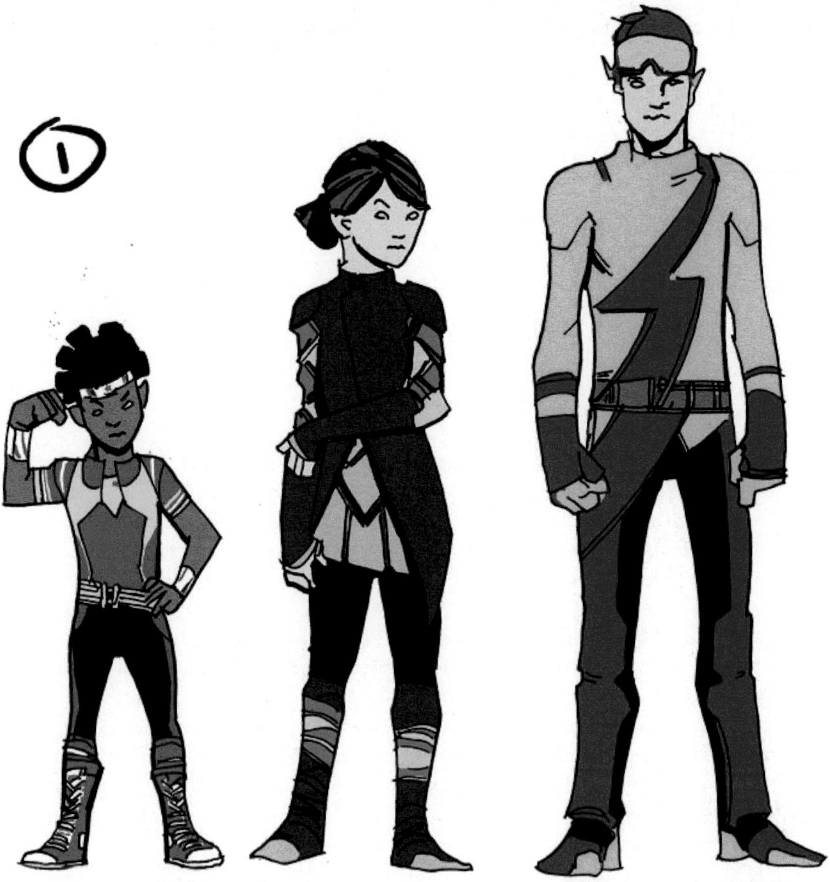
1

WONDER GIRL KOLE IMPULSE

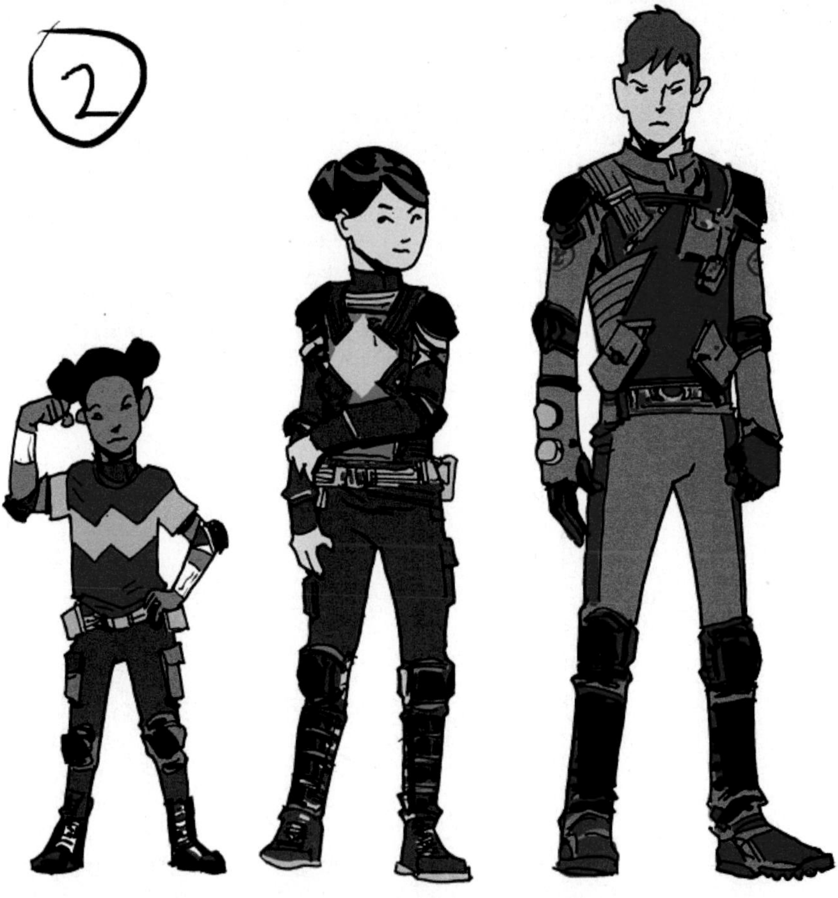
2

JEFF LEMIRE *New York Times* best-selling author Jeff Lemire is the creator of the acclaimed graphic novels SWEET TOOTH, *Essex County, The Underwater Welder* and the sci-fi love story TRILLIUM. His next original graphic novel will be *Roughneck* from Simon and Schuster. He has also written the monthly adventures of ANIMAL MAN and GREEN ARROW, among many others.

In 2008 and 2013, Jeff won the Shuster Award for Best Canadian Cartoonist. He has also received The Doug Wright Award for Best Emerging Talent and the American Library Association's prestigious Alex Award, recognizing books for adults with specific teen appeal. He has also been nominated for eight Eisner Awards, seven Harvey Awards and eight Shuster Awards. In 2010, *Essex County* was named one of the five Essential Canadian Novels of the Decade by the CBC's Canada Reads.

He currently lives and works in Toronto with his wife and son.

ANDY MacDONALD is the artist and co-creator of the cult classic series *NYC Mech*, as well as the artist of THE NEW 52: FUTURES END for DC Entertainment and *The Terminator* for Dark Horse Comics. In 2013, he adapted to comics the best-selling novels *Zoo* by James Patterson and *The Way of Shadows* by Brent McKee.

He lives in New York City with his wife and two cats.

BRAD ANDERSON, a native of Kenora, Ontario, Canada, began his comics career after attending the Joe Kubert School in 1996. Shortly after returning to Canada, he began coloring comics at Digital Chameleon, where he cut his teeth on some of the top characters in the business. After leaving as Art Director, he began working independently on a long stint with Dark Horse on *Star Wars: Legacy*, as well as CATWOMAN, BATMAN: EARTH ONE, and many other series at DC.

Brad currently resides in Winnipeg, Canada, with his wife, Kim, and two children.